The Tricks of the Trade

The Tricks
of the Trade

DARIO FO

Translated by Joe Farrell
Edited and with notes by Stuart Hood

Routledge · New York
A Theatre Arts Book

Manuale Minimo dell'Attore first published
in Italy in 1987
by Einaudi, Turin
Copyright © Dario Fo
The author has asserted his moral rights

First published in the United States
in this translation by
Routledge
29 West 35th Street, New York, NY 10001
by arrangement with Methuen Drama

A Theatre Arts Book

Translation copyright © 1991 Joe Farrell

Library of Congress Cataloging
in Publication Data available

ISBN 0–87830–007–4 (Hardback)
ISBN 0–87830–008–2 (Paperback)

The cover photograph is by Chris Harris

Typeset by Deltatype Ltd, Ellesmere Port

Printed and bound in Great Britain by
Cox & Wyman Ltd, Reading, Berkshire

Contents

List of Illustrations

All the photographs are from the private archive of Dario Fo and Franca Rame.

Introduction

In the original Italian, this book was entitled simply *The Actor's Mini-Manual*, and while it is entirely characteristic of Dario Fo to focus on the actor rather than on the playwright, the work itself covers a wider ground. It is a handbook of the range of skills that Fo himself has acquired in the course of his professional life and which he is anxious to pass on, but it is also a record of his own experiences, his thoughts and second thoughts on all topics theatrical, and a kind of unsystematic manifesto for the style of theatre which Dario Fo admires and which he has attempted to write and stage.

Manifesto may have the wrong connotations for a man so little inclined to abstract theory, and anyone hoping to find here a modern equivalent of Stanislavski or Brecht on acting technique, or the basis for a coherent overall view of popular theatre will be disappointed. It does, however, trace out an historically well-grounded approach to a particular style of theatre, and does debate the notions of culture which lie behind Dario Fo's own plays. His refusal to be bound too tightly by a rigid method is reflected in the structure of the book itself. It was not written by an author who sat down at a desk, having decided that the moment had come to convey a lifetime's experience to aspiring members of his profession. Indeed, it could hardly be said to be written at all. It is rather a collection of talks, workshops, lectures and conference pieces, some of which were delivered off the cuff, and all of which were recorded at the time before being written up, and edited, by Fo's wife and collaborator Franca Rame.

The closing section of the Sixth Day is entirely Franca's own work. Most of the work produced by the two of them in recent years has appeared under joint names, and has dealt with dilemmas facing women in the modern world. Franca Rame has a distinct viewpoint, not just because she is a woman but because of her own family background. Unlike Dario Fo, she comes from a theatrical dynasty who have over generations provided strolling players of exactly the sort Fo came to admire and celebrates here. In addition to working as an actress – a profession she claims to dislike – she has been actively involved in women's group since the early days of the feminist movement in Italy. If in stage works like *Female Parts* she dramatises the daily grind of ordinary women now, she has also looked into the unrecorded role of women in performing and writing for theatre in other ages. She contributes a female, and feminist, approach to the construction of their distinctive view on theatre.

The 'Six Days' structure recalls and parodies the literary framework used by classics of Italian literature such as *The Decameron*, but it is principally an attempt to reproduce the format and atmosphere of one particular week-long conference for drama students held at the Teatro Argentina in Rome. On that occasion Dario Fo covered much of the ground that seemed to him fundamental. His initial plan was simply to reproduce the proceedings of that event, but he later decided that the same topics had been treated with greater panache and success at similar gatherings in other parts of the world. Discussions, set pieces, question and answer sessions, demonstrations and improvisations held in places as far apart as Jutland, the Riverside Studios in London, New York and Bogotà were incorporated into what were by now purely fictional 'days' in a Roman theatre.

The tone of the book is thus conversational and informal rather than literary and formal. Fo is not on these occasions an elegant or fastidious stylist. His special gift is the ability to communicate recondite matters with a lightness of touch and with elements of zany fantasy and wit. The vocabulary he employs is colloquial, relaxed, slangy and anything but dictionary-bound. His idioms are enriched and embellished by an inventive humour, which, though a delight to the listener, is the despair of the academician; established jargon seems to Fo inadequate or colourless. In the course of one sentence, he can move dextrously from technical theatrical jargon into the slang of the moment, before launching into some purely personal flight of fancy or into plain gibberish. He will discuss Greek theatre in terms more appropriate to music hall, but will always insist that anyone who wishes to work in theatre in any capacity must acquire a mastery of the specialised language and tricks of the trade. Fo has no sympathy for the dilettante among theatre practitioners, much less for the half-hearted or lackadaisical.

Dario Fo toyed with the idea of calling this book *The Anti-Paradox of the Actor*, with the half-serious purpose of drawing attention to disagreements with Denis Diderot's celebrated work. And if he quickly jettisoned that notion, the idea was enough to stress that one of Fo's aims was to sketch the outlines of a philosophy of one sort of theatre. Its borders are reasonably clear. For Fo, Diderot will not do for his rejection of the actor's emotional power, Benedetto Croce for his obsession with the written text to the exclusion of all else. Brecht is viewed with guarded approval, although his theories of 'alienation' are of doubtful applicability from an actor's point of view. To the Elizabethans, Shakespeare included, Fo accords a genuine, if

2

decidedly idiosyncratic, respect, and while he venerates the Greeks, neither they nor the Elizabethans are really masters to be imitated today.

Pride of place in Fo's private pantheon is awarded to actors or writers in styles of theatre conventionally viewed as minor, or to performers who are more frequently regarded as purveyors of mere entertainment – strolling players, clowns, variety performers, farceurs and script writers for various popular carnivals and fêtes. There is nothing provincial about his preferences, any more than there is any limitation in time. Those whom he studies as masters of technique and holds up as models come from many ages in history and from countries as different as Iran, Bali and Sardinia, but all of them operate within the field of what can be termed popular theatre. Many are as nameless as the architects of the great Gothic cathedrals of Europe.

Terms such as 'popular culture' still make the bluff British critic cringe. The term is a fairly recent addition to theatrical vocabulary, and although a decision to work in that field was what distinguished writers of political theatre of the sixties and seventies from their predecessors in the inter-war years, it seems again to draw the ire of contemporary playwrights such as Howard Barker. It is still common to hear practitioners of theatre in Britain say in all solemnity that there are only two types of theatre – good and bad. Attitudes of this sort are hardened by a linguistic difficulty. The words *Teatro popolare* or *théâtre populaire* still retain some contact with the notion of people's theatre, whereas 'popular' has undergone a shift of meaning in English making possible such rough jibes as – Who's in favour of unpopular theatre then? The real opposite of popular theatre is bourgeois theatre, but this is another of those terms that the theatregoing public on both sides of the Atlantic are decidedly coy about using.

There is no such coyness in Fo, and not simply because his politics are uncompromisingly radical and left-wing. There is a breadth to his vision of political theatre which is uncommon among major theatrical personalities. Ultimately his commitment to popular theatre is only an extension into another dimension of his political beliefs and activities, although, the statement might be made more palatable if the order of the words were reversed. He does not limit himself to plays on immediate social or economic injustice, but looks at the cultural roots that permit such a situation. He is fond of quoting the Marxist philosopher Antonio Gramsci on the need to know where one has come from before establishing the way forward, and many of his views on culture, particularly on the existence of an alternative culture alongside the officially recognised culture, derive ultimately from Gramsci's Socialist writings.

Dario Fo is thus in a different category from those political playwrights, especially in Anglo-Saxon lands, who seem positively to boast of being rootless and bereft of all tradition, and who thus allow political theatre to be presented either as militant agit-prop or as something covered by that commonplace cliché which states that all theatre is willy-nilly political. Theatre, the notion runs, that is not positively challenging is an act of complicity with the status quo. The trouble with such a blanket denunciation is that whereas it may be all very well to make Aristophanes a Tory *ante litteram*, Goldoni a bourgeois militant or Beaumarchais a proto-revolutionary, to stamp as *ipso facto* reactionaries all those – from the writers of medieval mystery plays to latter-day dramatists like Pirandello or Ibsen – who have chosen to portray human beings as trespassers on the earth rather than as citizens, is a somewhat crass categorisation. It is not informative about the nature of the relationship between politics and theatre down the ages. One of the most valuable aspects of Fo's critical work is the challenge he issues to *bien-pensant* orthodoxies of this stamp. He has been willing to wander down some untrodden by-ways to locate forms of people's theatre that no one else considered worthy of notice.

Dario Fo is not merely a playwright for today, although there is here a paradox which he gleefully points out. The great playwrights, as decreed by the higher criticism, are those who ponder and reflect the human condition, while the political playwright is one who rages on the fringes, raucously drawing attention to a restricted number of issues but studiously ignoring others of more weighty, transcendental significance. The playwright whose principal interest is the politics of his day, in however wide or narrow a sense, is viewed as a creature circumscribed by his own time and not expecting, unlike the great immortals, to outlive it. In reality, those now accorded the status of classics were usually careless about future reputation and, like Shakespeare or the Greeks, wrote for their day and made no provision to ensure posterity's approval.

Fo has a territory of his own, marked out by a theatrical talent for setting his plays somewhere between Wonderland and the Wasteland, and by a critical desire to establish a new concept of culture. He is involved in a search to identify the relationship between power and dissent throughout history, to trace the various forms that it assumed in theatrical activity, to follow it into such unlikely areas as medieval religious drama, but always with the intention of finding roots for a style of pugnacious theatre that has value and appeal today. Anglo-Saxon observers may dub that kind of activity 'academic', but while academic, like intellectual, is not a term of automatic contempt in other countries, Fo's interest was always to see what could be rescued from the culture of other times and what was serviceable in the theatre of today.

There are two equal and opposing risks with Dario Fo – that of neutering him by leaving all politics out and reducing him to a farceur of the rank of Feydeau on the one hand, and that of harping on about his politics to the exclusion of his passion for theatre and entertainment on the other. There were various radical troupes – Het Werk Teatr of Holland was the most celebrated – established in the aftermath of the heady days of 1968, who used theatre as a means of struggle. The theatrical means were indifferent, for all that counted was the message to be communicated. Fo never had any sympathy for such an approach. His international renown may date from the big political plays of the sixties and seventies but he was already a man of the theatre through and through. It was no accident that his first work once he broke from – his phrase – bourgeois theatre to establish an alternative circuit was not *Accidental Death of an Anarchist*, which deals with the death of the anarchist Pinelli at the beginning of the terrorist campaign in Italy, or a play for today like *Can't Pay? Won't Pay!* which portrays moves by housewives in Milan who simply expropriated goods from supermarkets in protest against inflationary pressures, but *Mistero Buffo*, a reworking of a series of sketches by itinerant medieval minstrels.

Where is the tradition, he continually asks? His aim is always to establish continuity. It can hardly be surprising if Fo the all-round man of theatre operates in an explicitly Italian tradition. As an actor-author, he is, in the sense in which Ralph Waldo Emerson used the term, the representative man of Italian theatre. The central figure of Italian theatre has always been the performer rather than the writer. Ultimately, that is the only answer to be given to explorers undertaking the futile quest for the Great Italian Theatre to set alongside the Golden Century in Spain, the Classical Moment in France, the Romantic Era in Germany or the Elizabethan Age in England. The search is being conducted in the wrong places. Italian theatre is dominated not by authors but by performers, by improvising actors of the Commedia dell'Arte, by anonymous strolling players, by minstrel figures in motley from the Middle Ages who, to eke out their days and amuse their paymasters, devised their own scripts. To such figures the text was simply a tool of the trade, like face paint or props, and not a contribution to the literary treasure-house of a nation.

When Fo puts himself in this performance tradition, he is closer to the theatrical mainstream in Italy than might be the case elsewhere. Neapolitan theatre has produced several author-actors similar in inspiration to Dario Fo. Eduardo de Filippo, whom Fo describes as his father-figure in theatrical terms, is an obvious example from this century, but Eduardo Scarpetta and Antonio Petito could be cited from the nineteenth century, as could Ruzzante

5

(a Northern Italian) from the early days of Commedia dell'Arte. From this popular lineage, Fo creates a rival to the established great tradition, and is impatiently severe with critics who denied the independence of the popular tradition, as well as with figures such as Diderot or Croce who were unable to grasp the essentially performance-oriented nature of most theatrical texts. He has little patience with aspiring drama writers, for example Pier Paolo Pasolini, who were capable of producing nothing more than 'literature'. The inverted commas are *de rigueur*, and such a term is no compliment when used by Fo.

Although fascinated by Commedia dell'Arte in general and by the colourful figure of Harlequin in particular, Fo's favoured model is the medieval *giullare*. The *giullare* is a figure from Italian history, and it is not easy to find the exact equivalent in English. Etymologically, the word is associated with 'juggler', but the English term has now taken on a more limited meaning. The translation employed here is 'minstrel', although there are inevitable drawbacks to that word, with its sentimental associations with the musician figure with the harp on his back. The *giullare* was the street performer of his day, the busker of the Middle Ages, with something in common with the Shakespearean Fool, but nothing at all with the aristocratic pet who was the Court Jester. Of his very essence, he was the people's entertainer, but also the people's spokesman, giving satirical voice to resentments felt by ordinary people against authority. He made his living from what he could earn as he travelled from town to town, and he was willing to turn his hand to storytelling, to acting in the piazzas, to singing, dancing, acrobatics.

This figure has come to exercise an enormous fascination for Fo. Increasingly he has come to identify with him in every sphere, politically, culturally and theatrically. When making his break with conventional theatre in 1968, Fo announced that he was tired of being the minstrel of the bourgeoisie, and would aim in future to become the minstrel of the proletariat. It may be that he has reshaped the historical figure so as to provide himself with the model he was seeking, but the *giullare* has at least become a living being again rather than a figure from an antiquarian's notebook. Dario Fo gives a real sense to the over-used word 'tradition', and that in itself is an achievement.

Joe Farrell

The footnotes to the text that follows are by Stuart Hood.

First Day

Commedia dell'Arte

Our first talk is dedicated to Commedia dell'Arte. Once, I don't remember when, I heard the actor Carmelo Bene exclaim: 'Commedia dell'Arte? Give us a break! It never existed!' With his well-known taste for hyperbole and paradox, Carmelo Bene had in fact uttered an important truth . . . only he forgot to conclude the sentence with the words 'it never existed . . . in the form they always taught us'.

It is beyond all doubt that there has been such an enormous amount of nonsense spoken about the myth of the players risking all on a kind of magical tight-rope, about the lyrical rag-and-bone men who wore the masks, and such a general volume of down-market literature on the subject that it would make anyone want to scream 'Enough of this rubbish – there never was any such thing!'

Harlequin, the Whore-monger

The first time the name of Harlequin appeared in print (we are in the year 1585) it was to denounce him as a notorious pimp. The pamphlet in question, recounting the journey of Harlequin to hell, was drawn up in French. The Harlequin in this case was Tristano Martinelli, the actor who first wore the costume of the character. Harlequin descends to hell in an attempt to snatch from the clutches of Lucifer the soul of Mère Cardine, a well-known 'madame' and owner of a brothel which had achieved a certain fame in Parisian society. Martinelli was said to be a valued procurer for this business. The author of this trenchant tract was apparently a certain minor poet, devoured by jealousy because of the favour Harlequin enjoyed, not only with the man in the street but also, more especially, with men of culture in the city and even with the King and Queen of France.

Harlequin replied with a brief, excoriating piece of his own in which he turned the tables on his jealous rival. Harlequin descends yet again to hell, this time accompanied by his denigrator. The two, like Dante and Virgil (obviously the Dante role was taken by Harlequin) move through the various circles of hell, bumping into the great figures of French high society. Each

7

one gives proof of regard and affection for the son of the Zanni,* whereas the unfortunate poet receives nothing but kicks in the face, and ends up inside tubs of liquid faeces . . . pots of boiling cat dung . . . turned cold, which makes it even more disgusting.

They find themselves playing dice with Beelzebub: Harlequin-Dante wins, Virgil, cursing, loses and is tormented by the devils of hell. Harlequin saves him from being flayed alive by the enraged devils. Filled with gratitude, the wretched creature begs pardon and admits his guilt . . . magnanimously Harlequin gives his blessing. The two emerge 'to see once more the stars' . . . the poet in his delight slips on, of all things, a bit of wet dung: he tumbles to the ground . . . bangs his head on a priapic kerbstone . . . and lies still, dead! The poet's soul descends to hell . . . but this time without Harlequin.

The ending is not altogether authentic, since I have extrapolated from a script by Scala, the author of *Harlequin*. But it seems to me to fit quite well.

Following a well-established tradition of 'run these dirty beggars out of town', the Commedia players have had a hard time of it, so much so that there are certain authors of learned essays on the Italian Comedy who seem willing to use any stick to beat them with. They present the actors of improvised comedy as a flock of out-and-out vagabonds with neither dignity nor craft, or as performers and entertainers who lived by their wits, getting by from day to day, up to all kinds of deceits and frauds. To read some of these debunkers, it would appear that the strolling players did not even possess that much-vaunted, unrivalled art of inventing fresh pieces of dialogue or up-to-date situations there and then, before the very eyes of the audience. Far from it, they assure us, all that 'improvisation' was no more than a bluff, a cunningly pre-arranged device where the situations and snatches of dialogue had been committed to memory in advance. Which is absolutely correct, as far as it goes, but the evaluation of this fact is open to interpretation. My assessment is one hundred per cent positive.

A well-worked Bluff

The actors had at their disposal an incredible store of stage business, called *lazzi* – situations, dialogues, gags, rhymes and rigmaroles which they could call up at a moment's notice to give the impression of on-stage improvisation. This repertoire had been prepared and assimilated through the experience of an infinite number of performances, of different shows, of situations worked out directly on the audience, but the central fact was that the majority were

---

* Zanni – Venetian dialect version of Giovanni: the name given to two of the comic characters in the Commedia dell'Arte who played the part of servants. Hence 'zany'.

the result of study and careful preparation. Every actor or actress learned by heart dozens of 'tirades' on a variety of topics corresponding to the parts he or she might have to play; we have a long series of passionate and amusing monologues from the famous Commedia actress, Isabella Andreini, for a woman in love, expressing contempt, jealousy, spite, desire or despair; and each of them could easily be adapted to the most diverse situations, or even turned upside down and stuck into the middle of dialogue. For instance, the woman feigns contempt, but conceals an overwhelming desire . . . in the course of her outburst she pardons her lover, who in his turn declares himself offended and even tells of his hatred for the woman . . . who, cursing his faithlessness, throws herself on her lover . . . then breaks into a raucous laugh and delivers a piece of jeering doggerel against the young man, who repays the compliment and sneers at the woman he loves . . . who grows indignant, but in the end lets herself be cajoled and pacified. They laugh, together this time, at the memory of the little ploys they use to keep each other's interest. Sighing, caught between laughter and emotion, they embrace.

From this one sequence, it would be possible, by changing the rhythms and the development, to achieve a dozen variations. The players were past masters at dismantling and re-assembling the different elements, and in this style the most unlikely twists and turns could be extended over the entire script. Example: Isabella is in possession of a magic potion which sends anyone who drinks it mad with love. She offers it to her lover to stop him leaving her, but the potion is accidentally taken by the boy's father, Pantaloon. Pantaloon, wild with passion, falls in love with Harlequin, who, to further a ploy of his own, had dressed himself up as a woman. Harlequin is compelled by Isabella and her lover to maintain his disguise and to continue with the game, since, if he were deprived of the woman he loves, Pantaloon would die of a broken heart. The two go through an engagement ceremony. Harlequin throws himself wholeheartedly into the part and begins to have a bit of fun: his only thought is of rich clothes, jewellery and food. Pantaloon, in a frenzy of passion, desires to possess his fiancée, Harlequin, who manages, under cover of darkness, to have himself replaced by a plump serving-maid. Pantaloon, convinced that he has had his way with Harlequin, is now wholly satisfied with himself, and is more than ever in love. Harlequin is then forced by the young lovers to blackmail Pantaloon so that he will allow his son to marry Isabella. The circle is complete. Pantaloon is offered an antidote which will restore him to his senses, but Harlequin won't permit it, because he realises he is better off than he has ever been previously, so, to get the antidote out of the way, he gulps it down himself. He cannot know that the antidote, if not preceded by the original potion, has the power to drive people more insane than ever. At this stage the possible outcomes are limitless: Harlequin could fall in love with Isabella, with her lover, with Pantaloon, with the serving maid, or even with the chicken or lamb he had just slaughtered for the wedding feast.

Anyone who is at all familiar with the business could easily dream up other situations along the same lines. All that is necessary is to decide at the outset that the potion will be drunk by some young man who will then fall madly in love with Isabella, that Isabella should in her turn drink the potion and fall helplessly in love with Pantaloon, and that, in the comings and goings, Isabella's original lover should swallow the potion and fall in love with the servant. In the midst of this chaos, Harlequin could well give us one of his famous sniggers. Indeed it might be an idea to present him, the master mischief-maker, as the one who, by adding potions to glasses right and left, was responsible for the whole bedlam. It reminds me of the sequence of the couples falling in love with all the wrong people in Shakespeare's *A Midsummer Night's Dream*. This is itself a classical notion taken from Commedia dell'Arte. From an analysis of the structure of that comedy, the incredible number of possible variations that can be obtained from these exchanges becomes apparent. In other words, the players were in possession of an enormous repertoire of devices, as well as of great skill and craftsmanship.

The Rame Family and the Craft of Improvisation

Franca Rame, who was born into a theatrical family, had the extraordinary good fortune as a child of breathing the air of the real Italian-style comedy. They were all actors in her family, and generally performed in northern Lombardy. (The Rame family can be traced back at least three centuries.) So rich was the repertoire of this group in comedies, farces and dramas, that they were able to stay put in the one town for months on end, presenting a different play each evening. Franca recalls that they did not even require to revise their parts. The company poet, Uncle Tommaso, would gather the actors together, give out the roles, remind them of the outlines of the plot, describe the action scene by scene and then hang up in the wings a kind of calendar containing the entrances and exits, as well as the subject of each scene. On some occasions they would put on a completely new work based on a novel or on a report in that day's paper.

Uncle Tommaso, the poet, read out to the members of the company the outline plot, spiced with any specially piquant or vivid details he had prepared and then distributed the roles. There were no rehearsals of any kind; they came on stage, and after looking at his list of sequences and entrances, they did everything by improvisation. Everyone knew an enormous range of appropriate dialogues which obviously varied with the occasion, and in particular knew by heart the opening and closing topics, that is, the conventional words of gestures which alerted the other actors to variations, changes of situation, the approach of the close of the scene, of the act or of the play.

Plainly the knowledge of all the tricks of the trade in the world could never of itself be sufficient if the actor did not also possess the innate flair and that one gift indispensable for improvisation – the talent for giving time and time again the impression that he was saying something completely new, something which had just come into his head that very moment.

Origin of the Expression 'Commedia dell'Arte'

Before going any further, the first task is to establish the precise meaning of the Italian term, Commedia dell'Arte. *Arte* is normally translated as 'art', and the mere mention of that word is enough to release a flood of images, of grand stereotypes and clichés by the score: art as the sublime creation of the human imagination, art as the poetic expression of genius, etc. etc. In actual fact, in the present case the term 'art', or at least its Italian equivalent *arte*, is connected to the concept of craft.

In the Middle Ages, *arte* also meant guild, and there existed an *arte*, or guild, of woolworkers, of silkworkers, of masons and so on. These were, as is well known, combinations of craftsmen. The aim of these associations was to stop people employed in the same line from tearing each other apart, and to enable them to stand together against the power of the big merchants or the interference of princes, bishops or cardinals.

Rights and Privileges of 'The Market Place'

Commedia dell'Arte, then, means primarily comedy staged by professional actors. It involved an association with a statute of rules and regulations of its own, through which the actors undertook to protect and respect each other. Just as the major guilds concerned themselves with keeping their markets free from the competition of outside corporations, so the professional actors declared open war on any unauthorised company who invaded their 'market place', and they did not hesitate to seek the assistance of the local authority from whom they had obtained the initial monopoly rights for that dukedom or county.

In this way, freelance performers, groups of acrobats and tumblers and companies of occasional or amateur actors were literally chased off the 'market place'. On occasion, the professional actors themselves organised punitive expeditions against any groups of amateurs who, in spite of the official ban, insisted on acting in the privileged sites given to the recognised players. Often, a well-known company would not bother with the guild rules and simply swept aside the rights of their smaller rivals, as is shown by an extract from a letter by Isabella Andreini written in uncompromising terms to the Governor of Milan, Don Pedro Enriquez: 'since it is known that the aforementioned have put up a platform in the piazza to perform plays, or, more precisely to ruin plays, I beg you to write to the Mayor of that locality to have permission withdrawn'.

On another occasion, her husband, Francesco Andreini, went even further, writing: 'those governing the city of . . . should in no wise permit comedies and tragedies to be so execrably performed on a public platform but rather in a private place, with such honour and splendour as may be thought fitting'.

Regarding the label 'Commedia dell'Arte', we know of certain highly considered authors who assure us that there is no connection with the Italian term for craft or with the notion of a guild. Allardyce Nicoll, an excellent British scholar, believes that the word *arte* should be taken in the sense of 'quality', as in, for instance, 'the Shakespearan quality', and consequently 'dell'arte' would mean 'of skill'. On the contrary, Benedetto Croce agrees with the guild origins, but only to demonstrate that whereas the players of Italian-style theatre were no doubt capable craftsmen, worthwhile performers and entertaining mimes, they were certainly not artists: 'there is no trace of the presence of the gifted author'.

Croce and the Obsession with Script

Croce, who deserves full credit for emphasising the high professionalism of the players, was, nonetheless, obsessed with the dogma – 'no (literary-dramaturgical) script, no art'. But let us, at least for the moment, not be drawn into polemics. It is sufficient to underline one point which derives, not from a reading of the texts, but above all from practice: the Commedia dell'Arte is a form of theatre based on a combination of dialogue and action, on spoken monologue and performed gesture, and not on mime alone. In spite of what Croce asserts, if they had relied exclusively on a series of somersaults, dances, poses and moves, the players would never have been able to make anything work. We are by no means the only ones to advance that proposition.

Casanova and the Praise of the Spoken Word in Harlequin

Let us consider the judgement of the performance of a great eighteenth-century actor, Antonio Sacchi, given by no less a man than the famous Casanova, himself the son of an actress and a great admirer of Commedia dell'Arte: 'The substance of his witty speeches, always fresh and spontaneous, is so disjointed and confused, its strange phrases composed of such a collection of words suited for themes of an entirely different kind and so unexpectedly applied to what he is talking about, so replete with divers ridiculous metaphors, that it would seem as though the whole must prove a formless chaos; yet this method finds full justification in the very disorder of the style that he alone knows how to manage.' Reporting this comment, Allardyce Nicoll remarks: 'Casanova concentrated not on the performer's acrobatic skill but on his words.'

That is to say, it was not an arbitrary choice, but a question of method and style, and the final proof is given by another observation, once again from Casanova: 'This actor has the unique and inimitable gift of being able to make his audiences share in the entanglements of those speeches: he plunges in and emerges with the wittiest confusions of intricate rhetoric; boldly he goes on, appears so lost that he cannot get out again, then in a moment wriggles out of his predicament and issues from the labyrinth just as the most attentive spectator, duped by his desperate circumlocutions, is at last convinced that he cannot escape.'

Against the Notion of the Beggar Players

Regarding the role of the actor in the Commedia dell'Arte, I want to turn my attention to the nature of the dramatic quality and originality that distinguish this style of theatre from all others known to us. This dramatic quality and originality are not determined, as some people seem to believe, by the use of masks or by the appearance of the characters in fixed stereotypes, but by a genuinely revolutionary approach to making theatre, and by the unique role assumed by the actors. I am in overall sympathy with those scholars who would prefer to tag this kind of theatre not Commedia dell'Arte but 'actors' theatre'. The entire theatrical structure rests on their shoulders: the actor-performer is author, producer, storyteller, director; he will be required to pass from lead actor to supporting role at a moment's notice, and will astonish, with his continual twists and turns, not only the audience but also his fellow-actors.

It is only to be expected that this kind of approach will lead to occasional drops in tension, lapses in rhythm or the over-accumulation of gags that lessen each other's impact. Often the play ended up going nowhere, or became mawkish with the laughter an end in itself, but that all depended on how successful the actor-manager was in instilling a sense of rigour in his company; it depended principally on native talent, and on the understanding established between the company and the audience.

Diderot and the Anti-Actor Paradox

It was this particular problem of unpredictability which exercised Diderot* in his *Paradox of the Actor* (1773). The famous encyclopedist could not cope with the fact that the success of a play might depend almost exclusively on the actor, on his state of mind at a particular moment, on the fact that he was in a good mood one evening but not the following evening, on whether the audience established an easy rapport with the actors or whether they were sunk in a deep torpor from which there was no rousing them. Diderot asserted that an actor ought to be able to programme himself and check his own performance, that he should, without any scope for error, make a calculated forecast of the impact of each and every passage in the entire work. In other words; rationality and detachment from the emotions, nothing to be left to change or to accident, much less to a passing state of mind or of indigestion.

There is no doubt that Diderot was totally right to attack the half-baked 'just let it flow' school, or to berate the naturalistic nonsense of abandoning oneself to impulse, to the *frisson* of the moment, to sniffles, to shallow effects, to showy flourishes without method or rigour. 'The extremes of sensibility', he intoned, 'render an actor mediocre, while the absolute absence of all sensibility makes possible sublimity in an actor.' A deep paradox indeed!

Display Feeling at your Peril

Nevertheless, it is in his underlying assumptions that Diderot is, in my view, completely wrong. Diderot's reasoning is that of an author, of a man of letters and, in consequence, he claims that the written text is all-important: the text is sacred, the actor must adapt to it, serve it with the highest measure of discipline, if possible without discussion. Diderot prefers to overlook the strength a script acquires when it is performed night after night on stage. Oddly enough St Charles Borromeo† had no doubts on this score and warned his bishops to guard against the immediacy, freshness and irresistible appeal of improvised comedy. 'The words of writers', he declared in a letter, 'are dead, but the words of actors live.' You can be sure he did not have in

* Denis Diderot (1713–1784), philosopher, encyclopedist, novelist, art critic and dramatist.

† St Charles Borromeo (1538–1584), cardinal and archbishop, one of the most influential figures of the Counter-Reformation in Italy.

mind those programmed, drily rational actors of Diderot's imaginings. In fact, that style of theatre which the master of paradox proposed never did manage to attract even the smallest measure of popular support. One of the reasons was that while Diderot had a refined mind and a lively wit, he was incapable of writing a line of theatrical dialogue.

In my view, another handicap of Diderot's was the complete indifference he showed for the audience. Indeed, for Diderot the spectator does not exist. Intent as he is on his project of forging, in complete rationality, the figure of the actor, he ignores one small detail: that theatre is normally created for spectators as well. Further, his fixation with detachment, with emotional non-participation, has caused him to lose sight of the principal aim of theatre – entertainment. It is, of course, true that you can entertain yourself with the pure exercise of reason . . . but if you overdo it you risk boredom . . . and paranoia.

Every radical position leads to disaster: dialectics teach us how to make the most profitable use of the dynamic conflict of opposites. It is not true, as Diderot suggests, that it is impossible to feel emotion and to maintain a critical sense at the same time. It all depends on how well the individual has been trained to manage certain impulses, on his ability to attain a balance between the intellectual and the emotional, and to transform that balance into something not static but dynamic. In other words, in architectural terms, Diderot prefers a system of beams, fixed, immobile, with very little give; the players of Commedia dell'Arte prefer the overhead arch, with all the pressures and counter-pressures that are built into it. It is well known that at the first seismic tremor, the beams give way but the arch, miraculously, stays in place.

In addition, Diderot contradicts himself when, at the very opening of his *paradox*, he admits that an actor must be, above all else, an artist and must cultivate sensibility . . . and even goes so far as to talk about an emotional trance . . . but then, the love of paradox often leads to inconsistency. Personally, I find it happening to me one day, then the next, then the next . . .

Huguenot Terrorists

It is time to jettison another idea which once had wide currency, the picture of the strolling players as a gang of uncultured, uncouth, virtually illiterate comedians, probably pimps into the bargain. There are accounts that present them as acrobats and jugglers, eking out a day-to-day existence as best they might, held in contempt by honest, hard-working citizens, tolerated briefly at public fairs or in manor houses, only to be kicked out when the festivities were over, precisely as happens to whores at carnival's end.

This is nonsense. It is perfectly true that, leafing through certain chronicles on the life of the old players, you will come across some companies whose theatre had nothing to commend it. This, however, is not a widespread phenomenon. The theatre of Commedia, the style of work which made its mark on the history of drama throughout the whole of Europe for at least three centuries, was created by people endowed with a high level of culture, not to say modern tastes and education. That is not to deny, as we have already said, that in some cases they were willing to act in defence of privilege in a manner worthy of the worst of the medieval guilds. I would like to recount an anecdote that will, without further elaboration, illuminate the power and prestige that some companies enjoyed. It was written by one of the protagonists, and tells of the tragic journey of the famous Geloso company of Italian actors.* The King of France, Henry III, on his return from Poland, had attended in Venice a performance given by this company, and was extremely impressed. From Paris he sent a message, through his ambassador, to the Doge of Venice requesting the favour of having the Geloso company spend some time in his court. The republic of Venice organised the trip, put together a caravan composed of a substantial number of carriages and wagons, and the whole convoy made its way to Lyons, and from there to Paris. Halfway there, something unforeseen occurred; a gang of Huguenots (the Protestants of France) captured the entire company.

There is no need for me to go over the conflicts in the second half of the sixteenth century between the Catholics and the French Protestants, the most notorious incident of which was the massacre of the Eve of St Bartholomew (1572), when the Protestants were decimated. Some time after this slaughter, a gang of Huguenots set out to blackmail the king with what today we might call a terrorist outrage. They kidnapped the whole Geloso company and then sent a letter to the king in more or less the following terms: 'If you want your precious actors back in one piece, set free our brother Huguenots whom you are holding in the jails of France. Further pay up fifty thousand silver florins and ten thousand gold florins, otherwise we will only be able to let you have a bit of them . . . their heads.'

After negotiations which lasted two weeks, all the Huguenots were liberated, the money was paid over and the actors were able to continue on their way to Paris.

A contemporary commentator made the point: 'If he had been dealing with a Prime Minister, four of his Consuls and three Marshals of France, Henry III would not have hesitated to let them go to their deaths, ensuring only that

---

* *Commedia dell'arte* company founded by Isabella and Francesco Andreini.

High Mass, with suitable pomp, was celebrated in their memory.' However, the problem related to a group of actors who had come to France under the protection of the Most Serene Republic of Venice. In addition, the King had already issued invitations to the most important personages of the kingdom and to a group of foreign dignitaries for what was to be the biggest theatrical event of the century. He could not really present the heads of the company, neatly preserved in a sack of salt, so he had no choice but to give way. Could something similar happen today? Not really; the best you could hope for would be to see an actor elected President of the United States.

One other tragic event occurred to the same group on this unfortunate journey. On their way back from Paris to Italy, they stopped again at Lyons, and there Isabella Andreini, the great actress of the company, eight months pregnant, fell ill, had a miscarriage and died. The funeral, according to the chronicles of the time, outdid that of a queen, and no one was more astonished at the pomp of the burial ceremony than the actors who were accompanying her. Princes, poets and writers from all over Europe walked behind the coffin, laid out on a flower-laden carriage. During her life, Andreini had been, uniquely for a woman, accepted as a member of four Academies, and not for her beauty, but for her talents and the verve of her poetry. She was by no means the only cultured person among the actors of Italian comedy: the actors of that time counted among their number people who had the ability to write intelligent things in stylish prose. They were also on close terms with the finest minds of the age – Galileo Galilei (who wrote two Commedia scripts), the poet Ariosto, Pallavicini, several great architects and, just to round things off, Michelangelo and Raphael, another two great theatre lovers.

An Actor! Who Cares?

There is no denying that, just as there were some companies who flourished and enjoyed every respect and consideration, there were others who lived in virtual servitude. These unfortunates were looked on as the private property of their respective lords and masters, who were entitled to dispose of them as big football clubs today do with their players, except that the actors did not command a fat signing-on fee. Their treatment, even considering the conditions of the times, was extremely harsh. When an actor failed to respect the terms of his contract, even over a trifling detail, the grandee duke would have no second thoughts about throwing him into jail, without limit of time. His life was scarcely worth a second thought.

This is an interesting tale which illustrates the status of the actors. The King of France had heard people sing the praises of an elderly performer in the service of the Duke of Mantua, and decided that he would like to see him for himself in Paris. Unfortunately the actor in question was extremely ill, but the Duke ordered him to get out of bed and to prepare himself for departure. The palace doctor intervened and requested the Duke not to insist. 'His medical state is such that he could well die before reaching his destination.' The Duke would have no truck with such nonsense; 'I would sooner have him breathe his last than risk having the King of France think that I was unwilling to accord him the favour he solicited.' Even though in a fever, the actor was constrained to set off, and, exactly as the doctor had forecast, he died while crossing the St Bernard Pass. Courtesy had triumphed. The King of France was, no doubt, duly moved by the gesture of sublime sacrifice made by his generous vassal, the Duke. Generous with the life of an actor.

Masks not for Masking

Of all the elements which made up Commedia dell'Arte, masks are, if not the most essential, certainly the best known and most obvious. This piece of equipment is of such importance that it has come to represent, by itself, the entire theatrical apparatus employed by the Commedia characters and types, and it is even common to refer to these characters as 'masks'.

When we think about the mask, our mind jumps automatically to its natural context, Carnival. The carnival feast exists everywhere, in every time and place. I have been to many carnivals and have seen many others on film. I have even been to a carnival in China and recently went to a particularly fine one in the Asturias in Spain. At the origin of all of these carnivals there is invariably the celebration of an ancient rite, a mixture of magic and religion. Masks and, associated with them, the use of disguise date from the very dawn of human history.

Cave Men in Masks

One of the earliest pieces of evidence on the use of masks dates back to pre-historic times, to the walls of the cave 'des deux frères' on the French side of the Pyrenees. The painting, a hunting scene, has been drawn with astonishing skill and depicts a herd of wild goats grazing in a field. The group appears, at first sight, quite homogeneous, but, on closer inspection, it becomes clear that one of the goats has, instead of the cloven hoof, a man's legs and feet. And not four, but only two. The hands which can barely be seen from beneath the animal skin are gripping a taut bow and arrow. The creature is evidently a man, a hunter in disguise. On his face he has a goat's mask with horns and a beard, and the area from the shoulders to the small of the back is covered by a goat's skin. You could bet that he has smeared goat dung over himself to smother his own body odours.

There are two main reasons for this use of disguise. Firstly, as anthrolopogists explain, it serves to override taboos. Ancient peoples – the early Greeks are an example – believed that each animal was protected by a special divinity. With the use of disguise, however, it was possible to get round the vindictiveness of the god of the goat, who would undoubtedly have gone out of his way to make life a misery for any hunter who slaughtered one of his favourites, without the by-your-leave of a counter-taboo. The other, more down-to-earth, purpose was that once he had donned the disguise, the hunter could creep up on his prey without arousing suspicion. She-goats are notoriously superficial creatures and never take the trouble to examine the feet of their guests. He's got horns and smells like a goat? 'Come right in . . . must be one of us.' Feet are a secondary matter. In this way the hunter with a mask had every opportunity to wander up to the she-goat he fancied and, perhaps under the pretence of chatting her up, pick her up under his arm and out into the night without being noticed by the Daddy Goat. You know what the latter are like, what a primitive and possessive sense of family they still have, and how readily, with those great horns of theirs, they turn to acts of the most appalling violence.

This extreme zoomorphism, the transformation of oneself into an animal, plainly required a certain skill because it is never enough just to pull a mask over your nose or toss a smelly piece of animal skin over your shoulders. The real problem is to imitate the movements of the goat or whatever animal one is intent on capturing, and these movements vary according to the situation. The rite of dressing up in animals skins is linked to the culture of almost every race on earth.

The Mammuttones

I wonder if you have ever had the chance to see a documentary on the *mammuttones* of Sardinia? It is a very ancient ritual performance which can still be seen today in the centre of the North of the island. I was once privileged to be present. The *mammuttones* is a character of myth. Dressed in the skin of a goat or a black sheep, he has clusters of bells tied round his waist and along the full length of his leg and these make the eeriest and most alarming noises each time he moves. Over his face, he wears a black mask with protruding horns, suggesting a goat. The *mammuttones* never appears alone but in groups of five or ten, one of whom is selected as leader and establishes the rhythm and tempo of the dance. Their arrival announced by the beat of wooden clappers, the pack invades the village. The inhabitants flee, feigning terror, then reappear at the doors and windows of the houses. Meanwhile, the children of the place follow the *mammuttones* down to the piazza, where other animal-like masks, once again dressed in tanned skins and black dyes done up to resemble sheep and pigs, make their appearance. They dance together and leap wildly about producing terrifying guttural screams which are not, however, in any sense imitations of animal bleating, braying or bellowing.

The tale, or, more precisely, the myth that they recount, is now defective, reduced by time to a broken fragment of itself. This is hardly surprising; anthropologists assure us that these myths were, originally, sacred representations, that is, mysteries, dating back more than eighteen centuries.

Enter Dionysus

I once asked the curator of the anthropological museum in Sassari, in Sardinia, what a certain mask of obviously human appearance, with, moreover, light-coloured skin and aristocratic features was doing there in the midst of a group of animals. He replied that, in his view, that character had made his entrance at a later date with the arrival of the Phoenicians, or perhaps later still with the Attic Greeks, and that he represented a Phoenician deity or possibly even Dionysus himself.* Be that as it may, there can be no doubt that those ceremonies were linked to the fertility rites that every people organised, without fail, at the spring equinox and summer solstices and at the appointed date for the celebration of certain myths, like the Eleusian festivals among the Greeks.†

Dionysus in Thessalia

I once managed to attend a Thessalian mystery play performed by the shepherds of the region. The chorus was made up of pseudo-*mammuttones*, each attired in goat skins and horse-leather breeches. They too had collections of bells of various shapes and sizes round their waists and attached to their legs, the only difference being that, instead of goat masks, they covered their faces with horse masks. To be more precise, the mask had the form of a horse's face but without the skull. The bone had been removed and the skin treated in such a way as to make it shrunken and pliable, almost like the mythical masks of the Sileni, who escorted Dionysus at the primitive festivals.

On that occasion, the underlying sense of the myth was even more clear.

* A god of the fertility of nature who inspires poetry, music and drama.
† The Eleusian mysteries were the most famous of Greek religious ceremonies.

The central theme of the performance was the sacrifice of Dionysus who offered himself as captive to Pluto, the god of the underworld, who had snatched his sister, Koré, the spirit of spring. In exchange, he sought her return to earth for two-thirds of the year, to allow her to restore brightness, love and life to the whole of creation.

In the grand sweep of the spectacle, I recognised the child Dionysus in the arms of his mother Demeter, great goddess of the earth, the grim Pluto, god of the darkness, as well as an assortment of Sileni satyrs and bacchae, and later the fully grown Dionysus in the guise of a hermit. I also made out a scene in which a group of elders on a cart compelled the young men of the village to pull it and the women to push it. In the following scene the young men rebelled, succeeded in ousting the elders and in making other young men pull the vehicle. There was no change of role for the women, who were still condemned to push.

The closing scene, divided into two parts, presents the death and resurrection of the hermit Dionysus. First, the body is tossed into the mud, smeared with filth, then rolled in the slimy clay before being dipped in the animals' drinking trough. Water and mud restore life. In other versions of the ritual, Dionysus dies after being transformed into a goat.

Tragedy and Communion

To be more precise, his body is dismembered, pulled apart and devoured by all the participants in the rite. *Tragos* – the sacrifice of the goat, hence tragedy; that is, the rite of eating a god and drinking his blood, just as with Communion, which we still find in the mysteries celebrated by Catholics during Mass, in which Catholics feed on the body of Christ.

There are other legends which tell of a primitive rite expressed in a social art of unimaginable violence. Tribal unity, communion, was obtained in this way: at a pre-arranged moment in his leadership, the tribal chieftain was set upon by the entire community, and, during an official meeting, was literally torn limb from limb and devoured; thus through the dismembering of the leader the unity of the tribe was guaranteed.

There is, in my view, a lot to be said for the re-introduction of this usage in our own times. Instead of the familiar, boring collapse of governments at pre-arranged moments, with the equally familiar, and inevitable, spectacle of the re-emergence of the familiar faces in different ministries a few weeks later, we could, literally, make a meal of the outgoing Prime Minister.

To go back to the primitive rite, the tribal chiefs soon attempted to put an end to this somewhat inconvenient custom and substituted scapegoats. Goats for politicians, is that a fair swop?

Mask, rite, survival are the three constants of every primitive religion. Let us consider some examples of animal-design masks. One, from the island of Bali, has the face of a giant frog; another, from the Ganges in India is a monkey mask; there is another monkey mask, this time from Sri Lanka. Both have a hinged jawbone, which jerks with the movement of the chin. The lower jaw moves in time with the action the mouth when talking. There also exist masks of composite likenesses, made from the imaginary crossing of different animals or different species; paradoxical crossings, in other words.

Courtyard Masks

The mask of the Captain in Commedia dell'Arte is a mixture of a bloodhound, Neapolitan mastiff and man. He has many names: Spaventa, Matamoro, Dragonhead, Crocodile, to mention only a few. Similarly, the mask of Pantaloon or of the Magnifico becomes cockerel, turkey or hen and, in consequence, the gait and movements of the actor wearing these masks will imitate the mechanical and schizoid gestures of a hen. Another famous mask is the classical one of Harlequin, which is both cat and monkey. In certain cases, because of the evident similarity, it was called the Harlequin-Cat. The actor who dons this mask will proceed in a series of springs and jumps, lazily moving his arms and legs and occasionally leaping forward in a giant bound.

Almost all masks, then, including those of Commedia, refer to animals; in other words they are zoomorphic. To be more precise, they are taken from courtyard, domestic or tamed animals, so that, as we have seen, Harlequin is a mixture of cat and monkey, the Captain is the result of a cross between bloodhound and mastiff, while Pantaloon is born from the turkey and the cockerel, and so on down to Brighella, who is half dog and half cat and the Doctor who is pure pig.

The link with courtyard animals has a precise social significance, linked to the 'downstairs' society of that age. The 'downstairs' segment of society meant the servants, or those who made a precarious living attending to the wants of their betters. The 'upstairs' is always presented as a cross-section of human beings, and, as it happens, in Commedia dell'Arte the knights, lords and ladies never wear masks at all. The class orientation is beyond dispute: only those sections of society that did not exercise absolute power (doctors – universally regarded as scoundrelly quacks, shopkeepers – depicted as uncouth cheats, and those nobles who were penniless and down-at-heel) could be openly laughed at. No one dared cock a snook at the major nobility, at the leading merchants or at bankers. Anyone who tried was liable to be run out of town, with no more than a bloody nose to show for his exertions. It was only permissible, then, to make jokes at the expense of people and professions not to the liking of the nascent capitalist bourgeoisie who, at that time, controlled all culture, including the theatre. This society required its actors not only to treat particular themes, but even variations on these themes.

We know that the masks of Commedia dell'Arte have their more or less legitimate ancestry in the stock characters of Roman and Greek theatre. In its turn, it is known that Greek theatre has its roots in oriental theatre. There is, for example, a mask from Bali which is very similar to that of Pantaloon. It is the mask of an elderly man with the same look of dogged determination, the same sneer, the hollowed eyes, the bushy eyebrows and prominent forehead which give an air of importance. Then there is the monkeylike mask from India, with definite anthropomorphic connotations, which resembles the archaic masks of Harlequin. These similarities are sufficient to make clear the cultural transmigration from the Orient to the Mediterranean, from the ancient world to the world of Commedia dell'Arte.

In this context, I would like to draw attention to a further aspect of the subject. Many masks, from that of Harlequin to that of the Zanni, have on their forehead a kind of red stamp. A very similar sign can be seen on many oriental masks, perhaps under the form of a golden disk or of a coloured mark between the eyebrows. An instance of this last has been found on an Indian mask dating back almost a century, representing an individual from the lower classes, from the 'downstairs' society – a servant, in other words. Other masks indicate demonic figures, and sometimes even have a stone or a coloured crystal set in a swelling on the forehead. Evidently this is a kind of third eye, which allows the holy man, or demi-god or demon to see beyond the bodies of men and into the very depths of their being. The third eye can also be found in Chinese and some Japanese masks.

In most cases, this third eye serves to indicate the diabolic character of the mask. I have already pointed out how masks could, in their original form, serve to protect hunters from the force of a taboo, as well as camouflaging them as they crept up on the animal they were stalking. I would add that even Pan, the faun-like god who guarded the herbs, is, in his turn, a half-devil, half-animal creation. Harlequin himself, as I have already said, is a kind of faun-cum-demon, so much so that in the protuberance on his mask some experts claim to detect the remains of the broken horn of the Devil in the form of a goat. I have at home a Brighella mask which unmistakably carries the third eye. And let us not forget that the Egyptian god of death, Osiris, has on his head a disk of gold – the third eye once again – framed by two branches of palm, which produce the same plastic movement that we find in the mask of Harlequin. It may be no more than a coincidence, but it is worth thinking about.

Other personalities or types emerge, on the other hand, directly from aboriginal cultural forms, and recur both in carnival masks and in string and glove puppets.

Puppets

The early puppets did not wear masks in the genuine sense of the word, but their facial expression undoubtedly represented a grotesque characterisation not dissimilar to that of the masks themselves. I have a personal collection of old puppets that prove this point.

It has been pointed out that much of the mime and many of the gestures of the Commedia characters are closely related to the distinctive movement of puppets. There is no doubt about this, and I have become aware of it myself when executing one specific style of walk with swift about-turns where the sudden twist of the leg in the opposite direction is a classical imitation of the puppet twirl. The same could be said for the attempt to give an almost wooden quality to certain gestures, like falling and rising while maintaining a jerky movement of the head and shoulders. Does this not bring to mind Totò, the great Italian comic actor?* Totò invented an extraordinary mask from a reworking of various Commedia dell'Arte prototypes, and also dedicated much study to the disarticulated movements of puppets. From these elements he forged sequences of dance step actions, at times mincing about, at times leaping forward with giant strides, all the while flailing his arms in the air and contorting the whole upper part of his body into bizarre formations, to irresistible comic effect.

It is time to move on from the origin of masks to their use, and here we can make reference to the documents and texts in our possession. There is a great wealth of images preserved on Greek urns, and these permit us to formulate certain hypotheses on the function and role of masks. Let us begin with a consideration of one particular mask, which merits special attention not only because of its structure, but also because it was produced by the greatest mask maker of the Italian tradition, Sartori of Padua. The grotesque sneer is identical to what we find in characters from the Atellan farces,† one of the forms of farce from Roman times, but there are images resembling it even before that on Attic vases of the fourth century containing scenes from the comedies of Aristophanes. This is the character who delivers the harangues, the word-spewing troublemaker.

* Totò (1898–1967) a famous Neapolitan comedian, variety star and actor.

† The Atellan farces were the earliest form of Roman farces which used masks for stock characters.

Mask as Megaphone

The first task is to establish the reasons for the forms and designs of the masks. The mouth constitutes a kind of megaphone, an implement which, plainly, amplifies the voice. It is worthwhile recalling the sheer scale of the Greek theatre, which could hold up to 20,000 spectators. The voice was projected and amplified thanks to the funnel form of the open mouth. All masks are constructed in such a way that every form contributes, on the inside (by means of cavities which on the outside appear to be bumps), to the production of special, varied sound vibrations. I could show you a Zanni mask in which the megaphone is created by a mechanism which holds the lip in a raised position. If I put it on, thanks to the special opening which holds the frame a good three inches away from the mouth, the volume of my vocal output is increased twofold, especially in the deeper tones, because, to establish his personality, this character requires low, sinister tones.

Every mask is a musical instrument with its own particular echo chamber. With access to different devices, it is possible to manage a huge range of tones, from the falsetto to the sibilant, and, obviously, to link them to different physical types, from the Zanni to Pulcinella.

The Harlequin Faun

Take the original mask of the Zanni, forerunner of Harlequin. It is a mask from the late sixteenth century, unlike the other which dates from the mid-seventeenth century, and this early Harlequin mask too is stronger in the production of bass tones of the general level of animal grunts, because the early Harlequin was a more oppressive character and an impetuous savage. He made extravagant leaps and bounds, but, even though acrobatic, never danced those balletic steps that will be identified with the later Harlequin-Cat of the eighteenth century.

Big Mouth, Aristophanes' Agitator

I must return for a moment to the caricature of the haranguer, for whom there does not exist a precise name in English (or Italian). The Greek word indicates the charlatan *par excellence*, the one who spews out high-speed diatribes. This character was employed in the theatre of Aristophanes as a 'breath-drawer' – in other words, his appearance allowed the other actors to draw breath.

He came on stage at the interval, insulting the audience, telling lies and chattering at top speed – a veritable Big Mouth. That is more or less the correct term for this character, who has his equivalent in the Roman farces.

The character from Commedia dell'Arte who most resembles Big Mouth is the Zanni; at times Pulcinella assumes the same role.

Big Mouth was brought on to upset the audience. In *The Birds*, for example, there is a monologue in which the haranguer appears on stage, starts off cajoling the audience but then gradually overturns the situation and ends up yelling at them, accusing them of being ignorant, empty-headed and incapable of grasping even the most obvious satiric allusions. Then he notices that someone is laughing, so he launches into a routine on people who laugh too loudly in all the wrong places. He ridicules people who have come to the theatre with a slave dressed up as a woman (slaves were normally forbidden admission to theatre); what's the slave for, he wonders, if not to explain all the satirical barbs to the slow-witted owner?

The value of these harangues lay not so much in the written script as in the speed of delivery, in the rhythm and timing with which the routine was performed. Obviously the mask, with its brazen aggressiveness, helped a great deal.

Masks Hurt

Incredible as it may seem, there is for me something magical in the fact that wearing a mask, after an initial moment of awkwardness, allows one to see more clearly and to act with greater liberty than with the face completely uncovered. I would like to remind you of an anecdote. Marcello Moretti, the father-figure of all the Harlequins of the last half-century, for years steadfastly refused to wear a mask. He daubed his face with a solution of black make-up with a wax base – I remember it well from my own early days starting out at the Piccolo Teatro in Milan. He had two reasons for refusing to don the mask, and, having personally undergone the same experiences, I have a lot of sympathy. Firstly, wearing a mask can, in an actor, induce anxiety deriving not so much from the use itself as from the fact that the mask restricts both the visual field and the acoustic-vocal range. Your own voice seems to be singing at you, stunning you, ringing in your ears and, until you master it, you cannot control your breathing. The mask feels like an encumbrance and can easily transform itself into a torture chamber. It is not too much to say that it removes your powers of concentration.

That is the first reason. Then there is a second which is mythical, magical almost. A singular sensation afflicts you when you take off the mask – this, at least, is my reaction – the fear that part of your face has remained stuck to it, or the fear that the face has gone with the mask. When you remove the mask after having it on for two or three hours, you have the impression of annihilating yourself. Strange as it may seem, after ten years or so, when

Moretti was totally on top of the requirements of the mask, he was unable to perform without one. He made every attempt to play other roles in other works, but was driven to the verge of despair because he was convinced that his face had lost the necessary pliability. I will tell you why.

Hands Off the Mask

For a start, the mask imposes a particular obligation: it cannot be touched. Once you lay a hand on that thing drawn over your face, it vanishes, or appears contaminated or nauseating. Seeing hands on a mask is damaging and unbearable. You cannot permit it. While you speak, the gestures you make seem to have become amplified. It is the value of the body which decides the weight of the mask. In other words, if I take a step forward, the mask takes on a certain value but if, all of a sudden, I change position and walk at a different pace, the mask's value changes. Underneath, my face remains impassive and expressionless because it is the body which gives all expression to the mask. This habit, when continued for hour after hour, year after year, destroys the mobility of the facial muscles. Any contractions are of a completely different type from those which express theatricality. Never allow your native agility, your comic impulse to be buried under the excessive use of the mask. I address this remark above all to those young people who tend to use masks without discernment and reason. Every so often, it is necessary to toss the mask aside and forget all about it.

Since we mentioned Moretti, I would like to digress a little so as to be able to provide some kind of answer to those who, on many occasions, ask me for my opinion on Giorgio Strehler's* famous production of *Arlecchino, Servant of Two Masters* by Goldoni.† The objection I most commonly hear advanced about this work is that it has little of the savour of improvisation, but rather that it goes like clockwork, like a comic mechanism with pre-programmed timing, or alternatively that it has too much precision and too little liberty of imagination. These are matters people believe to be not in keeping with the reading of Commedia dell'Arte most congenial to me.

First of all I would like to say that to be dealing with a piece of comic mechanism which does go like clockwork is already quite extraordinary, and by no means an everyday matter. Before being too specific, however, I would have to preface my remarks by saying that the Commedia dell'Arte with

* Strehler was the actor-manager of I Picolo Teatro in Milan.

† Carlo Goldoni (1707–1793), Venetian playwright whose reforms ended the era of Commedia dell'Arte.

which Strehler occupied himself was Goldoni's, in other words that late-eighteenth-century model which bore the marks of the comings and goings of two centuries, from 1580 to 1780. In the early stages, there had been an exodus towards France, with a particularly happy exercise in cross-breeding with French popular culture, and even with that vein of the more learned culture inspired by Rabelais and the *fabliaux*.* In the first half of the seventeenth century, several of these companies made their way back to Italy. The return had a stimulating effect, not least because certain of these comic actors had gained considerable notoriety. A transfusion of fresh blood was secured by the encounter with Neapolitan companies, who had prospered in the meantime as a consequence of the success of *opera buffa*.† This continual to-ing and fro-ing was the mainspring of the process of permanent renewal of Commedia dell'Arte, and of that exceptional longevity which is without parallel in the history of theatre of any age.

Goldoni, too, had a go at transmigration, but the results were not exactly encouraging. It was Voltaire‡ who insisted that he give up his theatre in Venice and move to Paris. Voltaire had an enormous regard for Goldoni, whom he considered the only man of theatre worthy of comparison with Molière.§ The invitation had tragic consequences, because after the first moments of euphoria, applause and compliments, Goldoni was abandoned and left to rot . . . not unlike some less illustrious pensioners of today.

Any discussion of Goldoni and his view of Commedia dell'Arte must start from the premise that the author of *Arlecchino, Servant of Two Masters* was a man strongly linked, in modern terms, to his own times. Those times were marked by the new mercantile culture, which meant that the ledger books, no matter how crooked, had always to appear in order. His purpose was to impose order on the chaos of the actors' handbooks of outline-plots and to rid the theatre of an ever-present crudeness, or, put more simply, his purpose was to implement a programme of reform. The reform he had in mind could not be merely structural but must also be moral and political. Goldoni believed in the entrepreneurial class of his time and had no intention of denigrating them by any form of satire, even if, at a later stage, in a mood of disappointment if not rage, he wrote some works in which he fulminated against the acquisitive bourgeoisie he had come to view as cynical and mean-minded.

* *Fabliaux*: French medieval verse tales, mocking, anticlerical, often misogynist in tone.
† Comic opera.
‡ Voltaire (1694–1778), poet, historian, philosopher, dramatist.
§ Molière (1622–1673), great comic dramatist, creator of French comedy.

28

Giorgio Strehler openly faced Goldoni's early ideological position, and, rightly, attempted neither to disguise nor distort it. Goldoni's Harlequin, unlike those created by Martinelli (1585) or by Biancolelli (from 1627 onwards) is something of a fiend, all cunning and pliability, but quite free of all trace of any brutal, obscene or disturbing inner turmoil. Needless to say, I personally prefer the first two but I have no hesitation in saying that for those of us who work in theatre, Strehler's production of *Arlecchino, Servant of Two Masters* has been an object-lesson in directing as well as in the use of rhythm, of the cadences of comedy and, above all, of style in the staging of a play. Strehler worked on it with enormous enthusiasm and a sense of fun; he constructed and reconstructed, assembled and dismantled with that stubbornness which is his alone and, perhaps for the only time in his career, collaborated with his cast, leaving them considerable scope.

Body as Frame for the Mask

We must turn to analysing the mime as back-up to the mask. It is all a question of the particular style of gesture imposed by the mask: the action and movement of the body are continually all of a piece and almost always go beyond the swaying of the shoulders. Why? Because the whole body acts as a frame for the mask and transforms its inertness. There are gestures which, by a variation of rhythm and dimension, modify the significance and value of the mask itself. It is exhausting to perform for and with a mask, because you are obliged to spin round continually with the external part of the neck and to execute rapid turns – left right, up down – to the point of producing the effect of animal-like aggression. For this reason, when wearing a mask, a specific choice of rhythm of word and content cannot be avoided. It is essential to put yourself through this type of exercise until you attain a near-natural roundness.

Matching Trade and Gesture

The question is – what gives rise to the technique that produces these movements? Are they merely random or mechanical sequences, or even arbitrary choices? Let us consider one aspect of the problem: Plekhanov* believed that the style of gesture of every people derives from its relationship with the need to survive. A very great researcher, a Russian anthropologist who was a contemporary of Lenin's, a close friend of such artists as Meyerhold and Mayakovsky, Plekhanov had, from his studies into the

* Georgi Valentinovich Plekhanov (1857–1918), Russian Marxist philosopher, author of *Art & Social Life.*

gestures of hundreds of different peoples, discovered that the rhythm and timing of the essential acts in the performance of jobs or trades indispensable for survival determine the general contours of human behaviour. They are responsible for the general attitude which is then applied in other areas that could be considered accessory to life, such as dancing, singing, playing. All these activities are linked by the style in which they are conducted to the basic occupation practised to earn a livelihood. In this context, the dance of the rope-spinners in Sicily is of some interest.

Until a few years ago, the Syracuse rope-spinners used to work inside enormous caves when twining the strands of the cables used for mooring boats, since the constant climate prevented the material from undergoing alteration. The spinners would line up, five, six or seven of them on either side, depending on the strength the rope was to have. One of them would crouch down in the middle with a drum to beat out the time and the rhythm. To make sure there were no knots, they had to wind the strands together, pass them one under the other and then, with five on either side, stretch the cord taut. The whole process was accompanied by a chant which the spinners sang so as to keep in time with each other. It would be more precise to talk about alternating intonations rather than a choral chant as such. The verse ran:

> Sciuri, sciuri, sciurite tuttu l'anno*
> Il su mi . . .
> Sunnu iunnu a, ghenna iunnu e . . .

The last line replaces the order to pull all together. The order of movements was then more or less as follows: one, two, three – turn, raise the arms and twist – one, two, three – wait till the strand is passed along and wind it in – and so on. It is a step similar to the tarantella and many other dances of southern Italy and Sicily, all based on the non-stop movement of the pelvis and the back of the leg.

Sing as You Row

The most explicit link between dance and work is undoubtedly a song that accompanies the rowing movement of the inhabitants of the lower Lagoon – obviously I am referring to the vicinity of Venice. In the lower Lagoon towards Polesine or in the stretch of water near Grado where the water can be as shallow as a few feet in depth, they use a special type of boat with a long hull and low sides. Normally it takes three or four people, using long poles, to row

* 'Flowers, flowers, flower all year long . . .'

it. The boatsmen stick the poles on the bottom of the Lagoon, and propel the boat forward: one, two, three – out, up, down, push – one, two and so on.

These rhythms and exclamations are indispensable if the rowers are to stay on their feet. If only two people are rowing and one makes a mistimed move, the boat, which is extremely light, will capsize. The men row standing up, precariously balanced, and need to keep in time by making synchronised movements beaten out by the rhythm of a song.

Let us take as an example a famous song with the title 'Canto de Barca de'Stciopo'. The title refers to a type of boat (*Stciopo*) whose name was derived from the firearm used in hunting ducks. The weapon, the culverin, was loaded with nails, so it was possible to strike whole flocks of ducks in the water. In other words, the *stciopo* was a very light craft that could move silently over the water to the spot where the fowl were gathered. Here is the song:

> E mi me ne so' andao
> dove che feva i goti
> i jogando bele done ed altri zijoghi
> E mi me ne so' andao . . .

(I sailed off to the spot where they made glasses, and where the beautiful women and others played different games.)

It continues in the same rhythm. The first verse gives the theme which is then developed with its account of the journey through the various islands of the Venetian Lagoon, from Burano to Murano and on to Torcello etc. It is the first line which interests us. 'E mi me ne so' andao.' Note one detail – E mi. Like all the other lines, it begins with a vowel and not with a consonant, permitting an intake of breath. There is an inflection of the voice and a lowering of tone. Why? In this way, the rower has the abdomen compressed, forced as he is to bend forward while pushing the pole against the sea bed. The lowering of tone is due to the reduction to the minimum of his vocal power.

> E mi me ne so' andao. . . . *then break*
> (*Stands upright*)
> Dove che fe. . . . *no further obstacles, the move is complete*
> Dove che feva i goti. . . . *release of maximum pitch*
> I jogando. . . . *once again starts with a vowel, because needs to draw breath*
> I jogando bele done ed altri zijoghi . . .

No need to labour the point that each time he takes the strain and has not much breath, he lowers the note, while when he raises the pole he draws breath and raises the voice. Let us look at the gesture: one, raise the pole, lower into the water, push, change – one, two, three, four – breathe – raise again, lower, push – one, two, one, two – move to the right, pull out the pole. . . . Through a series of variations, the rowing motion is transformed into a dance. And there is another interesting fact – the metre, with its employment of the septenarius.*

Oarsmen Imitating Poetic Metre

This is no other than the classical septenarius which we find in the *strambotto*† or in the *contrasto*‡ of the earliest Italian poetry, so the question immediately poses itself – who was the first to employ this metre? Was it the oarsmen or the poets? The poets, maybe? So one fine day the oarsmen cried out in unison – 'What a splendid metre! Let us invent a style of rowing that will allow us to plough the seas, singing and rowing in time to the rhythm of the septenarius! It cannot be done with the ordinary oars, with us seated in twos, so why don't we all move to the Lagoon, where punting along causes no difficulties. Poetry before all else!' Maybe it did happen that way.

I could spend any amount of time illustrating the various forms which derive from the septenarius, the hendecasyllable, the octosyllable, the *strambotto*. All of them are metres which are, amazingly enough, to be found among song styles and reflected in work movements. To find confirmation, consider the kinds of chant which accompany rowing or the threshing of wheat, or indeed the various means of keeping time while hauling a net ashore. In all cases, different forms of movement and activity are involved.

Work – with Style

In 1977, I was invited to a conference in Zante on the theme of culture and popular art in the Mediterranean. Several well-known European experts in the field of popular culture were in attendance. I planned to speak about my own experiences, and was struck by the number of speeches based on the work of Plekhanov given by Turks, Greeks, Romanians and Bulgarians. All concentrated on the value of dance as a ritual instrument in peasant labour, in craft-work and in the small, grand gestures of weaving. The problem of the application of a style of a specific manner of harvesting wheat and other cereals was also discussed.

It was as though the gestures, considered as a live expression of human

---

* A Latin verse of seven feet.
† A satirical poem.
‡ Poetic dialogue.

need, respected the economic principle of the 'golden mean'. A man at work expending energy has to produce the maximum result with the minimum effort, otherwise he will burn himself out. In this way, balance, which is a system of compensating forces, determines both in individual and even more so in collective actions the optimum value of gestures used as a visual symbol of what is being undertaken. They operate from the standpoint of other people – which is a way of saying that they assume the role of other people.

A worthwhile example is provided by the oarsmen who help each other by a process of symbolic interaction. The five on one side intone a rhymed chant whose purpose is to encourage the others and avoid capsizing the boat, which would have disadvantages on both sides. This system of interaction, characterised by cadenced movement and vocal intonations, constitutes a sort of dance regulated by ritual forms.

As a boy, I learned the movement of cutting the grass with a scythe. At the beginning it seemed easy, so I ended up cutting my foot. For anyone who knows the trade, the movement is executed by changing balance during the work. The trick is to shift position and support, to find balance and then go off-balance in the course of a swinging action, with one hand pushing on the rest and the other pulling the handle. If you do not manage this level action, as I failed to do, one foot will get stuck making you trip, with the risk of bringing the blade down on the other. It is not merely a question of rhythm and timing; the half-fall forward of the body produces the pressure necessary to give the blade that gliding, cutting action. The movement comes not so much from the arms as from the hips and from a back push of the legs. If all the power came from the circular movement of the arms, there would be a risk of breaking them after a time from sheer fatigue. The whole body must play its part by a continual curving action, as though in a dance.

While in Zante, I attended an exhibition of dancers from the Cyclades who began with a silent mime based on the rhythms of wheat-cutting, and progressively transformed those movements into dance steps. So, how should those of us who work in theatre, with our everyday gestures, go about rediscovering traditions which suggest harmonious movements suitable for dance? None of us rows across the Lagoon or cuts wheat in the Cyclades, so we do not have that advantage in a search for gestures and rhythms with a base in tradition. Where are we to locate the origins of our system of gestures?

Making the Moves (Gesture – as Extra)
A brief preamble to what follows: you have no idea of the disasters that can ensue when you are surrounded by a group of mime artists and have to produce a show which makes use of mime on a large scale. I was invited to put

on a work for La Scala, which would later go on tour to Rome, involving thirty-two mime performers who were all graduates of the Piccolo Teatro school in Milan and of various other schools in Italy and elsewhere. The thirty-two had been hand-picked from a huge number of candidates all trained in the techniques of classical mime.

When it came to actually performing, they had no idea where to put their hands, their feet, their arms or even of how to move in a broadly acceptable way. They jerked around the place like a spluttering engine. There were some who seemed to topple over as they walked, throwing their body ahead of their legs and giving the impression of being permanently on the verge of collapse, while others simply flopped on their bottoms. Some were incapable of bending their legs, so one leg remained continually stretched out in the style of an ostrich which has gone rigid at the knee, and others again seemed to droop at every limb, or else they slouched, skidded or walked as though they were under water or had a gale-force wind in their faces.

Decroux, the great French master of mime, has a display of different styles of walk which lasts for no less than three-quarters of an hour. Each one of us has an individual gait. I am aware that I have a very unusual way of walking, a cross between a horse and a flamingo. Everybody should get to know their own walk and basic gestures, not only to correct them, but also to capitalise on any which are potentially valuable.

In the situation in which I found myself with that group of young performers, the hardest part was to get each of them to become aware of their individual style of movement and gesticulation so as to be able to modify or emphasise it to the best effect.

See no Gestures, Or the Side Salad

Once I was giving a lecture at a conference on the relationship between audience and production. There had been a whole host of speeches so when it came to my turn I decided to improvise and went on to the platform and gave imitations of all the speakers who had preceded me. For some of the caricatures I simply used mimicry, for others various kinds of *grammelot*.* I showed up the varying peculiarities and all the different ways of pointing fingers, waving arms, leaning forward with head and shoulders. One man sawed the air with broad strokes, another built up piles of odd-shaped volumes; there was yet another who fought out a private duel with one hand, only to stop suddenly and flutter the other about, finally free and at peace.

* A method of producing the semblance of a given language without adopting real or identifiable words from that language.

The odd thing was that none of the caricatures was recognised by the subject himself! 'No, I don't do that!' All the rest immediately chorused: 'It's you to a T!' They grinned while the victim looked around in amazement. The fact is that we are blithely unaware of the gestures we ourselves produce. We read our words, we are careful about our pronunciation, and would be enraged with ourselves if we were to split an infinitive or misplace a pronoun. On the other hand, we are indifferent about the gestures that accompany our speech, even though they could be every bit as coarse, inelegant or uncouth. How is this to be explained? What makes us believe that gestures and movements are the side dish, the salad, while the word is the main course, the meat? This notion has been inculcated into us all since our schooldays. Ever since nursery, the pronunciation of each and every word will have been corrected, but no one will ever have bothered about the accompanying gesture. By the same token, gestures have been relegated to a secondary position in the actor's vocabulary.

Gesture and Gesticulation

Learning how to move the limbs and the trunk with unaffected elegance and awareness ought to be the first element in the training of the actor. An apprenticeship in the movement-related techniques of breathing, right up to performance in acrobatics, ought to be the central plank of our profession, even more than voice training. I have seen several highly rated directors break down in tears when confronted with the awkwardness of some actors who were simply incapable of controlling their gestures. There are actors who try to hide their sheer lack of naturalness by sticking their hands in their pockets, by fidgeting with their cuffs and lapels or by continually smoothing their hair.

There are actors, like the Americans of one particular school, who, in order to avoid the problems of on-stage awkwardness, have created a kind of mimic-gestural repertoire of a level which is, in my view, positively subnormal. Obviously I have in mind the products of some of the great schools like the Actors Studio, where gestures are fired out in a sequence of paranoiac twitches, all too often bereft of any connection with real life and intended to display purely abstract virtuoso flourishes. You know the kind of thing I mean: rubbing eyes and noses, scratching heads with greater or lesser vehemence, sticking hands into pockets to incredible depths, and so on.

The real problem concerns the matching of the gesture to the mask. What is the purpose of the mask? To magnify and simultaneously give the essence of the character. It obliges you to widen and develop your gestures, which must not be arbitrary if you want the audience, your immediate mirror, to

35

follow you and to grasp the flow of the piece, especially when dealing with a gag, a routine or a comic situation.

Concerto for Squeaks, Coughs and Chocolate Wrappers

In comic theatre, one problem I would like to touch on is the programmed or 'telegraphed' laugh. The phrase is common in theatre. To telegraph gags or, on the contrary, avoid telegraphing them means to reveal or avoid revealing the comedy of a situation before time. It is a way of masking the point of arrival or, on the contrary, preparing people for the final comic solution.

All this is preliminary to the fact that it is impossible to articulate grimaces, make funny faces or give winks when you wear a mask. The mask does not allow any facial mobility, so you must be content with the one identical fixed sneer, but, as we have already said, with the assistance of the gesticulation of the whole body, you can bring mobility and expressiveness to the mask.

First Lecture on Synthesis

The mask, in bringing the movement of the whole body into play, imposes the need to identify the essence of a gesture, because if, in order to heighten a particular effect, a multiplicity of senseless gestures are performed, the result is to destroy the value of the original gesture itself. It is crucial to select gestures in full awareness of the choice. The movement, the general attitude, the positioning of the body must be duly pondered and reduced to the bare essential.

Finally we arrive at the topic which underlies both Commedia dell'Arte, and, strange as it may appear, a substantial part of oriental theatre. The moment anyone puts on a mask to play a stock character in Commedia, he realises that the entire performance hinges on the pelvis, the source of all movements. For instance, the figure of the old man is characterised by the springy forward stretch of the pelvis. The eighteenth-century (supposedly classical) Harlequin moves with his belly protruding to the front and his buttocks to the rear, and so is forced into a position which imposes a continual, bent double dance with occasional hops.

Pelvis – Centre of the Universe

The early or seventeenth-century Harlequin, on the other hand, positions himself on his trunk, moving 'off-balance' with a hip movement which is, however, walked, not danced.

This hip movement has, however unlikely it may seem, an equivalent in eastern theatre. In Japan, *kaza*, for example, means 'hip' or 'stomach' and *kabuki* is a composite expression which stands for 'theatre of the hip'. The same definition could be applied to the theatre of Commedia dell'Arte – theatre of the hip, theatre of a unified approach, linked to this essential fulcrum. Only continual exercise with the mask can convince us of the truth of this definition.

This implement not only imposes a quest for the essential but also forces the wearer to eschew all form of mystification. Bernard Shaw once said: 'Give a hypocrite a mask to wear, and he will be rendered incapable of further lying.' Perfect; the mask obliges people to tell the truth. Why? Because the mask cancels the prime element – the face, with all the expressions we formulate and employ with such ease – used to give expression to any form of mystification. When the face is removed from the equation, people are compelled to speak in a language free of formulas and of fixed stereotypes – in the language of the hands, of the arms and of the fingers. No one is accustomed to lying with their body. We never bother to check the gestures we make while speaking. If you pay sufficient heed, and if you know the language, you are bound to notice that many people say one thing with their mouth which they contradict with their hands and arms, thereby revealing themselves as liars. In other words, Bernard Shaw hit the nail on the head. The use of a mask is an extraordinarily effective means of checking your own gestures. A word of warning, however; never place yourself in front of a mirror, because the results are likely to be unfortunate. To gain a reflection of your own gestures, it is better to use your imagination, and to bear in mind that the best mirror of all is an audience.

No Cheetah Dance – No Revolution

We have left suspended Plekhanov's thesis on the relationship between gestural movement and expressiveness, between craft and survival. I wanted to emphasise the particular value these origins assume even in our memory.

Once while I was in Cuba I attended a festival of African cinema, and saw a splendid documentary on the process, from struggle to final liberation, through which an enslaved people has to pass to attain consciousness of their situation. The title was *Angola and the Consciousness of a Subject People*, and it portrayed the extent to which this nation, who had been under Portuguese domination for more than three centuries, had lost, with the passing of time, all links with their own history and origins. At the opening of the colonial era, Catholic priests had abolished all the native rites and feasts and had introduced Catholic ceremonial without so much as attempting to adapt them to local rites and myths. Further, they suppressed – and here they showed themselves extemely intelligent – all tribal festivities that had, according to a European way of thinking, no connection with religion. They did away with puberty initiation dances, village hunting celebrations, and the drums and other musical instruments previously used in the feasts of propitiation for an end to drought or for a plentiful harvest.

The Portuguese colonists succeeded in making the Angolans, to quote the Sicilian poet Buttita, 'a people without voice, without eyes, without movement', in other words a dead people. They were on their knees to the point that even had they had the will, they would not have known how to rebel. In consequence, the first organisers of the rebellion, a group of European-educated Angolans, understood that what was lacking in their countrymen was a relationship with their own times, their own actions and their own origins. A people with no culture has no dignity of its own, takes no interest in its own roots, and in consequence has no desire to liberate itself, much less to struggle.

The first move of this group of educated Angolans was to attempt to revive primordial ritual, and one of these concerned the preparations for the cheetah hunt. As everyone knows, the cheetah is the fastest beast of prey on earth and can even chase monkeys on the branches of trees, as was illustrated in this documentary. It also showed a mime sequence executed in the village clearing. All the characteristics of the cheetah, its speed, courage and swiftness are pressed into service to give colour and emphasis to the initiation dance a man is engaged on. The aim is not only to prepare him for the appallingly risky enterprise he will have to face, but also to enable him as an individual, through timing, rhythm and, above all, the aggressive impulse, to increase his capacity to harmonise his own movements. The body acquires awareness, then, through the rites of movement, becomes an expression of balance, of invention and of harmony. All these elements are part of the rites taught to the boys, over time, by old hunters who live like hermits in the savannah. Outlawed by civilisation, they return like masters to a subjugated and dying community. Gradually, by waving spears, crawling on the ground, leaping on to branches of trees, plunging into rivers, they re-establish links with their own ancient styles of movement.

On the surface, all this has nothing to do with a war fought out with machine-guns, anti-tank devices, bazookas, 20 mm cannons and the like, but the leaders of the Angolan resistance knew that if they were to form reliable cadres, their first task was to rediscover the keys that would unlock their own courage and identity. Now, we who live in this modern technological society, what have we managed to save in the way of gesture?

Marble and Chorality

The last expressions used as part of day-to-day living that I have managed to observe were – and this is astonishing in itself – in the marble quarries in Massa and Carrara where Michelangelo, Donatello and Bernini came to extract the marble they used for their masterpieces.

The marble is removed in various stages. Firstly, the marble is sawn out of the quarry with a steel wire. Once the block, which is of considerable size, is cut free, the workers start sliding it down into the valley, but before the transport operation can get under way, they have to file off all unusable or superfluous parts so that the boulder is reduced to a geometrical shape. Some of these blocks are of such dimensions that they would dwarf an average sized theatre. The blocks slide down the mountainside on rails, and are held in place by winches.

Some quarries are, on account of the roughness of the terrain, inaccessible to machinery even today, so there is no alternative to the time-honoured methods with ropes and manually operated levers. Hundreds of men have to be employed, some laying down the poles on the mountainside, others hauling ropes attached to the huge marble block and letting them out slowly as it slides over the runners on its way down the slope. Plainly this work requires careful coordination of the movements, which have to be executed with speed, safety and litheness. It would be a catastrophe if one team were to slip up. Many days' work would be lost and a disaster of incalculable dimensions could result.

The task of imparting the exact rhythms of the operation is entrusted to a foreman, who takes up position on foot on top of the marble and releases the instruction in a sequence of articulated shouts, each with its own rhythm and volume, just like the syncopation and breaks of a song. The sounds indicate the movements which the different groups must execute one by one.

This chant, vaguely similar to the cries of sailors as they unfurl the sails, has its origins among the mountain people, and can be traced further back to Upper Lombardy.

Prefabricated Cathedrals

From the early Middle Ages, entire populations of stone cutters and sculptors made their way to Carrara and Massa. They were known as *comacini* from the Latin *cum macina*, that is workers who had organised and trained themselves to carry out building works with machines, be they mobile towers, adjustable centring devices, cranes or manoeuvrable platforms. The *comacini* came from the North of Italy and took up residence for the entire period necessary for the construction of a particular edifice. The columns, the capitals, the thousand and one pieces of stonework needed for the design of a church or palace were cut and worked entirely on site in the quarry so as to

39

avoid the problems of transport which were, in the Middle Ages, a major problem. A block of stone of the dimensions needed for a capital would weigh twice as much as the finished article and could easily split during the sculpting. In other words, the whole team of workers, stone cutters and sculptors had to stay near the quarry, and the construction would be carried out bit by bit in the same place. Once completed, the work would be transported by sea and mounted in the assigned spot.

The area was for centuries a melting pot of languages and dialects, and these people maintained, generation after generation, the nuances which differentiated them, to give us the linguistic archipelago which the Massa-Carrara zone is even today. The guttural sounds belong to the medieval dialects of the Upper Po valley, and the traditions, the rhythms and the sounds are equally ancient. The choral effect is a consequence of the harmony of questions and answers which the two groups exchanged while placing the runners and letting out the ropes.

A Chant to keep the Feet in One Piece

The workers whose task was to drive in the stakes in Venice had a similar chant. Everyone must know that Venice is built, for the most part, on artificial islands made up of wooden stakes driven into the bed of the lagoon, and that these are still, for thermic considerations, used in preference to steel pylons in reinforced concrete. Machines are now used, but once they had to get four or five men to drive in the stakes. They used enormous trunks which were raised up and then brought down with great force. The rhythm and the timing was fixed by one man who stood outside the group and gave chanted orders. The trunk had a series of handles in its side, and the singer coordinated the movements and kept the workers in time, since any loss of rhythm would have caused difficulties, especially to the feet.

> E jeveremo la bandiera bianca (We will raise the white banner)
>   ehhee . . . bang
> bandiera bianca e segno di pace (White banner is a sign of peace)
>   ehhee . . . bang

Obviously the 'bang' refers to the thud of the pole, while the 'ehhee' is the chanted reply of the workers. It is the fall.

A Word against Facile Classifications

Many more examples could be presented, and Plekhanov himself uncovered a case concerning the oarsmen of the Nile estuary, which had many analogies with the rowers in the Venetian Lagoon. The Nile oarsmen employ a rhythmical motion and accompany themselves with songs and scansions very similar to those in use around Venice. Where the environment is similar, the gestures will be similar and so too will be the means of producing the rhythms and the accompanying song.

The transcription of the working gesture into dance or mimic gesture comes naturally, and culture and the historical period have their weight too. Clearly any attempt to match up similarity of gesture with similarity of environment *tout court* would produce false and facile answers.

Many times gestures have been modified for reasons that have nothing at all to do with the urge for survival, and in some cases it is simply impossible to rediscover the original style of gesture. Over the course of time, as a result of the competition of gestures copied from other ethnic groups, the dominant or the subject peoples (see the impact of black music and dance on American culture) alter their gestures and movements and transform their own physical language into something unpredictable and unclassifiable.

Attached to the Production Line

What is our problem today? It lies in the difficulty of unearthing anywhere around us live expressions and natural gestures representative of a primitive state long since crushed by a fixed and stereotyped system of life. This system of life does no more than produce moments of dull silence alternating with deafening din, and a deadening of all the creative faculties. And yet, even in the midst of all this senseless clamour, some people have managed to express with art the joy and anger of their own times. It makes good sense to seek to understand why one particular environment in Liverpool, that of the working class, gave birth to a style of rock music which was, almost immediately, taken up in some American circles, only to be sent back to Britain and to find an avid following in an ambience which was still overwhelmingly popular. I want to remind you that the Beatles are from Liverpool, the industrial city *par excellence* of England, and that various other groups of rock stars come from similar backgrounds, Manchester for instance, and that they belong for the most part to a suburban way of life, distinguished by particular styles of life and of self-expression.

Some have suggested, after seeing me perform a parody of mass production, that the soul of rock resides in that form of robotisation of gestures which, in the work place, are reduced to simple repetitive mechanisms.

Gestures and Masks

In discussing the differences which exist between performing the same piece with or without a mask, I will take as my reference point a monologue I first performed in Rome some years ago, and which was subsequently seen on television. It deals with the hunger of the Zanni.

The *grammelot*, which dates from the late sixteenth century, tells of a starving Zanni, who, on the point of despair, dreams of eating himself. It is important to have some idea of the historical and social origins of the Zanni. Zanni is the nickname given by the Venetians in the fifteenth century to the peasants of the Po valley, and especially to those from the valleys round Bergamo. The name is derived from the name Giovanni or John, and is connected with an important moment in Venetian history. Here, in the early years of the sixteenth century, something extraordinary occurred – the birth of modern capitalism.

Very few people are aware that capitalism was born in Italy. It is something we ought to be proud of. When I mention this outside Italy, people are amazed, because they have an idea of Italians as mandolin players, spaghetti guzzlers, latin lovers, and nothing else. It is a source of extraordinary pride that capitalism, thanks to the banks, that symbol of our Renaissance civilisation and pride of the upper bourgeoisie, was born among us. The Magnifico, with whom the grotesque mask of the impoverished nobleman had its origin, was a banker. The most important families of Florence were banking families. It is no accident that the man who appropriated to himself the title of definitive discoverer of America was a Vespucci, scion of a banking family who, having subsidised the second, third and fourth expeditions of Christopher Columbus, dispatched their son Amerigo to make sure that the Genoese adventurer was not doing them out of the profits. It is significant that America carries the name of a banker.

Through the brilliance of the bankers of that age, the *maona* was invented in Venice. The *maona* was the share offer made to the citizens, and, for the first time in the history of mankind, wars were not organised by the captains and the kings but by the banks, who, obviously, involved all the citizenry with the cash and the courage. Every citizen became a participant and, more importantly, an instigator of war. The wars in question were wars of colonisation. At that time, Venice increased its territory considerably. Citizens of the republics of Venice and Genoa found themselves obliged, on account of the vast expanse of land acquired, to emigrate to Turkey, the Middle East, Greece, Iran, Iraq, Syria, Lebanon and so on.

These people managed to develop the economy of their homeland thanks to the revival of slavery. Foodstuffs arrived in the markets of the whole of Italy at greatly reduced prices, with the result that the peasants, the Zanni, were brought to the point of bankruptcy. Being unable to sell their products, they had no option but to abandon their lands and emigrate in large numbers to Venice and Genoa. According to some calculations, ten thousand moved to Venice in one year alone, a quite incredible exodus when you consider the limited population of those times. Ten thousand men, with a further ten thousand women with no option but to follow their own Zanni.

The Zanni are Coming!
These 20,000 souls poured into a city of little more than 100,000 inhabitants, and obviously their presence disrupted the balance. They met with resentment and contempt, and were treated as objects of derision, as is normal. They provided convenient scapegoats for every mishap – the fate of all minorities. They had no command of the local language, they committed gaffes, were continually hungry and some of them had the misfortune to die of starvation. Their women took the humblest jobs, including that of prostitute, because there was a glut of servants on the market.

Such was the supply of these services at that time that the expression common among Venetians, 'your whore of a mother', dropped out of currency. The reason no one said it was that it would draw the reply – 'Yes, you're probably right. And yours?'

The Starving Zanni
The character I wish to present is a Zanni talking about his own hunger. In despair, he imagines himself eating his own foot, hand, testicle and buttock. At the end, he plunges his hand deep into his stomach, pulls out his entrails and devours them too, suitably cleaned up. Then, realising there were spectators present, he looks up towards the audience and decides there would be good eating in some of them too. He grows angry with God, makes a number of quite explicit comments which there is no point in my warning you about and ends up with a gargantuan tirade which is his final nightmare.

The principal interest of the piece for me lies in the fact that it illustrates the difference in gesture which requires to be made depending on whether the mask is being worn or the face is uncovered. For *The Starving Zanni* the language I use is *grammelot*, which is an onomatopoeic device based on the use of sounds, where real words make up roughly 10 per cent of the whole and the rest is a *mélange* of seemingly senseless noises which, however, contrive to indicate the meaning of the situation.

I'm starving. Never been so hungry . . . oh God . . . (*Series of onomatopoeic sounds*.) I could eat a foot, a knee, I'd chew up one ball, then the other ball, I could devour my prick then I'd get stuck into

43

one buttock, then the other; can you just see me with one buttock in my hand, and the other. . . . damn. . . . I'd chew all my insides, I'd stick a hand right up there and out would come the guts. . . . (*Onomatopoeic sounds. Mimes feeling great pain in backside.*). . . . I've torn my arse apart. . . . (*Babble of sounds. Mimes hauling his intestines from his stomach. Blows on them to clean them up a bit. Series of raspberries.*) All that shit. . . . damnation what a world. . . . aaah. . . . I'm ravenous . . . (*Further tirade. Stops short. Goes forward to front of stage.*) What a lot of folk! Nice people! Could tuck into one of you! (*Onomatopoeic munching noises.*) God, am I hungry! I'd eat a mountain, I'd suck the sea dry (*Stops, looks up.*) And just as well for you, God, that you're not here, otherwise I'd eat your triangle, with all those little cherubim fluttering round about . . . scared, eh? (*Removes the mask.*)

While performing this piece, I have always avoided placing my hands on the mask or even putting them close to it, but if, in the version without the mask, the character is to be fully rounded the need to touch yourself, almost to reconstruct yourself and, so to speak, to fashion your own face, shoulder, body and hands become paramount.

In the final part, the Zanni, after having dreamed about swallowing a pot of polenta with chicken, meat and so on mixed in, wakes up to face a very different reality. He then grabs hold of an imaginary pan . . . filled with polenta complete with chicken, meat and so on. In his rush, he cuts off a section of his finger and eats that as well, without bothering. We are at the point where he picks up the pot and swallows the big wooden spoon.

(*Long series of onomatopoeic sounds, shakes the pot, swallows the leftovers, licks the spoon, swallows it too, shakes himself a bit to break up the spoon in his stomach and help it digest. Enormous final burp.*) Pardon me. . . . damn. . . (*Sobs.*) . . . you haven't eaten a thing. (*Grammelot, sobs and outbreak of rage. He seizes an imaginary big fly. Stares at it in his fist.*) Lovely . . . good and plump . . . don't move . . . what a beast! (*Mimes pulling a leg off the fly.*) Just look at that little paw . . . could be a pig's trotter . . . the wings, the wings . . . hey, I'll eat the lot (*Gobbles up the rest of the insect, uttering little cries of delight, like a gourmet.*) Oh dear me, what a feast!!!

The Camera in the Brain
The real difference, mask or no mask, arises from a particular psychological attitude which on different occasions compels the spectators, almost as though they were using a series of lenses, to frame the images produced by

the actors in different ways. The decisive factor is the way the audience is persuaded by an actor to focus on one detail of the action, or on the totality of the action, by the use of lenses unknowingly stored in the individual brain. Let me explain.

While performing *The Starving Zanni*, I create a wide space around myself, allowing my whole body to be kept in view. At a certain point, this body is, as it were, forgotten, insofar as I deliberately freeze the lower half, thereby eliminating all interest in it, and I induce the audience to do a close-up of my face alone. My gestures are limited to a circumference of no more than thirty centimetres and are never allowed to stray outside that imaginary framework, because this would lead to a loss of concentration on the part of the spectator. Concentration must be built up progressively, not in leaps and bounds.

In this atmosphere of mounting tension, one passage which is especially worthy of note is the one which begins with the vision of the wooden spoon being swallowed, going down the throat and through the body, leaving the body itself to twist, turn and spin in a kind of belly-dance. All of a sudden, attention is turned to the sobs, that is, to the face. Next the lament assumes a sharper sound and is transformed into the buzz of a fly which is annoying the Zanni. He turns one way then the other, which makes the space widen out a little, but it is immediately narrowed in again when he seizes hold of the fly. The frame is now bounded by the nose with converging eyes, staring at the fly. Here the spectator is compelled to restrict his own range of vision right down to a micro-frame, centred on the fly whose wings and legs are being pulled off. The progression, which is obviously calculated, must be executed with the utmost precision, must possess a precise rhythm and must give the illusion of a space which, if opened out or narrowed too much, would produce fatigue and a loss of attention.

The frame which includes the mask cannot, on the contrary, be excessively restrictive, because the movements of the shoulder and the bust are competing for attention inside it. The actor who is speaking with the mask over his face requires, as a minimum, the upper part of his body to express the things which, were his face uncovered, he would be able to communicate with the slightest movement of his eyes or mouth. That is not to suggest that acting in the natural state gives advantages or better results than using a mask.

Let us now analyse a piece from Harlequin's repertoire illustrating the sensual approach, or, more precisely, eroticism with deliberately obscene elements.

Harlequin – the Devil!

The piece is of French origin. As is well known, the Harlequin character is the result of cross-breeding between the Zanni from Bergamo and farcical, devil-like characters from the French popular tradition. We first find Harlequin in Paris towards the close of the sixteenth century on a stage run by an Italian Commedia dell'Arte company called the Raccolti. The actor who played Harlequin was Tristano Martinelli, a native of Mantua.

The name Arlecchino, or Harlequin, comes from a medieval character, Hellequin or Helleken, or in later forms, Harlek-Arlekin. Dante refers to a devil by the name of Ellechino. In the French popular tradition of the thirteenth and fourteenth centuries this character is described, appropriately enough for any self-respecting devil, as scurrilous and villainous, but also as impish and much given to tricks and practical jokes. The character also gets crossed along the way with the 'homo selvaticus' or 'sebaticus', who, depending on the season and locality, went clad in animals skins or in leaves. He comes in different guises, at times showing the cunning of a fox, the agility of a cat and the violence of a wild bear, at others simply uncouth, naive and foolish. All these characters, including the devil Harlek, are lumped together to produce the Arlecchino of Tristano Martinelli – a kind of faun who rants in a Lombard language typical of the Zanni, but dotted with expressions from French slang. The first Arlecchino wore no mask, contenting himself with black paint marked with red wavy lines. Only later did he appear in public with a mask of brown leather wearing the sneer of an anthropomorphic monkey, complete with heavy eyelashes and a great lump on the forehead. The costume was of rough cloth, with leaf-shaped forms scattered on a white base. The leaves were green, yellow, beech red and brown. The reference to 'homo selvaticus' is unmistakable. The lozenges and the traditional multi-coloured patches with which we are familiar came sixty years later with another great Arlecchino – Domenico Biancolelli.

Both actors resorted to all kinds of provocation. They would wander on stage, assaulting the audience with obscenities and acts of unheard-of scurrility. Martinelli, in the middle of a love scene between a knight and his lady, dropped his trousers and, in perfect peace and tranquillity, began to defecate on the stage. He then picked up the result of his labours with both hands (they were, nearly always, roasted chestnuts) and hurled them at the audience, with a loud chuckle: 'It brings good luck! This is your chance!'

Other provocative acts included pretending to urinate over the audience, falling headlong over the people in the front rows, throwing objects at the stalls, firing with culverins and aiming murderous rockets at the spectators.

There is one script which describes the collapse of the entire set including the rostrum and flats, all of which go crashing down in the direction of the people in the stalls. At the last minute, the scenery is held back by ropes which, obviously, had been put in place in advance. The effect of terror was guaranteed.

King Henry III was enamoured of this new style of theatre, especially of the Harlequin of Tristano Martinelli, who was a frequent guest at court. The King showered gifts on him, and gave him ample proof of his affection. The Queen acted as godmother for his children. Harlequin, secure in the knowledge that he could pass unpunished, took full advantage of the King's favour to ridicule and satirise the politicians, prelates and aristocrats of his time. The fact that political satire is a component of Commedia dell'Arte is unknown to many specialists. At the time of Molière, Biancolelli dramatised many inconvenient issues, such as the problem of justice and injustice. There are two plots extant in which Harlequin plays the part of an avaricious judge and of an inquisitor who is both fanatical and hypocritical.

The Expulsion of the Players

Around 1675, all the Commedia dell'Arte performers were expelled from France, and certainly not on account of their rollicking comic style. It was their satire on the customs, the hypocrisy and the politicking of the age which was considered remiss. Power cannot put up with the laughter of other people, of those who are without power. Throughout the whole of the seventeenth century, the Italian comedy triumphed all over Europe, and some companies made their way back to Italy to revive the style of Commedia dell'Arte there, where it was in a state of decline. Enriched by their encounter with other cultures, they created new characters and fresh comic situations and were immensely successful. Some companies, including some of the most prestigious, continued wandering around Europe and turn up in Denmark, Holland, Belgium, Britain and even Russia. The fearless comings and goings of these groups, with the history of their alternating fortunes and disasters, will form the subject for another day's discussion.

I would, at last, like to move on to the passage in question, which comes from the popular French tradition of the *fabliaux*. This tradition was taken over lock, stock and barrel by the actors of Commedia dell'Arte. The *fabliaux* are a typical expression of the theatre of medieval storytelling, and are based on continued obscene allusions. In the Middle Ages, as well as in Commedia dell'Arte, the obscene always played a liberating role, even if in other social contexts it could be an end in itself. The comedies of Cardinal Bibbiena* are the very apotheosis of the obscene and of the libertine spirit, but they have

---

* Cardinal Bibbiena (1470–1520), Italian poet, author of *La Calandria*, a famous comedy.

nothing in common with the approach used in the piece I am about to perform, which carries with it an explicit denunciation of phallus worship. The title itself in indicative – *L'Arlecchino Fallotropo*, that is, exhibitor of the phallus.

This is the story: Arlecchino is instructed to perform an errand for his master, the Magnifico. Magnifico is an ironic title, since this master has nothing of the splendour of Italian courtiers of that period. He has fallen on hard times, is down on his luck, penniless and decrepit. Into the bargain, he has fallen in love with a prostitute who is out to fleece him and rob him of the little he has left. The prostitute arranges to meet him at her house, where they will finally make love. However, the Magnifico is devoured by the fear that sexually he will not be up to the job, and that it might all be a terrible anticlimax, so he turns to a witch and asks her to administer a potion which will bestow the necessary vim and vigour. Arlecchino is dispatched to collect the flask containing the miraculous liquid. The witch warns him that if his master swallows more than one teaspoonful of the concentrated potion, his penis will be liable to explode. While still in the witch's house, Arlecchino haggles over the cost and succeeds in beating down the price to about half of the agreed amount. With the money left over, he goes to an inn and orders a few bottles of wine, which he proceeds to down. He bursts into song, laughs merrily and, in his drunken state, finishes off not only the wine but also, as he realises with horror, the magical potion. He feels a warm sensation moving from the lower part of his stomach towards the upper reaches. He notes that something unmentionable is growing out of all control and that his trousers are suddenly uncomfortably tight; the buttons fly off and the belt gives way. At that moment, some women turn up, and Arlecchino finds himself unable to mask that inconvenient hump. He sees a cat skin hung out to dry and throws it over the 'growth'.

One of the girls expresses a wish to stroke the cat, but Arlecchino pushes her away. A dog comes running on, barks at the cat and tries to bite it. Arlecchino tosses the skin away, and the dog immediately falls on it. Another group of women come along, and Arlecchino once again faces the problem of concealing the monster. Some strips of cloth were hanging on a line, so he wraps them round the 'beast' as though it were a baby. He even finds a little bonnet. He does not know one end of a baby from the other, but pretends to sing a lullaby. The women, charmed by what they believe to be a new-born babe, attempt to take it in their arms and cuddle it. Once again Arlecchino has to chase them away. The women resist, tugging the baby this way and that. Arlecchino is close to despair.

The piece should begin with a *grammelot*. Arlecchino enters, singing a drunken song, but fully aware that he has taken the potion.

(*Singing.*) Oh, what gorgeous wine, red as the rose and bubbly. Warms the insides, belly, balls and prick . . . (*To the audience.*) Seventeenth-century song from Bergamo, for drunken soloists. (*Onomatopoeic sounds.*) Oh God, the potion, the potion, where is it . . . I've drunk it, I've downed the lot . . . oh, oh, oh . . . I'm not feeling well . . . what's that . . . It's getting bigger, it's breaking out . . . stay down, you idiot . . . (*Mimes the attempt to arrest the enormous growth of the phallus.*) . . . I've got a hump in front of my stomach . . . (*Onomatopoeic sounds.*) How in God's name am I going to hide this damn bump? What's that? . . . a cat's skin . . . (*Mimes wrapping a cat's skin round the phallus.*) . . . nice pussy . . . there, there, there . . . lovely pussy, miaow, miaow . . . if you like pussy cats, oh . . . pussy, pussy . . . (*Sits on a stool and tries to cross his legs but the encumbrance of the phallus and its cover prevent him.*) Bloody cat! (*Onomatopoeic sounds.*) What's wrong? No, miss, I am sorry, but there is no way you can be permitted to lay a finger on this cat . . . and that goes for you too, dear . . . it is wild. Off you go now, go away, leave it alone . . . OOOOO . . . (*Mimes being attacked by a dog.*) AAAAAAA . . . what a wild bloody animal! Get away! OOOOhh that was sore. . . damnation . . . (Mimes throwing away the cat's skin.) A baby's shawl, the very thing . . . (*Mimes seizing a shawl from a non-existent clothes line.*) . . . Women! Never here when they are needed . . . where is Mummy? Daddy'll take care of baby . . . always Daddy's little baby . . . hush, hush, hush . . . (*Mimes wrapping the clothes round the baby.*) . . . what a pretty little bonnet . . . which is which, the top or the bottom? (*Moves along and sits on the stool.*) . . . Good evening to you, Madam . . . my little baby, yes . . . yes, no . . . I'm not sure if it's a boy or girl . . . must be a boy . . . of course I'm the father, and the mother. You think it looks just like me? What's that? I'm not holding it the right way . . . why, what are you supposed to do? You sit still with the baby in your arms, rocking it gently from side to side. You see how I love this baby. (*Mimes being set upon by the women, all desperate to hold the baby for themselves.*) Leave it alone . . . it's not yours . . . go away . . . AAAAAAA . . . Oh God, the baby's blown up, it's exploded . . . I'm castrated . . .

At this point, I would swear I could hear a voice complaining – 'And what about Pulcinella? Is he not a character of Commedia dell'Arte as well?' There was, however, a polemical, almost resentful, edge to the voice, as though the real statement was: 'It's the old story. Even when discussing Commedia, they still discriminate between the North and the South. So far all we've had is talk about Northerners. What about the poor Southern Italians?' All right, let's get on to Pulcinella.

Some authorities place the birth of Pulcinella, the 'white hunchback', some time between the thirteenth and fourteenth centuries, while others push it back much further towards Roman comic theatre, in other words to the Atellan farces or the Fescennine verses.* It is well established that Neapolitan theatre in its totality has very ancient roots and was already known and important, with a distinctive character of its own, in the era of Magna Grecia. Lucian of Samosata records that during the Dionysiac feasts in Naples they danced on stage and used mime and the grotesque even in tragedy. He also writes that they used dance forms to perform drama and comedy – the only known case in the Mediterranean. It was in Naples, in the view of many experts, that mime, understood as a genre of total theatre employing voice, body, dance and acrobatics, was born, and these are the essential elements in the composition of Pulcinella, that most Neapolitan of characters. However, there are facsimiles of Pulcinella to be found all over the Mediterranean: Karakochis is a Turkish and Greek comedy character who dates back to the third century AD and who has the same scowl, the same hunchback, the same aggressiveness, the same taste in lies and paradox. The art of living on your wits, of doing anything needed to survive, was undoubtedly an invention of Pulcinella.

Pulcinella is a close relative of Arlecchino, and we often find these two scoundrels squabbling with each other over the best parts. They turn up in identical scenes, with the same role played by now one, now the other. The gags, the routines are the same and the only difference lies in the language and the style. Pulcinella, with that little head of his squashed in between his shoulders, his back weighed down by the hump, moves as though crushed by an enormous sack. He stretches out his arms and flaps them about like wings, as if he were trying to achieve balance and volatility. And he succeeds. What never fails to amaze in this clumsy, S-shaped clown, with the drooping belly of the eternally starving poor devil protruding on the one side and the hunchback on the other, with that famous neck topped by the black skull peeping out of his carcass like a tortoise's head, is the lightness with which he moves and the grace of his various jumps, turns and pirouettes.

Nevertheless, in comparison to Arlecchino, the feature which distinguishes him from all other Commedia characters is his cynicism. I refer to the cynicism of the Cynics,† to that particular philosophical frame of mind, born

---

* The Fescennine verses were ribald and obscene pieces in early Roman times.

† A school of philosophers of the 5th century BC in Magna Grecia, which included Naples.

– and this cannot be a matter of mere chance – in Naples and its surroundings. The early Pulcinella as he appears in the first scripts loathes and rejects all forms of pathos and rhetoric. Undoubtedly, like the unscrupulous scoundrel he is, he will play on these feelings, act the part right up to the hilt, proclaim the passion or the despair of the lover and wear a bleeding heart on his sleeve. He will swear that nothing could be further from his mind than lining his pocket or filling his belly, while all the time working for his own ends, only – once again like the born cynic – at the very last minute, when success is in his grasp, to be moved by some unpredictable, perhaps aesthetic urge and throw it all away. Privilege and power irritate and mortify him. It is better to start out afresh, for freedom of spirit is worth more than a king's throne! Only one other character can be as pitiless and hard as Pulcinella – the English Punch, a lineal descendant of Pulcinella.

In closing the work of this first day, I would like to widen the question of creativity on to two specific cases which I am often asked about. The first concerns children: many people ask themselves why it is that children playing with dolls manage to cradle them in their arms, turn down bed covers, feed them and, in general, imitate grown-ups in every way with total naturalness. On the other hand, this spontaneous ability has vanished by the time they have become adults, and can be rediscovered only after research, exercises and special study.

Taming the Child

Any reply has to address the overall process of creativity in the child. Some time ago, I took part in a discussion between psychologists and educationalists all involved in research into the causes of the deadening of creative faculties in children. All pointed out that as the subject matures, a sense of shyness develops in the adolescent which invariably leads to a block in his gestural and expressive faculties. There are young children who do stupendous drawings, who can use colour in bold and original ways, but who lose these abilities once they have passed their tenth birthday. With the years, a systematic destruction of the mental freedom of the child takes place, which eliminates all possibility of seeing and describing things with imagination and fantasy. A programmed scheme, with a sequence of rules, takes the place of fantasy.

We live in a society in which school-teaching is programmed and organised according to cage-like systems. We are forced to write inside lines and boxes, to follow the established precedents. I myself attended the Faculty of Architecture and I remember the anguish, the mental blocks and the constrictions created for me by the exhaustive classification of the architectural styles of the Greeks and Romans, made up of tables of models and relationships. It was a typical device for carving learning and knowledge on blocks of stone. I brought this personal experience of the negative impact of rules with me into the theatre, so that every time I find myself confronted with young people asking advice on how to get ahead in the profession, I always reply: 'The first rule in theatre is that there are no rules.' That does not mean that you can go on the rampage; it means that each individual is free to choose a method that will allow him to attain style, that is, to attain an effective, dialectical rigour. And in any case, order is a word which calls to mind an unpleasant family of terms – established order, social order, law and order, not to mention religious orders.

Design, in the sense of the portrayal of emotions through signs and non-codified spots of colour, is crushed out of us by orders such as: 'No, that tone is not quite right; first, attend to the outlines, then fill in the colours. No, don't spread colours with your fingers! Look at that blot! You've made a mess!' On the contrary, that blot could become a moment of inventiveness. Picasso said: 'An imbecile painter is painting. Colour drops from his brush. A gaudy stain spreads over the page. The imbecile painter, in despair, tears up his sheet and starts over. On the contrary I am, if I may say so, a painter of talent and as the stain spreads, I smile, look hard at it, turn the sheet over and over again and, deeply moved, begin with sheer delight to take advantage of that accident. It is from the blot that inspiration is born!'

Any child who spills paint over his paper is normally criticised by his teacher and held up to his classmates as an example of what not to do. In an environment where there were no rules and oppressive schemes, but, on the contrary, where freedom was the norm, you would never hear cries like 'Out, you're a dirty little so-and-so!' Rather you would hear an explicit invitation to preserve creativity at all costs and by any means: 'Get yourself dirty, draw with your hands, with your nose; splash on all the colour you want, use water, milk, coffee, anything you like. The important thing is that what comes out at the end should be authentic, alive, and, if possible, amusing and witty!'

All too often at school, the teacher sticks to the stereotypes laid down by the educational system, so that even if he is a person of some imagination he limits himself to telling the children to reproduce in their own jotters familiar images of the well-known types, e.g. Santa Claus with his sleigh, queuing up respectfully with his reindeer waiting for the traffic lights to change. Just imagine the scene if some child were to cover his jotter with drawings of Zorro, or, even more likely, with some punk star done up in outrageous make-up, with a balloon coming out of his mouth containing the words 'How about it, doll, oh yeah!' He would be required to present himself at the headmaster's the following day, in the company of his parents.

To avoid problems of this kind, the child who would be perfectly happy drawing twelve-eyed monsters firing rockets from its belly button, or naked women, or an armoured car with a willy instead of a cannon, is reduced, tamely and limply, to drawing brainless little flowers and to paying heed that the colour does not spill over the fixed margins.

The same process of inhibition, reinforced by parental authority right from the tenderest years, contaminates gestures. 'You mustn't do that; that's not nice. Stop making funny faces, don't make so much noise, don't sit on the ground, don't get yourself dirty!' How is anybody going to tackle mime without falling to the ground, rolling about, getting their clothes crumpled up? And God help you if you kiss a baby, male or female. How could it ever be possible to present passionate feelings or situations without being able to touch? Have you ever heard of *cordon sanitaire* mime? All games invented by children breathe the air of total liberty. They have a feeling for the grotesque, for subtlety, for joy, but the moment an adult says: 'Anyone like to act?' that sense of liberty is choked off and everything takes on a forced air. Nothing remains except that weary movement redolent of senseless and arbitrary rules which makes theatre nothing other than a poor copy of the downright obvious, a stereotype bright and shining like a plaster cast and as full of the sparkle of imagination as a lump of smoked Mozzarella cheese vacuum-packed for export.

The other subject I wish to tackle concerns women. Often they put to me a question in more or less these terms: 'In Italy, what form of theatre is possible for us? In this country, women are still in a state of subjection. They are trying desperately to free themselves but they are not succeeding, and this makes impossible the emergence of a theatre created by women, which would reveal their real face, so long hidden behind a mask imposed by society.' I reply by recounting my own experience of not so long ago. It concerns the writing and production of a play *Elizabeth: Almost by Chance a Woman* put on in 1984, with eight performers. In it, I played one of the minor characters, with Franca playing the lead.

No Self-pity
I have to confess that the gestation of this work was difficult and painful, for the very good reason that Franca upset me time after time. The first draft was completed in 1982, and as soon as I had got it done, I sat down and read it to Franca, who listened with great attention. I must preface these remarks by saying that the play has a firm basis in history, but that it also, by way of a

series of twists in the plot, deals with recent events in Italian politics. It is the story of Elizabeth I of England, a woman forced to make choices between the private and public dimensions, between femininity and power, between her own free sexuality and the logic of the 'Virgin Queen' image required of her by the ruling culture: a dilemma that was both tragic and grotesque at the same time.

Franca told me with great sincerity that although she found the play very interesting and full of scenes of high theatricality, overall it failed to convince her. Now then, let's have no beating about the bush: I defy anyone to write a play, work on it for months on end (as I did in the present case) only to have someone tell you: 'Yes, very interesting, but it does not convince me.' I took her by the lapels:

– No, no, no, you've got to say where it does not convince you, and why not.

– I don't exactly know. I just feel that it doesn't have enough drive.

– What do you mean – not enough drive?

– I don't know, it just doesn't have the drive!

– I'll tell you where you're driving me! I've no time for these vague, airy-fairy, emotive criticisms.

In other words, it ended up as a bawling match. My final request was peremptory: 'I require a detailed, itemised, point by point list of criticisms. Don't give me any of the stuff you get from one of those reviewers who doze off during the performance because they've been out on the town before-hand, and then slam you because their digestion is bad and they couldn't manage a good belch to round it all off.'

Franca would have been entitled to tell me to go to hell, but instead she took me at my word. I had on my desk, in artistic disorder, a pile of essays on the Elizabethan period which I had used to gather data and information on the subject. She picked them up one by one and set about reading them. About three weeks later, she returned with an armful of notes and launched into a thoroughgoing, point by point critical lecture on the historical clarity of the various characters, on the unfolding of the situation, on the presentation of the sequences, and above all on the dialectical evolution of the characters, as well as on the comical-satirical mechanism at work in the play and rounded off with a few remarks on whether or not it was working. Winding up, she dropped a hint that it might be an idea to start out afresh.

Undaunted, I set to with a will, rewriting the whole thing from start to finish. The second draft received Franca's approval and we proceeded to the staging, but another storm, worse than the first, was brewing. The character of Elizabeth herself, which had seemed to work wonderfully well at the reading, came over on stage as distorted, riddled with unjustified and gratuitous contradictions and as nothing more than a pretext for satirical comedy. At this point, with a wealth of biblical oaths (this may be something of a euphemism) I dropped the whole thing: 'Sort out the character for yourself!'

She did. She picked up the papers which I had so gracefully distributed around the room and threw herself into the task of reading, re-reading, cutting, introducing variations and glosses. She let me calm down a bit before she proposed a possible alternative progression of scenes, a different approach in some speeches and an adjustment of some of the dialogues. I stood my ground with a certain irony and detachment: 'This woman thinks she can give lessons to me . . . ME . . . if I give way on this one, she won't even let me write a Christmas card.'

The following day, in absolute secrecy, I glanced at Franca's notes. I gave some of the most fanciful scowls in my wide repertoire, but a few moments later I found myself following some of Franca's suggestions. I have to admit that the character began to work much better, and this was not, alas! an isolated experience. Any day at all, she can shoot me down, now that she has developed a taste for it.

Now why, you may ask, am I recounting this personal, or rather family, tale? It helps me reply to the female complaint I started out with. The moral is: it is not sufficient to act the part of Cassandra, or to denounce society for oppressing women and leaving them too little space. To obtain space and credibility, perhaps the remedy is to get on with it yourselves, conceivably even, if it is of advantage, in collaboration with men, and to persuade them to address the question and to force them to face up to the problems which confront women – as Franca, in her own small way, has done. If you women manage to free yourselves totally from mere males and do productions of your own, so much the better. Forgive me if I sound as though I am sermonising, but I believe it is essential for you to liberate yourselves, more than anything else, from ritualistic moans and from weeping into your handkerchieves.

With this little telling-off, here endeth the first day.

Second Day

Wordless Speech

I would like to begin with a discussion of *grammelot* and this will provide a means of dealing with the history of Commedia dell'Arte, and also with a very special problem – the problem of language and its application in practice.

I will give a demonstration of *grammelot*, using a piece from the classical repertoire to show how it should be done. *Grammelot* is a term of French origin, coined by Commedia players, and the word itself is devoid of meaning. It refers to a babel of sounds which, nonetheless, manage to convey the sense of a speech. *Grammelot* indicates the onomatopoeic flow of a speech, articulated without rhyme or reason, but capable of transmitting, with the aid of particular gestures, rhythms and sounds, an entire, rounded speech.

Granted this standpoint, it is possible to improvise or articulate *grammelots* of all kinds in the most diverse lexical registers. The prime form of *grammelot* is that devised by the incredible imagination of children, when they believe their babbling (which among themselves they understand perfectly) is ordinary speech. I once overhead a Neapolitan and an English child chattering away to each other, and I noticed that neither of them hesitated a moment. For communication, they did not use their own languages, but another, invented one – a *grammelot*. The Neapolitan pretended to speak in English, and the English child pretended to speak Southern Italian. They understood each other perfectly. With the help of gestures, tones and infant prattle, they had constructed a code of their own.

As for ourselves, we can, after a minimum of application, of study and practice, speak all the *grammelots*, be they Spanish, French, German or English. I will have a few technical suggestions to make, but in this context it is impossible to lay down or endorse rules. The only way to proceed is by intuition and by an almost subterranean knowledge, for in this field no definite, comprehensive method can be prescribed. However, by observation you'll get the idea.

Let's take as an example Aesop's fable of the crow and the eagle, which many of you will know. First frame: the eagle soars through the skies in huge circles, when, second frame, all of a sudden, it notices a lamb, slightly lamed, a short distance from the rest of the flock. Third frame: it circles round, swoops down, seizes the lamb in its claws and carries it off. Fourth frame: the shepherd comes running up, shouting at the top of his voice, throwing stones; the dog barks but it makes no difference, for by now the eagle has flown off. Fifth frame: a crow perched on the branch of a tree. 'Ha! ha!' it screeches in excitement. 'I never knew it was as easy as that to snatch a lamb. All you have to do is swoop down on it! What's stopping me doing the same? I'm as black as the eagle, I've got claws too and they're every bit as strong, my wings are nearly as big as hers and I can circle and swoop just like her.'

No sooner said than done. Sixth frame: the crow starts circling and is about to swoop down on a lamb standing on its own, as he had seen the eagle do, when he espies a flock of sheep feeding a little further on. 'What a brainless fool that eagle was! With all these fat sheep around, what's the point of going for a mangy lamb? No flies on me. I'm going for the biggest, juiciest sheep of them all , so that in one go I'll have enough to keep me going for the rest of the week.' He swoops down, sinks his talons into the sheep's fleece, only to discover to his dismay that making off with it is harder than it looked. At that moment he hears the shepherd yell out and the dog bark. In terror he flaps his wings wildly but cannot raise the beast, nor can he even disentangle himself from the animal's hide. He pulls and tugs but all to no avail. It is too late. The shepherd arrives on the scene, strikes him a blow with his wooden club, the dog pounces on him, seizes him by the neck and throttles him. Moral: black feathers, a firm beak and a wide wing-span are not enough. If your trade is lamb-snatching, you have to be born an eagle. A further moral is this: the real problem is not getting hold of your prey – making a getaway without getting a knock on the head is. So, make do with the underfed lamb and leave the succulent sheep for the day when you have a jet engine attached to your hindquarters. This variant does not feature in Aesop.

Let's now consider how one would set about recounting in *grammelot* the parable in question. I am doing it off the cuff, so improvisation is of the essence. At this point, I can reveal some details of method. To perform a narrative in *grammelot*, it is of decisive importance to have at your disposal a repertoire of the most familiar tonal and sound stereotypes of a language, and to establish clearly the rhythms and cadences of the language to which you wish to refer. It may be that we wish to use a pseudo Sicilian-Calabrian dialect and to construct a *grammelot* on the basis of that sequence of sounds. What are the fixed or decisive points that need to be established to make this possible? First and foremost, it is important to inform the audience of the subject that will be discussed, as I have just done, then it is vital to elaborate, through sounds and gestures, the key elements that characterise the crow and the eagle. Obviously I will only be able to hint at the dialogues, allow the audience to guess their nature, rather than set them out in their entirety. The greater the simplicity and clarity of the gestures which accompany the *grammelot*, the greater the possibility of comprehension. To recapitulate: onomatopoeic sounds, clear and clean gestures, the correct timbre, rhythm, coordination and above all a firm grasp of the techniques of summary:

His performance begins with small gestures and the conversational tone, but increases in rhythm and incisiveness. He conveys stage directions in 'throwaway' lines of babble. He widens out the gestures, passing rapidly from one frame to the next. He accelerates the dramatic pace by raising the tone of voice and the cadences.

Every so often, in the course of the delivery, I was careful to throw in a couple of easily recognisable terms to assist the listeners. Which words did I pronounce clearly, even if with some distortion? Eagle, shepherd, crow, and then, with the aid of gestures, I picked out certain verbs like howl, bark, run. The key to the whole exercise resides in that connection with one decisive, specific word that we have agreed on together. 'The eagle circles in the skies,' or else 'the dog barks and growls' – these are images that must be conveyed clearly and precisely. This is the key phase of exposition in the onomatopoeic procedure that is *grammelot*.

Another important means of communication is the correct use of gesture. When portraying the flight of the bird, when attempting to reconstruct the efforts of the crow to rise from the animal's back, I must stand side-on towards the audience in the stalls, because it is vital to present the exertions of the subject as it beats its wings, and this is more evident when my body is entirely visible, in silhouette, rather than when it is turned directly towards the audience. I could perform the same scene facing the audience, but the results would be substantially different.

The positions of major impact should be repeated, using the identical image on the occasions that are decisive for one of the variations of the theme. To explain: first frame – the eagle: I take up position side-on, lean forward, wave my arms, spin round as though about to soar off. Second frame – the crow: the important thing is to repeat everything in the same way, but bringing out the clumsiness of the operation. In the first case, the spectator will be invited to note the ease with which the eagle takes off and flies through the skies with the lamb in its claws, whereas on the second occasion he will witness the bungling efforts of the crow as, all ungainly and maladroit, he struggles to extricate himself from the sheep's fleece. The repetition of the terms of the action in both cases must be, if it is to work, meticulous, almost as though the one were overlaid on the other. This focus on a few central points conveyed by stereotypes and clear variants constitutes one of the techniques used in the narratives recounted on Greek and Etruscan vases, as well as in Giotto's frescoes for his sequences of images on the life of St Francis or of Jesus – sequences which some people consider the finest cartoon strips in the history of art. Similarly, the sequence I have just executed could be easily translated into comic strips.

In this context, one other observation may be of some value. Many people will have gone to see an opera performed in a foreign language, and will have been surprised to discover that they could follow much of what was going on, and that at certain moments the whole thing was absolutely clear. Plainly gestures, tone, rhythms and above all simplicity all play a part in ensuring that the foreign language does not become an overwhelming obstacle, but of itself that is insufficient as an explanation. It is impossible not to become aware of something subterranean or magical which goads the brain to grasp, by a kind of instinct, matters that are not completely and clearly expressed. Who has not had the experience of being dimly aware of acquiring, over a period of time, a number of vague linguistic notions, with variants that stretch towards infinity? The hundreds of tales stored in our minds, from childhood nursery rhymes to stories garnered from cinema, from theatre, from cartoon strips, from television all contribute to enabling the brain to make sense of a new story, even when recounted without intelligible words.

Theirs Not to Reason Why

There is no better example than Charlie Chaplin of the way in which an artist can play on all the deepest memories filed away, perhaps in complete disorder, inside our minds. A great man of the stage, an extraordinary storyteller, Chaplin knew how to make use of all conventions and stereotypes at the most appropriate pace and in the most effective way. The same could be said, at least in part, for the Italian star Totò.

On the other hand, too many comic actors perform without any awareness of the factors that make an impact in comedy, an impact that can be decisive for their own success. I have often spoken to them and have been struck by the fact that they never asked themselves why a particular gag got a better response when, for example, they stood side-on rather than facing the audience, when they raised the tone, or when they stepped up or reduced the pace of their delivery. They never bothered to analyse the question because, thanks to their astonishing memory for effects, they had mastered an approach and acquired the right pace. Later, quite instinctively, when they found themselves facing a similar situation, all they did was repeat their act, with tiny variations, as to the manner born. They never asked themselves –

how did I get here? A word of warning: people of this stamp have a short life, because they lack the capacity for renewal. At the first shift of taste or fashion among the public, they are destined to find themselves, without fail, on the street.

I always tell anyone who is interested in the theatre, whether as actor or as director-author, that it is valuable to learn how to analyse, constantly, with rigour and imagination, the situations and impact of every performance. It is essential to stop actors from merely repeating the lines or gestures they have acquired. There is a type of actor who delivers himself into the hands of the director, without ever giving anything of himself, except his knowledge of the business and a portmanteau professionalism. The director says – Go there, then over there, then come here and speak your line: 'Oh, the blessed day will dawn when men will carve out their own destiny, their own being.' And then lean against that tree trunk, and stick your hand in your pocket – and there really is no reason why he shouldn't stick his finger up his nose, or anywhere else.

This habit of doing things straight off without ever attempting to understand the reasoning behind it can be carried to ludicrous lengths. I could recount a somewhat malicious anecdote, but no names. I once went to congratulate the lead actor, a friend of mine, for his performance as Macbeth. I jumped up on to the stage and showered compliments on him. 'Well done, you were marvellous. You grasped the whole momentum of the no-holds-barred denunciation of power present in every breath of the play, especially in the historical allusion to the character of Anne Boleyn. You really brought out her criminal manoeuvres, the skulduggery of her politics, its cruelty, cynicism, malice – all those allusions which are just as valid today. Congratulations above all for suggesting that slavish, almost supine, attitude of his towards his wife, Lady Macbeth. You've obviously found a director with whom you can see eye to eye.'

At this point the acclaimed and famous actor peered at me with utter astonishment: – When?

– What do you mean, when?

– All this stuff about alluding to historical reality. And me being slavish toward Lady Macbeth? Look, you've got it all wrong. It never so much as entered my head.

– Of course it did! It could not have been more clear!

At that, like the born fanatic that I am, I launched myself into an exposé of all the allusive passages that he had brought out with such clarity. I pointed out the parallel situations, the references that were so obvious as to leap out at you from the page without any critical sleight of hand. I dwelt on the way one connection had been deliberately forged so as to lead on to another, and just as I was coming to my peroration, what did I hear but the voice of the director bawling in a paroxysm of rage. – Dario Fo, I'll kill you!

– Why, what have I done?

– Come over here! You got me into this, now you get me out, he whispered in my ear, shoving me into a corner.

– I don't know what you mean.

– Don't you see? You have explained to him what he is acting! You've landed me in it up to the neck. Tomorrow, he'll never be able to utter one single word that makes sense!

Maybe now you have some idea of the way certain directors view actors – a group of robots, nothing more; people to be trained, not educated. It is a dangerous outlook.

One of the reasons I recounted this anecdote was to illustrate the sheer panic some directors feel at the mere thought of clarifying the guiding principles of the production. They quake at the prospect of cramming an actor's inadequate brain with too many ideas.

The Actors' Diaspora

How was the *grammelot* born? Why did the actors of Commedia dell'Arte feel the need to produce that babble on stage, or to imitate a *mélange* of words in every language? The reason is obvious, more or less.

It is an established fact that the great exodus of the players took place in the century of the Counter-Reformation, when the decree to dismantle all the theatrical spaces, which were regarded as an outrage to the Holy City, was promulgated. Pope Innocent XII, under pressure from the most backward elements of the bourgeoisie and of the upper clergy, issued an order in 1697 for the destruction of the Teatro di Tordinona, whose stage, in the view of the moralists, had witnessed the greatest number of obscene displays.

In the same spirit, Cardinal Borromeo, operating in North Italy, dedicated himself to the redemption of his 'Milanese children'. He made a clear distinction between art, a vital force in spiritual education, and theatre, a manifestation of the spirit of profanity and vanity. In a letter addressed to his collaborators, which I quote from memory, he expresses himself in more or less these terms: 'We, anxious to root out this evil plant, have prepared bonfires of scripts with offensive material, have spared no effort to extirpate them from the memories of men and have, at the same time, determined to pursue those responsible for their publication and circulation. Nonetheless, it has become clear that while we were asleep, the Devil has been at work with renewed cunning. How much more deeply does that which the eyes see penetrate into the soul than that which is read in the pages of a book! How much more grievously does the word uttered by the voice and supported by gesture wound the mind of the young than the dead word printed in books! The Devil, through the work of the actors, spreads his poison.'

One of his collaborators added: 'These performers have learned the art of making themselves understood by all and sundry, be they male or female, matron or simple artisan. These dialogues of theirs spoken in a language clear and graceful – this was the exact term employed by Borromeo too – never fail to touch the mind and heart of the watching public.' He then closes by delivering, quite unwittingly, the warmest eulogy to Commedia dell'Arte ever given: 'These players do not repeat by heart written sentences, as do children or actors who perform for pleasure. These last invariably give the impression of being unaware of the significance of what they repeat, and, for that reason, fail to carry conviction. The players, on the contrary, do not employ the same words in every performance of a new work, but prefer to invent on each occasion, learning first, by a series of cues and headings, the substance, then playing by improvisation, thus training themselves in a free, natural and graceful style. The result is to involve the audience to the highest degree. That effortlessly natural style kindles passion and emotions that are a grave peril, since they offer approval of an amoral celebration of the senses, of lasciviousness, of the rejection of sound principles and of rebelliousness against the sacred laws of society; these are matters that create great confusion among simple folk.'

Down with Actors! All that Fantasy!

The majority of companies, especially the better-known among them, were compelled to leave and seek work elsewhere, causing a real actors' diaspora. The Gelosi, the Accesi, the Confidenti moved to France and Spain. In the early stages, the main problem was communication, because even if some of their number were acquainted with French and Spanish, not all of them were capable of making themselves understood with ease. For that reason, they pushed mimicry as far as it would go, and set about inventing ingenious devices to guarantee the greatest level of rapport with the audiences. Today these devices would be termed 'gags', that is, a series of rapid turns based on paradox, on nonsense, on knockabout and slapstick. The need to develop the standard of the gesture and the agility of the body so as to attain a high level of expressiveness received a boost with the invention of an onomatopoeic babble which, together with mime, brought about the happy birth of an unrepeatable and unparalleled style – Commedia dell'Arte.

It pains me to have to deliver a blow to Italians' patriotic sentiment, but the phenomenon of improvised comedy, with gags and *grammelot*, was born in this country only in embryo. It developed and grew almost entirely outside Italy. It was elsewhere in Europe that it enriched so wonderfully the fantastic extravaganza of its repertoire. It may appear paradoxical, but it was thanks to the Counter-Reformation that a completely new and revolutionary theatre was able to develop. At times the most hypocritical and moralistic of the clergy assist in theatre. Between the late sixteenth and early seventeenth centuries, troupes of performers of Italian-style comedy were formed in France, and these companies then found themselves in demand in Spain, Germany and England. Shakespeare was well aware of the new art of comedy, and had no hesitation in borrowing from it. There is no doubt that he knew several of the greatest Renaissance satirical texts, such as Machiavelli's *Mandragola* or Giordano Bruno's *Il Candelaio*, and it is beyond question that it was from these early Italian sixteenth-century works that he learned the use of stage machinery and from the same source that he acquired the idea of the use of disguise and of mistaken identity.

Keep the Censor in the Dark

Returning to the question of *grammelot*, I want to turn to the speech which bears the name of Scapino* and Molière. The anecdote is based on the undisputed fact that Molière, at the height of his career, performed in the Hôtel de Bourgogne, a royal property which he shared with an Italian company, La Troupe des Comédiens Italiens du Roi. The two companies took turn about. Molière frequently found himself at odds with the censor, who turned up at every production to flick through the text for any offending material. On the subject of censorship, some historians have tried to demonstrate that the apparatus of censorship predated the birth of theatre, and that it was the censors themselves who invented theatre, so as to have some means of making themselves useful to the power of the day.

Molière was protected by Louis XVI, the Sun King, in person, and he was always prepared to help him out of a tight corner, even if at times, faced with the onslaughts of the French clergy and the right-thinking bigots who attacked him on the moral and cultural plane, even he kept his distance. On those occasions, the Sun King, to reduce tension, would pick on someone to carry the can, and as often as not Molière provided a handy scapegoat.

The extract I wish to perform is taken from the outline of a play which brings together two other famous works – *Don Juan* and *Tartuffe*. The main character is a young man whose father, a banker with political interests, had

---

* A resourceful rascally valet in Molière's *Les Fourberies de Scapin*.

recently died. This notion of bankers interfering with politics and of politicians who meddle in economics is an idea specific to the French seventeenth century. It is completely foreign to us in the twentieth century. It is well established today that politics and banking are two completely separate worlds, and never the twain shall meet.

Balancing Bankers

There may have been the odd case of a banker entering the political arena, but the results have invariably been tragic. In fact, they tend to end up performing unusual balancing acts on bridges, such as Blackfriars in London. Not only that, but these eccentrics insist on trying out highly dangerous and exciting games (for anyone with the misfortune to watch them) involving sticking rocks into their jacket pockets, winding lengths of rope round their necks, and tying one end on to the girders above to stop them, should they happen to fall into the Thames, from getting their feet wet.*

In any case, our young orphan finds himself out of his depth, ill-equipped for the task of succeeding his father in the conduct of business. Regrettably, he has until now lived a wasteful and happy-go-lucky life, with no thought of mastering the delicate craft of making his way in the world of finance and politics. It becomes evident that drastic measures are needed and his family has the bright idea of entrusting him to an extraordinary master – a Jesuit. The satirical intent could not be more obvious, but in France at that time you could only go so far with jokes about the Jesuits. It is not like Italy today, where even children at primary school are allowed a giggle at the expense of the Jesuits. The censors came down on Molière's script immediately, with shouts of – Do what you please with the troglodytes, but hands off the Jesuits!

Molière, pig-headed as ever, refuses to give in, and has an ingenious idea. Why not bring in Scapino? He decided, in other words, to resolve the problem with an *escamotage*, to replace the prelate with a comic character from the company working in the same theatre. The actor who played Scapino was an expert in *grammelot*, capable of delivering a whole monologue in phoney French, using no more than a dozen genuine words and filling out the rest with onomatopoeic inventions. Molière decided to give Scapino the part of the master who taught the tricks of the trade to the young gentleman. You can imagine the plight of the servant of law and order who turned up to confirm that the censor's edicts have been respected and to file the appropriate report.

* A reference to the Italian banker, Roberto Calvi, found mysteriously hanged under Blackfriars Bridge in 1982.

He must have been desperate as he strove to decipher, without being able to make out even one, the words spoken by the actor on the stage. At the final curtain, you can imagine him tearing up his notebook and storming out of the theatre, and possibly out of the police. The whole thing worked like a dream.

Wigs, Lace and Cloaks

Scapino, master *extraordinaire* of the part of ageing domestic, a man of great experience and wisdom, laid down the laws of good conduct in society, beginning with style of attire. It was the fashion of the time for noblemen to don extravagant wigs, cut in styles that were, to say the least, grotesque. You must have seen portraits of the Sun King, in one of those enormous canvases: there is a tiny head in the centre and all the rest is wig. On either side of the picture there are other, tinier works, put there exclusively to gather up the curls that overflow from the main portrait. Scapino's advice was to the point: 'No wigs, no ribbons, no frills. You must appear modest and humble, so gather up your hair behind your neck, and there is an end of it.'

They tended to go over the score in Molière's day with frills and *dentelles*, or lace. *Dentelles* were used to decorate the clothes of the nobles, starting from the *jabots*, those cascades of lace on the chest which were meant to give colour to the shirt. Lace peeped out from under the waistcoat, while bows and ribbons were tied round the calves of the legs. Some even went so far as to have slits cut into the sleeves all the way up to the armpits to allow more lace to be glimpsed. Just imagine what a drama a visit to the toilet must have been for the nobles of the day. Covered in fripperies as they were, they had to rummage around to locate the correct instrument . . . only to find nothing but lace coming out. At the end, in annoyance, but with great dignity, they had no option but to do it over themselves. Hence the famous walk of the French aristo.

Scapino was insistent with the young gentleman: 'Have nothing to do with this nonsense. Don't wear all this gaudy attire, get rid of these *dentelles*. All you need is a plain black, tight-fitting suit with buttons – and be careful about the cloak!' At that time, princes and gentlemen in general weighed themselves down with cloaks of such extravagant dimensions that to put one on required considerable physical strength. It seems that court dwarves owed their success with noblemen to the secret help they gave by concealing themselves among the folds of the clothing to support the weight of the cloak.

The real problem with these cloaks arose when a strong wind caused them to be filled out like sails, dragging the poor aristos off their feet and frequently carrying them off into the clouds. Many of them were heard of no more. People in France, before venturing outdoors, used to look up to the sky and ask: 'Any aristos in view? No? A calm day, quite safe for a walk.' Scapino's rule was firm: no cloaks.

The wise servant proceeded to impart a lesson on the art of oratory. It is well known that nobles in that age, in conversation, were given to waving their hands and arms in the air as though they were engaged in a fencing match. Scapino taught them an appropriate, mannerly and elegant style of gesture, suggested that they avoid the crowing and bragging typical of the upper crust, and that they tone down their arrogance and bombastic talk. He demonstrated how to put on an act of humility, how to behave like a shy, timid soul, terrified of the things of the big, bad world – all the better to stay in power. It may be that Scapino's lessons suggest parallels with certain personages in contemporary politics, but that depends on the malice of the individual spectator.

Finally, Scapino will provide information on the correct use of justice, understood as a legal mechanism for the destruction of one's enemies and rivals. It will be shown, to general amazement, that even religious rites can be pressed into service to manage and control power. I intend to perform this piece both with and without the mask, to afford you the opportunity of understanding the vast difference in action and gesture between the two styles.

Masks Breathe

Firstly, I want to use a mask which is very similar to that used by Scaramouche. It is a leather mask fashioned by one of the greatest mask-manufacturers in the business – Sartori. It was made using a plaster cast of my face, or, more exactly, on the basis of measurements of my face, including the nose, because it is no joke working round a protuberance of that kind! Of the many masks in my possession, there are several I simply cannot wear, because they were not made to measure, so they crush my face, stop me breathing and above all give a false tone to my voice. The mask is like a shoe – if it is not comfortable on you, you won't walk.

The leather of every mask is fashioned by beating it out on a wooden outline. First of all the prototype is modelled in terracotta, then a gypsum mould is created, with the face form reproduced by chiselling on a block of hard, resistant wood. A thin sheet of leather, softened by soaking in water, is stretched over the form and is made to stick to it by being beaten with briarwood clubs. The modelling process is continued by the use of special tools – some sharp-pointed, others with a grained surface. Once the mask is formed, it is left to dry before special waxes are spread over it to make it at the same time hard and elastic, and most especially, able to 'breathe'. This expression, 'to breathe' is not an abstraction. The mask must be able to absorb your sweat as well as to live in symbiosis with your body heat and breathing rhythms.

Later, I will try the rhinoceros-nosed mask named after Razzullo, a Neapolitan mask whose comic effect can be guaranteed, and the black Magnifico mask, complete with bushy eyebrows. This mask, even though it has the typical frown of the Magnifico, could serve my purpose very well, because, in spite of the pointed nose, it has the down-to-earth grimace of Scapino. The important thing is to find a style of gesture which gives the right idea of the character. The Magnifico is the prototype of the character of Pantaloon, or Pantalone dei Bisognosi,* the Venetian merchant who moves and gestures in that peculiar way which manages to be both gangling and rigid, like a cockerel. There he is – all sudden starts and upraised knees, jerking his feet forward from the heels and stretching out his arms like a turkey flapping its wings. And his speech – 'Curses on all women, with their weeping, simpering and affectations' – marked by nasal tones and chicken-like starts, with the neck jerking back and forward and, as a result, the shoulders keeping time, like any farmyard fowl worth his salt.

The mask of the early Magnifico, on the other hand, has a quite different physiognomy – it is highly stylised, with prominent features, deep rings circling the eye sockets and two round holes for the eyes – and the character himself is much harder and more sullen. The Magnifico character emerged some hundred years earlier than Pantaloon and had enormous importance in the field of satire, not only in Spain but also in Italy in the early years of the seventeenth century. He is the Roman mask *par excellence*, honed by Cantinella, a performer of some flair. This Cantinella used to wander on stage, pulling on the costume and mask of the character as he went. His function was to caricature the great Renaissance lords, celebrated for their magnificence of wit and speech as much as of culture. Bullying, aggressive, mean-minded, all trace of the magnificence of his forebears had vanished, leaving only a pauper who had squandered his dignity along with his cash. Always on the prowl, he could be termed a Beelzebub of sex. Any woman who happens to cross his path becomes at once an object of winks, leers and nudges.

Reduced to its bare bones, the overall mimic and vocal range of the character is as follows:

Puts on the mask and parades up and down in a series of showily self-important struts, trips, trots and sudden halts. The display is accompanied by an outburst in

* *dei Bisognosi*, 'of the needy people'.

Venetian grammelot, *carrying the hint of gratuitous obscenity, of insolence of speech and of the miaowing of a chronically over-excited cat on heat. At certain stages, he transforms himself into a barnyard cockerel, then wraps himself in his cloak like a silkworm in a cocoon.*

This is the character I wished to discuss. Now I will put on the same mask to play an entirely different style of character, in an attempt to demonstrate how the mask and its own personality shift in relationship to overall body poses and to the gestures one produces. In the performance of the Magnifico character, the position of my body made for balance of the bust, through a loose, forward and backwards swaying movement, chest stuck out, pelvis retracted, arms swinging and haughty movement of the neck and head. On the contrary, with Pantaloon's walk, even though the same mask is employed, I proceed with the neck held forward like a turkey, shoulders upright swaying in time and, most importantly, a voice pitch which is as far removed as possible from the pitch and tone of falsetto. In consequence the two masks, no matter how similar they may be, assume, in either case, an opposing physiognomy. A further proof is provided by the performance of the piece in *grammelot*.

Lesson of Scapino in French *Grammelot*
(*First part with the mask of the Magnifico.*)

He introduces himself in the classical pose of the aristocrat, all polish and refinement, presenting himself as though he were a tailor's dummy. He starts off with a mimed description of an enormous periwig covering the head, drawing attention to the presence of rows of curls and ringlets, keeping up a commentary in semi-intelligible sounds which recall French speech. He details the operation of combing out the wig, which, as he proceeds, swells out until it becomes as big as a large ball, whose weight and awkwardness make him lose balance. The wig snaps shut over his face like a trap-door. He pulls out hair by the handful, hauls the wig this way and that, heaves a sigh, picks hairs out of his mouth and eye and exclaims peremptorily: 'pas de perruques!' He mimes the act of ripping off the wig and hurling it to the ground.

He proceeds to present his own dress embellished as it is with lace, ruffles and assorted frills – an absolute riot of lace! Unfortunately, the subject is attacked by an unbearable itch in every part of his body. He rips the lace from his ankles, his neck, his wrists, screaming 'pas de dentelles!' He seizes a cloak in mid-air, tosses it over his shoulders, but drags it forward with some difficulty since the cloak becomes continually heavier and bigger. With a sweeping, commanding gesture he takes hold of a hem and wraps himself inside the cloak as though in a cocoon. From the inside, he cuts it open with a blade. Freedom! He mimes the wind blowing up and making the cloak swell out like a sail. With a counterpoint of oaths and squeaks in *grammelot*, he describes his flight, as he is borne aloft by the crazed cloak. He is in mid-air, he is being carried further and further away into the clouds, when all of a sudden, the words ring out 'Fotu! Pas de manteaux!'

(*With face uncovered.*)

Mimes putting on a modest jacket, then launches into a speech of uninhibited bitterness. He moves his arms and pulls himself upright into the pose of some overbearing, sneering individual. He interrupts himself and screams out: 'Non!' Then, by contrast, he makes his gestures, especially the hand gestures, smaller: he makes a sign of the cross. 'Ça suffit de se signer!' He opens wide his eyes to represent the self-certainty of the truly insane. Gives a wink, imitates someone afflicted with short sight. Walks clumsily and awkwardly. Kneels down and crosses himself. Speaks, still uttering incomprehensible words but opening and closing his jaws and making expressions which are the caricature of the most fanatical of orators. Further adjustment, narrows the space between his lips until he ends up speaking through his nose.

(*Different mask, with the large Razzullo nose.* *)

He transforms himself, once more, into a character of immense conceit. Mimes a quarrel with an imaginary person who challenges him to a duel. With the same attitude of hauteur, he cuts the air with his sword, utters a few casual jibes and, at the end, with a grand sweep, runs his challenger through. He twists the blade in the wound, pulls it out, licks the blood and comments: 'Pas mal!' In the same breath, he abandons the character of the haughty criminal to resume the part of the wise old servant who, in a state of indignation, makes the audience aware of the incivility of that murderous conduct. 'Non! Ce n'est pas possible! Nous sommes des hommes, pas des bêtes!'

(*Mask of an ape-like Zanni.*)

Performs the mime with the aid of *grammelot*, recounting an assault mounted against an imaginary foe in the darkness of the countryside. Mimes stabbing him and tearing out his still beating heart. Proceeds to comment on the action with disgust, miming a cordial conversation with an adversary towards whom he displays understanding and friendship. All of a sudden, his moods turns to rage which mounts to the point of hysteria. He calms down, puts his arm affectionately round the shoulders of the other man, strolls a

* Razzullo was one of the clowns in the Commedia dell'Arte.

little at his side, listening to him as he chats and remarks: 'La dialectique! Ah j'aime la discussion, le raffront. Oui, j'écoute. Oui, je suis d'accord!' Then, in a swift movement, he stabs him. He lays out the body with care, pulls out the dagger and repeats: 'Oui, je suis d'accord.'

It is important to underline the diversity of behaviour and performance corresponding to each change of mask. Adapting oneself to the mask is a result of exercise and attention, of technique but equally of instinct. The feel of a mask of a certain structure on one's face, of a mask which forces one to assume a particular appearance and a definite character, involves the choice of precise models of gesture. The various masks which I wear during the piece on the lesson of Scapino compel me to continually change rhythm, timing and, in some cases, even vocal tonality. Further, I find myself obliged, by awareness and instinct, to heighten or diminish the value of those creatures and attitudes by a shift in the rhythmic progression – pushing on to the legs deliberately but with suppleness, moving and balancing the limbs, or jerking forward while keeping the legs rigid, after the manner of puppets. At times, your arms come up, swing round or move slowly, depending on the mask being worn.

Accidents and Big Noses

I would like to enlarge on a matter that has arisen because of an accident. During that piece of mime, I unwittingly knocked my arm against Razzullo's huge nose. The whole audience noticed, and I bet they were all convinced it was a deliberate gag. In fact, it was the merest chance, but I did not let the opportunity go by. I went on repeating a whole series of smacks on the nose of the mask, setting up a kind of comic dialogue between the nose, the arms, the hands and the sword, in such a way as to condition the duel by creating a copy in grotesque alongside it. I repeat: it was pure chance. I had never previously played that piece wearing that enormous nose, but once the accident occurred, I felt the need to make the most of the incident and to incorporate it into the scene. Therefore, a piece of universal advice: never miss the unexpected . . . and never let yourself be put off by it.

Since we are on the subject, allow me to digress and to discourse on the theatrical science of the accident. To exploit accidents, to make the most of chance happenings, is part of the tradition of Commedia dell'Arte and, even earlier, of the theatre of the minstrels. (Commedia dell'Arte and minstrels' theatre are two styles which fed off each other. There is no way of knowing exactly when the activity of the minstrels was replaced by the activity of the Commedia players. There is no date to mark the changeover.) What interests us is that certain basic comic mechanisms are to be found both in the space occupied by the minstrels and in that occupied by the players of improvised comedy, and so on down to clowns and variety theatre.

The most important, indeed fundamental, aspects, common to all genres of comedy, are improvisation and the accident. If we were to examine a Commedia script, we would have a hard time grasping the comic mechanisms sketched out in it. It is known that the authors of the scripts, from Scala to Biancolelli, made use of a veiled and at times deliberately secret style, as though attempting to stop outsiders to the family or the company from understanding the sense of the annotations.

I have myself had the good fortune, through Franca, my wife, who is herself from a theatrical family, to hold in my hand huge bundles of scripts belonging to the Rame family dating back two or three hundred years, and I have only been able to make anything of them because the present generation of the family still have some idea of the code, and so were able to work their way through the abbreviations and initials towards the subject matter. They have the special fortune of being able to summon up from the recesses of memory hundreds of comic situations and gags which they have themselves performed or seen performed from their earliest years. Among the various initials and abbreviations, the Rame family have pointed out a number which indicate accidents which happened or which were to be made happen. The players and minstrels immediately seized hold of these situations to work them for all they were worth, or to stand on their head any tired moments in the performance. Sometimes the accidents were manufactured in such a way that the spectators were made to feel they were the lead players in the show.

The Comic Wasp

There is an anecdote concerning Cherea, which has a symbolic importance for anyone interested in the attention the players gave to accidents. Cherea, a great actor of the same period as Ruzzante,* halfway between the minstrel figure and the Commedia player, was a person of wide culture. He was the first to translate and, more importantly, to stage, the Roman comic dramatists Plautus and Terence.

It is said that Cherea was in Venice performing one of Plautus' plays. The production was no more than mediocre and in spite of one or two lively passages, the play as a whole simply had not taken off. In other words, there was not much laughter from the audience, but one evening, just as the lead player was coming on to recite the prologue, a particularly peevish wasp had a go at him and started buzzing about furiously. Cherea edged away nervously,

---

* Il Ruzzante (1502–1542), famous as both actor and dramatist.

71

without letting the audience see his unease. He launched into the prologue, but the wasp, an unusually tenacious little creature, managed to get inside his ear. He chased it away, but it crawled up his cheek, then flew up a sleeve. The actor grew more and more agitated, striking out wildly. He gave himself a solid blow in the process, but never managed to make contact with the wasp. The effect was exhilarating. The audience, fully aware of the humour of the situation, fell about laughing.

Cherea, like the natural creature of the stage he was, instead of getting confused, threw himself heart and soul into the situation of the battle with the wasp. He redoubled the effects, pretending that the wasp had got in through the neck of his costume and was crawling up his back. He leapt about, he scratched himself furiously, he jumped in the air as though stung under the arm; he pushed his hand up his sleeve and held it there as though it were stuck and could not be got out. In that impossible situation, he carried on reciting the prologue. The audience could not make out a word, engrossed as they were by the *fou rire*. But Cherea had not finished yet. He pulled his hand forcefully down the sleeve, ripping the shirt in the process, and started groping around inside the tunic for the by now imaginary wasp. He hauled off the remnants of his upper costume, and rummaged inside the breeches. He mimed being stung on the buttocks, and on other more delicate parts of the male anatomy. The wasp had long since flown off, but Cherea had no difficulty in making the audience believe that it was still there, as insistent as ever. When the play itself got under way and the other actors came on, they too, having been tipped off, pretended that they were persecuted by the wasp. As if that were not enough, Cherea mimed a wasp-hunt which took him off the stage, down among the audience in the stalls where, quite nonchalantly, apparently trying to catch the wasp, he gave some members of the audience a slap on the ear. The play, needless to say, went to the dogs, as the saying is, but the success of the evening surpassed all expectations.

The Spoof Accident

The following day, the company met for rehearsal. With the aid of some horsehair and the addition of tiny pieces of material decked out with little feathers, a couple of nearly perfect wasps were manufactured. The incident of the troublesome wasp was encored in every detail, starting with the prologue. The wasp was even worked into the love scene. In the middle of a quarrel over a question of honour, the buzz of this nasty little insect makes itself heard. Everybody leaps to their feet, gets excited and jumps about in a kind of wild dance. At the end of the process, the comedy had lost its Plautine title to be rechristened *The Wasp's Comedy*. An external accident had become the mainspring for the renewal of the mechanism of the comedy.

However, accidents of this sort are useful not only for reviving worn-out schemes, but even more for destroying another pernicious scheme – the one that reduces the spectator to the role of *voyeur*. At this point, allow me to explain myself more clearly.

Breaking Down the Fourth Wall

A substantial part of theatre, including modern theatre, is conceived in such a way as to lull the viewer into a state of total passivity. It begins with the darkness in the auditorium, a precondition for a kind of psychic vacuum, but which, on the contrary, has the effect of producing attention of an exclusively emotional order. People find themselves following events unfolding on stage as though they were themselves on the far side of a curtain, or of a fourth wall which permits them to see – while remaining unseen – a succession of intimate stories, of private, at times downright brutal, incidents, which they, in the unlighted hall, have been trained to listen to in what can be described as a 'cover of darkness' state of mind. They have the impression of being spies engrossed only in some morbid pleasure of their own – the classical attitude of the peeping Tom.

The intention of doing away with the idea of the fourth wall was already an obsession with the Commedia players. Molière himself conceived the renewal of French theatre in terms of the genuinely revolutionary intuitions of the Italian actors. I have already explained how his master was Scapino – a mask which Molière himself played in his turn – and with the experience gained in Commedia circles, Molière grasped the importance of the involvement, including the physical involvement, of the spectators. As a first move, he had the proscenium pushed forward. When many theatres were first built, the proscenium came up to the line, today a purely imaginary one, which ran between the first two boxes outside the scenic arch. This was the ideal position for an actor performing works that were not of the intimate variety but were, on the contrary, epic and popular, since they required him to project his voice towards the stalls, beyond the scenic arch, to where the audience were seated, that is, outside the framework which delimits and marks off the stage in its strict sense. This space is called the front scene, and Molière brought on his actors – in both senses – here.

Molière was fond of repeating: 'A talented actor has no need of special supporting elements – complicated scenery at his back, sound effects, special background noises. If you are actors of sufficient sensitivity and with sufficient mastery of the craft, and if the text is strong, your voice and your body should be enough to convey that it is dawn, that it is raining outside, that it is windy, that the sun is shining, that it is warm or that there is a storm blowing up – just you by yourselves, without any need of equipment, of light effects, of clanging sheets of metal to suggest a storm or of rolls of drums accompanied by flying grains of sand to give the impression of wind and rain.' Molière had a deep hatred for all those props of the 'nearly real' variety. Personally, I believe that many directors today should learn to do without the sophisticated stereo consoles or the 'star wars' style lighting equipment. Braque used to say to his painter pupils: 'Too much colour, no colour.'

The Frontiers of Empire
Before moving on, I want to round off my remarks on *grammelot*. I have already shown how performers in other ages used this onomatopoeic device, but no doubt some of you will be wondering – 'How can this *grammelot* be put to use nowadays? Where, how, in what situations?'

Some years ago, faced with this problem, I managed to work out a *grammelot* with American overtones. Today, English, particularly the version spoken in the United States, has become the language of the Empire. There is no avoiding the reality; it is the dominant language in absolute terms, and this fact has led to an outbreak of lexical plagiarism in Italy. You can observe it in scores of journalists who, gurgling with delight at their own intellect, never fail to introduce into each and every article they write at least fifty-five terms from American slang – look, scoop, mood, network, match, meeting, feeling, workshop – the list is endless. This imbecility indicates that we inhabit the frontiers of Empire.

In this empire, without indulging in hysteria, we are moving unconsciously towards a 'star wars' situation. Under the 'balance of forces' pretext, they are continuing to pack arsenals with missiles that are getting more and more sophisticated and murderous. The atmosphere and the stratosphere round the earth are jam-packed with probes, satellites, sophisticated apparatuses and control stations. Every so often, a missile breaks free, collides with a passenger aircraft or crashes on to some inhabited area. It is the price to be paid for the progress of science. Every other day, you hear talk of how real is the risk of all of us being blown sky-high. Nevertheless, our political masters assure us that the situation is under control, that we can sleep peacefully in our beds – the generals and the scientists are reasonable people. That is the point – it is precisely these people's way of reasoning – which comes so close to stupidity – that I cannot trust.

Thinking about this environment and these characters, I had the bright idea of attempting a monologue in sophisticated American *grammelot*, featuring a high-level scientific conference where an illustrious nuclear electronic physicist is holding forth. This great technocrat would be explaining the science of robots with the relevant, comparative description of circuits, of relays, of computers, before proceeding to an account of the history of human flight, detailing early propeller planes with the internal combustion engine, and then going on to reactors and long-range missiles, like those installed, for our security, in Comiso in Sicily, even if it seems likely that they will gradually be planted all over Italy, tastefully disguised as bell towers so as not to spoil the effect. I hope they will put a few in the Vatican as well, just to give encouragement to the great traveller – you know who I mean – John Paul II, a man I love deeply for his exuberance, his panache, his love of the land in the primary sense of the term. I cannot get out of my head the kiss he bestows on the soil of every country where he sets foot.

The Kiss of the Flying Pope

I saw him some time back in Spain. I was performing in Madrid and went along to the airport specifically to see him at the moment he got off the plane. The airport was crowded with the faithful, and at a certain point the Pope's aeroplane was sighted among the clouds. It was a DC 10. You know the kind I mean? The DC 10s have a habit of dropping engines, wings, undercarriages as if they were sieves. Not the Pope's plane. Never lost a cog. It radiated a stupefying sense of wholeness and power. All tense, in yellow and white with a little skull cap on the top, so much so that one member of the assembled faithful, moved by a mixture of fanaticism and short-sightedness, pointed a finger and shouted out – 'There's the Pope!' Someone tried to put him right – 'No, that's not the Pope; it's just the aeroplane carrying the Pope.' The other was having none of it: 'It is him! It's Pope John Paul flying.' The rest of the bystanders joined in: 'It cannot really be the Pope. John Paul doesn't have all those little windows along his side.' Our friend did undergo a moment of perplexity, but I never was entirely certain that he was convinced.

The great jet came down on the runway, edged forward towards an open space and immediately a huge staircase with twenty-five steps was rolled over to the plane. The door was flung open ... usually, when important personages touch down, the aircraft captain, air hostesses, secretaries and various minor ministers make an appearance first ... but with John Paul, the door was opened wide and there he was, in person, first in line, in all his splendour – silver hair, shining eyes, snub nose turned up, powerful neck, magnificent pectoral cross, muscles and abdomen perfectly firm, sash tightly tied round his waist, red cloak hanging down to his feet: Superman!

He began to rock back and forward, one, two ... just as if he was working himself up for take-off. All around, the Spaniards held their breath. Some knelt down: 'The Pope is flying!' You could already picture the scene: Vrooooom! and there he was, floating free, arms outstretched, soutane aflutter, yellow and white smoke issuing from beneath the soutane, writing in the skies – God is with us, by God! Unfortunately, a spoilsport of a cardinal . . . (What can I do? I am recounting a true story, and one seen on television screens.) Everybody witnessed it. There he was leaning forward, and at his back a cardinal without a care in the world, chatting away with someone else, his foot firmly planted on the hem of the cloak. The Pope, unable to move, was nearly asphyxiated but – and this demonstrates the real strength of the man – he dilated his neck muscles (never forget that he was once a mason, a working man) and undid the tie of the cloak. He bounded down the steps at an unbelievable pace . . . no other human being can equal our Pope over a short burst of airport steps . . . A mad descent . . . but then something totally unexpected, devastating occurred: he missed the last couple of steps! So overcome was he by the longing for that kiss that he simply did not see them! The scene was cut both from the live recording and from the later edited version but I was there to savour it! He went headlong! Ended up face down! He made contact with the ground, his two eye teeth literally ploughing into the earth: a furrow three metres long. Then he kissed the ground. It was worth waiting to see the extent of sensual energy, of overwhelming voluptuous eroticism that went into it! The earth itself began to tremble: 'Nooo'. A tremor, an orgasm surpassing fantasy! There was the suggestion of an earthquake, of floods, of the wrath of God. That Pope John Paul, what strength!

Silence! Technocrat on the Podium

Let us leave him for the moment and pass on to the lecture on high technology given by the great man of science to his pupils and peers. I will play the part of the lecturer, and the spectators will have to think themselves into the part of scientific eggheads able to follow, without exerting themselves, a speech laden with mysterious, abstruse, technical terms, delivered in that elevated jargon so dear to experts. At the outset, as I have said, I will talk of robots and computers, and there you will understand every word, since – maintaining the fiction of you being illustrious scientists – everyone knows what they are and how they work. Then, with a giant leap backwards, I will go on to describe the aeroplane fitted with the internal combustion engine and, next, the rocket in which the scientist himself will be fired out into the stratosphere and then . . . but let's wait and see.

Now, as regards the exercise of the *grammelot*, which terms and words require to be clearly enunciated? I have no knowledge of English, apart from those expressions used by the most troglodyte of tourists – Good day, good evening, how are you, how much is that, I am sleepy, I am hungry, and that's the lot. In this case, however, I have, in keeping with the ideas I set out when discussing the *grammelot* of the crow and the eagle, learned a dozen terms. It is important to pay particular attention to this aspect. Anyone who is interested in this technique can try various experiments, perhaps at home with friends, and he will notice that as soon as he gets the feel of the thing, provided he has managed to articulate credible sounds and cadences, he will have no bother in persuading his listeners that he is speaking a genuine language. Let's have a go at the lecture of this distinguished technocrat, addressed to an extraordinary audience of great minds:

Places himself in front of the audience, with a beaming smile, radiating the impression of a man cocksure of himself but anxious to please. He casts a glance over the entire company, as though desperate not to overlook anyone and to have an individual greeting for everyone present. He delivers, in a subdued tone, his opening remarks, which appear to be words of welcome to those who have taken the trouble to come. He plainly perpetrates some gaffe, as can be gathered from the speed with which he corrects himself, gives an embarrassed laugh, and apologises. He proceeds, giving long lists of complex terms which, in his anxiety not to be misunderstood, he repeats, spells out, pronounces carefully. He allows himself the odd pun as he goes and, in a state of self-satisfaction, laughs delightedly at his own jokes. His countenance turns serious again as he describes a complicated piece of machinery. He draws in the air devices made up of lengths of piping, control relays, compressors, and tapes whirling at high speeds. He calls attention to the various noises, whistles, hissing sounds, scratches, crackles, bangs and small explosions which it emits, and, at the end of the sequence, pulls from the core of the machine a card which he proceeds to read. He rips it up, evidently disappointed. His commentary is interspersed with a series of different sounds. He pauses, gazing intensely at the audience, before asking, in clearly articulated words – Did you understand?

He returns to his mid-air designs, sketching out a flying machine with flapping wings, of the kind known to Leonardo. Mimes climbing aboard and pedalling like a madman. He gives the impression of lifting off. He floats, glides, rises up again and crashes with a dull thud. Mimes, with rage and contempt mingled with sarcasm, a single bolt taking off and hovering in the air. Laughs at the idea. Sketches out a new machine, this time a monoplane equipped with combustion engine. He outlines its dimensions, shape and appearance, not omitting the rudders and the propeller, which he indicates with correct English name. Gets the engine started by turning the propeller, all accompanied by appropriate noises . . . rrrrraaaaaa. Mimes cranking up a starting handle. The engine splutters into life: proooo too teeeeee . . . repeats the sound produced by the propeller – rrrrrrraaaaaa . . . then the engine sounds – prooooo tooo teeeeeee. Scolds the engine as though it were an impudent child, refusing to do what it is told. He tells it (still in *grammelot*, obviously) 'No, the propeller goes rrrrrrraaaaaa, you're supposed to go proooo tooooo prooooo not prooo toooo teeee. Let's all try hard to get it right, shall we?'

Has another go, first with the propeller then with the starting handle. This time the correct sounds issue from the engine, but not for long. The engine jams, stutters, coughs out a variety of odd noises, dies out, flickers back to life before falling completely still. The technocrat, in a state of some apprehension, urges it on, treating it delicately, as though it were a child stumbling over its first words. He fondles and strokes it, addressing it in a soft voice. The engine kicks back into life. Ecstasy of the expert. In the general euphoria, the engine delivers a few bars of a triumphal march, then, without warning, misses a beat, splutters, groans, and, to the consternation of our expert, breathes its last. Gives a final heave and gasp, squirting drops of boiling liquid in the face of the enraged scientist. Then issues a sound like escaping steam, gradually winding down to a wheezy death-rattle. The engine folds in on itself, lifeless. The technocrat bursts into tears.

After a few moments, he perks up. Mimes removing the cap of the fuel tank. Peers in, sniffs. 'No wonder it didn't work. Dry as a bone! Not a drop left.' In a rage, he turns to an imaginary assistant, hurling in his direction strings of insults, made up of a sequence of guttural sounds mixed with some of the most frequent English swear-words – Damn it, shut up, fuck off, bastard. The overall drift of the speech should be clear. 'Bloody idiot, how is the propeller to make its rrrrrraaaaa and the engine its proooo tooooo prooooo if you are too lazy to give it its petrol, imbecile, murderer of innocent engines? I'll boot you out on the street. Do me a favour, keep your mouth shut.' Still muttering aggressively to himself, he mimes seizing the petrol-pump hose, sticks the nozzle in the tank and turns on the pump. The liquid flows in to the last drop. He peers into the tank to check. Screws on the cap. Turns the starting handle, setting the propeller in motion. As the propeller starts up, the engine splutters into life. Thoroughly satisfied with himself, the technocrat points out the beauty of the rhythmic sounds – proooo tooo proooo. It begins to take on something of the beat of rock music, when, once again, something goes wrong. Further bangs, heaves and gasps: pot-pitpeeee-pet-put-to-ta-tii . . . the scientist urges, encourages, stammers in time with the engine which is now on its last legs. Final gasp, squirting water on his face. The engine runs down, with a hissing sound of escaping air – sssssssss.

The scientist looks round in despair, and in a gesture of annoyance aims a kick at the engine. Immediately, the rhythmic beat starts up – prooo tooo proo. The scientist cannot hide his delight, mimes pushing the plane out towards the runway. He orders everyone out of the way. Ready for take-off! Turns to the audience with gestures and tones of voice which suggest a measure of concern. He seems to be saying: 'Everyone down! The danger's not passed. While taking off, the plane will pass close above your heads, and might cut off one that sticks out above the rest.' The plane taxis out and takes off. Proooo tooooo proooo . . . the banging sound is converted into the real engine roar. The technocrat mimes the rise of the monoplane. He turns full circle, face up, watching the movement of the aircraft in transports of delight. Return of the banging noise, which changes into a kind of whine rising, falling, fading into the distance. Silence. Moment of panic. The whine comes back into range. The plane swoops headlong, as though about to crash. Gains height after having almost touched the ground, then comes sweeping back and again, in the middle distance, almost touches the ground. The professor throws himself headlong on to the ground, picks himself up and follows, turning his head to right and left, the mad gyrations of the plane. The plane makes itself heard once again. Will it gather height? No! Crash! smashing to pieces on the ground. Final proooo toooo and it is all over. The professor seems on the point of a hysterical outburst, but succeeds in containing himself.

He regains control of himself and issues a peremptory order to the mechanics to prepare the big rocket. Mimes a collective action. The missile is mounted on a ramp. The supertechnocrat mimes the climb up a long ladder. In a state of euphoria, he climbs at top speed, speaking rhythmically as he goes. His utterances change tone into a triumphal march along the lines of America, America. He interrupts himself once he gets to the top of the ladder where it reaches the cap of the missile. Looks down for an instant but is nearly overcome by vertigo. Secures himself to the steps by a belt and mimes opening a door in the missile cap. Observes the controls inside. Checks, still describing each step in scientific *grammelot*, the various instruments, moves the levers and turns the handles. Closes the entrance, makes his descent sliding down the steps fireman-style.

Begins to tog himself up like a diver. Puts on first the trousers, zipping himself up to the stomach. The zip sticks near the groin, catching a particularly sensitive and delicate member concealed in the undergarments.

79

Yells of agony. Undoes the zip with immense care. Succeeds without further mishap. The dressing ceremonial is complete. Pulls the helmet down over his head, opens the forward door, breathes with voluptuous delight. Closes it behind him. Takes hold of some pipes and places them in the appropriate openings, one in the chest at the level of the heart, one in the helmet next to the mouth and one lower down between his legs. The fastening operation is accompanied by groans denoting a mixture of apprehension and dissatisfaction. The final pipe is fixed uncompromisingly between the buttocks. He opens his eyes wide in terror. Makes a miaowing sound. Heaves a deep sigh. 'Oh yes!' Mimes having himself secured in the command capsule and seated in the captain's chair. Plugs in the various pipes and tubes. Carries out a routine check of the instruments – presses the buttons, manoeuvres the levers. The lights go on, sounds and whistles are heard and a cuckoo clock appears. The phone rings. Picks up the receiver. It is his mother! – loving dialogue of the classical all-American boy – deeply moved, delighted, bashful, grinning, anxious to be reassuring.

Sequence of almost syncopated sounds at each move of the supertechnocrat as he presses a myriad of buttons. The sounds become increasingly harmonious to the point where they are transformed into jazz music, complete with double-bass and trombone. The professor has another go. The cuckoo, in a decidedly bad mood, makes a reappearance. Quick as a flash, the professor pulls out a gun and shoots it dead. All in order. AOK. Prepare for lift-off. Count down under way. Our astronaut's heart is heard thumping loudly, the beat faster and faster. Excitement. Two, one, zero! Lift-off. Explosion! Bumps. Shudders. Trembles. The supertechnocrat mimes loss of consciousness. Feels himself crushed and crumpled under the weight, but recovers. The missile slides forward, bouncing as it goes. All is not going as per programme. A bang. A piece of the missile flies off, followed by other pieces. It begins to look like Guy Fawkes Night. The professor, scared stiff, observes the break-up of the machine. In a sequence of bangs and thumps, of whistles and whines, the whole thing falls apart. Blim! Ramp! Strump! Slim! Slam bin bon spom pim tung straaapooom patrac ooooo, rounding off with a low – phut phut phut . . . fading away to nothing. Final scream of our technocrat, who rushes off, arms outstretched, announcing the ultimate calamity.

Grammelot – Live Broadcast

I have to confess to a secret dream. I often long to sneak into a TV studio, seat myself in the newsreader's chair and deliver the entire bulletin in *grammelot*. I bet no one would even notice:

Yessay, a speachpour us Mrs Thatcher wole abse missiles wom
ranner is gorge near . . . Mr Reagan fud num intaras moo initiatives
dan mosco per intercess intle noo Afghanistan . . .

It would be easy to continue uninterrupted for a good half-hour.

Let us get back to the actions and gestures of the Commedia players. No
doubt some of you will already be wondering – Why is he paying so much
attention to the Commedia dell'Arte?

Study to Believe . . . With Reservations

It may seem a somewhat carping question, but less and less so the more you
think about it. There are authors, actors and directors who look down their
noses at this style of theatre and who will happily declare it inconsistent, or
the product of someone's fevered imagination. As I studied and analysed the
phenomenon with the aid of researchers and scholars I became convinced
that this superior attitude towards Commedia dell'Arte was due in great
measure to mere ignorance. There is nothing more typical of many theatre
people then this arrogant willingness to fire off judgements in all directions,
or to deal with everything from hearsay, delivering high-minded clichés
without ever running the risk of checking the facts or seeking them out for
themselves, let alone chewing them over and, hopefully, digesting them with
the aid of practice. At any moment of the day, they can be heard issuing
verdicts on any theatrical subject under the sun. It is a cretinous frame of
mind, just as it is cretinous not to take an interest in your own historical,
ethnic and anthropological roots. 'I am alive today, I am thoroughly modern,
so what do I care about what went on before me?' A certain Signor Gramsci,*
now somewhat out of fashion, had this to say: 'If you do not know where you
come from, it is hard to understand what you are aiming for.'

As regards Commedia dell'Arte and its language, I have discovered that it
is not enough to rely on the standard manuals on the subject. To decipher the
play-scripts – which are themselves legion – thorough research and a
comparison and contrast of the scripts among themselves are essential,
particularly if the *lazzi*, the set pieces, which are for the most part puzzling,
are to be interpreted. This has enormous implications for the comic output of
the so-called minor theatre – the popular farces of the nineteenth and
twentieth centuries, variety theatre, curtain-raisers, clown shows and even

---

* Antonio Gramsci (1891–1937), Italian Marxist philosopher, imprisoned under
Fascism.

the sketches of silent cinema. No small part of Commedia dell'Arte material ended up in these forms of comic enterprise.

In conclusion, practice is the best means of learning to read any theatre text, and in theatre practice involves not just staging plays personally, but also going to see how other people, particularly performers of talent and experience, set about the business. I myself acquired the basics of the craft by standing night after night in the wings, spying on the more seasoned practitioners in the variety companies I worked with. I would urge this course of action on young actors – go and watch every move, if necessary from behind the wings, even if the stage manager throws a fit and threatens to kick you out. Position yourself in a spot where you can follow the actor who knows the business inside out, the 'old pro'. Try to understand how he gets out of tight spots, how he achieves his effects, how he develops a feel for an audience, how he rearranges the script according to audience response, how he creates and shapes his rhythms, how he controls his pauses and timing. Believe me, this is the best theatre academy anyone could hope to attend.

To Swim like a Violin

The actor who has the audience eating out of the palm of his hand is like the virtuoso violinist who no longer has to watch his fingers as he plays, nor even keep an eye on the bow. He feels the notes as they leave the violin, and listens to them as they float back. You will never see a great maestro of violin or piano with his eyes fixed on the keyboard or on the instrument: the instrument has become part of him. In the same way, a skilled mime has no need to watch his own hands or to check their movement. The same should be true of a great actor with his voice or his body.

It is also important to bear in mind the need to keep the level of spray to a minimum. By spray I am not referring to anything produced by the excess of salivation or by pronouncing with excessive emphasis the letters P and B, because in me, for example, that level can be extraordinary. There are people who have been known to refuse a seat in the front rows when I am performing, while others have been known to catch a cold from the astonishing shower issuing from my mouth. There's no need for concern; it's an honest salivation. In any case, spitting is a part of our profession; indeed it is an essential element of it. The actor who does not produce much saliva has problems; he will strain his voice easily, he will have difficulty changing tones, he will find himself prone to stammers or stutters; he's like an engine without lubricating oil. However, it was not my intention to discuss plant watering.

I was really referring to producing spray as in the art of swimming or rowing. In Italian theatre slang, the verbs 'to spray' or 'to splash' are used to describe actors who declaim and roar on stage. The expression derives from an analogy with bad swimmers, splashing about madly with their arms and legs, producing as much spray as a small motor boat. The real swimmer can push himself forward in the water without producing needless commotion. He appears to do everything effortlessly; he glides lightly and rapidly, without making a single splash. His power comes from co-ordination and economy of gesture: on the other hand, the unfortunate amateur waves his arms as though they were windmill sails, and beats about wildly, as though whipping several bowls of mayonnaise at the same time. And does not move forward one inch; indeed, he is more likely to drown. The same is true in theatre.

Those who do not know how to act yell, and go in for a great deal of arm-waving. Those who have no sense of the stage strain their voice, and risk completely losing it. They rely on strident falsetto and nasal tones. In addition, they can hold neither time nor rhythm, and recite their part without heed to other actors, much less to the audience. The effect it produces on anyone listening is appalling, since, among other things, it gives the impression of an inhuman effort. In theatre, performers must give the impression of achieving everything effortlessly and in total relaxation.

This is not the same as giving less than your best, or performing lazily. On the contrary, it is vital to learn to act with perfect control and balance, rising to a crescendo in a planned, sensible progression, cunningly arranging pauses and breaths so as to give the impression of ease. I have seen an actor, who shall be nameless, but who had an uncanny resemblance to Vittorio Gassman, walk off stage after a performance and collapse into the nearest chair, completely exhausted, and yet had you seen him on stage at any point during the evening, you would have sworn that he had no problem in the world. That is what talent and a command of the craft mean.

So, to sum up: to get on top of this business, with dignity, to become a worthwhile man or woman of the theatre, the key is to work hard to acquire those elements of knowledge we have been discussing, and these come from study, from direct observation and from practice. In short, shun prejudice, avoid following fashion if you are keen not to end up on your backside. Be involved with your own times even when dealing with stories from other times. Reject definitions and classifications which purport to give lists of importance – in other words categories of the Aristotelian type, which would set up a scale of values with tragedy at the top, followed by drama, then comedy and so on down, down down to puppet theatre, acrobats and clowns.

Hamlet or the Fool

In the days when I was beginning my theatre career, everything to do with clowns was relegated to the level of theatre for minors – in every sense. Faced with this idiotic categorisation, I was tempted to throw everything up. Personally I did not come into theatre with any ambition to play Hamlet, but with the aspiration to be the red-nosed comic, the clown . . . but seriously. Around that time, in Paris, I had the fortune to attend an event which lasted three days and involved clowns from all over Europe. They performed their most outrageous routines, but I later discovered over half of the acts I had seen there were in the texts of the old minstrels, in the Atellan and ancient farces.

Jugulares Scurrae

So what exactly was a minstrel, or *giullare* in Italian? He was a mime who, in addition to gestures, expressed himself in word and song but who, for the most part, would not bother to write out his own scripts. He improvised and worked from memory, so the tradition was transmitted orally.

The extant minstrel scripts were hardly ever written out by the minstrels themselves, but by clerks, clerics or lawyers who relaxed by transcribing the ballads, the poems and rhymed disputes which they had heard. The volumes that collect together the greater part of these transcriptions are called codexes (e.g. the Laurenziano, or the Papafava) and are actually legal tomes, collections of contracts and laws. On the back of these acts, contracts and deeds, the clerk or the lawyer himself often scribbled out, for his own satisfaction, pieces of poetry he had heard the day before in the piazza or in some courtyard. At times their memory was less than reliable. In different codexes, we can find different transcriptions of the same text due, plainly, to differences of memory in different people, or to some little clerk's inclination to share in the process of poetic creation. The point is that these texts have not come down to us as a result of some conscious decision to transmit poetic works to posterity but only by pure chance, simply because the reverse side contained a document setting out the terms of a contract or a will. God bless lawyers and all their acts!

The minstrels almost always performed as themselves, by themselves, with no other actor on the board – or table – even when they produced 'two-handers' or dialogues between two people. Indeed, their special trick was to perform scenes where dozens of different characters made an appearance. They each used one eccentric costume of their own, but they had a penchant for disguise. In the course of market day, for instance, they would jump up on a bench, in the guise of a guard, a doctor, a lawyer, a priest, a merchant and the performance would get under way immediately.

Role of the Minstrel

Since we have mentioned schools, and since they have not been generous on the topics that interest us, I would like to flesh out their teaching with a few words on the role of the minstrel and *giullare* in the Middle Ages. In his *Social History of Art* , Hauser deals at length with the distinction between minstrel, wandering cleric and troubadour, providing neat categories – minstrel, storyteller, cleric and juggler – although, in my view, rather too schematically.

I do not believe that the differences were so marked. There were certain minstrels who were employed as couriers for the court poets, or troubadours, and their task was to go to other courts to recite or sing what the prince, perhaps in his troubadour guise, had written. Each chose the tone which came naturally to him – lyrical, ironic or simply coarse humour. There were others who had no difficulty over being simultaneously troubadour and minstrel. An example was the thirteenth-century Sienese writer, Ruggero Pugliese, a man of high culture, if also of extremely caustic irreverence. For his brashness, he found himself in the dock and came close to being burned at the stake. He used his trial as material for a rhyming song, which managed to be both tragic and joyful. In another ballad, he listed all the things that a good minstrel must know how to do: sing, pay court, swindle, ensnare, work the scales, make calculations, poke fun at suave gigolos, cheat at cards or dice, swear to all kinds of falsehood, deliver swooning – or tart – serenades, speak phoney Latin or genuine Greek, pass off what is true as false and false as true. Ambiguity, with a denial of all established values – that was the real minstrel.

I would not like this discussion of the minstrel in his early period to give rise to misunderstanding. Some people might go off with the idea that the minstrel was the symbol of never-ending revolt against authority, a stimulus to consciousness-raising among ordinary people, a kind of full-time intellectual dedicated to the cultural formation of the exploited classes.

No, no . . . please. The minstrel is not at all to be seen as the activist given over heart and soul to the emancipation and education of the people. There were minstrels who took the people's side, but there were others who were reactionaries and conservatives, shoulder to shoulder with the powers that be; some were agnostic, others burned to throw up the barricades; there were some on every side. In other words, it was all a bit like today.

Minstrels in the Peasants' War in Germany

Katrin Koll, a Danish-German scholar who has carried out important researches into medieval theatre, has managed to put together an impressive body of documents on the behaviour of minstrels in Germany during the Peasants' War of the sixteenth and seventeenth centuries. There are extant records of trials against minstrels who were sent to the gallows for abusing the passes which allowed them to move freely around the country, and who chose to act as go-betweens for the various groups of rebels operating as far apart as Swabia, Bavaria, Austria and the Tyrol, not to mention Croatia and Bohemia.

From the court records, however, it transpires that far from sticking to the task of acting as message bearers, they carried out propaganda work. In their performances they railed against the organised theft of the great landowners, against the merchant class, against the corruption of the Roman clergy and against the hypocritical opportunism of the new Lutheran ministers. In the trials, to establish their guilt, one can find, duly documented, the themes and grotesque humour developed in their performances, and the court archives include some of the illustrated leaflets, complete with lithographed caricatures, satirical sonnets and irreverent captions, handed out to the audience during the performances. An edition of these leaflets, beautifully reproduced, was published recently in East Berlin, and I am the proud possessor of a copy.

From other sources it is clear that some minstrels went to the other extreme and placed themselves at the service of the police. They moved from place to place, passing themselves off as sympathisers with the peasant revolt, while all the time gathering the information that would lead to the arrest, with the inevitable hanging, drawing and quartering, of the rebels. Every so often these bastards would be uncovered by the people, who were not as a rule inclined towards mercy.

In her anthology of historical documents on the minstrels, Dr Koll has come across one which sees them raised to the highest point of public esteem and approval. The incident to which the document refers occurred in Berne. The city, part of the Swiss Confederation, was autonomous, and in the early years of the sixteenth century was attacked by troops from Burgundy. The city's army, composed largely of citizen volunteers, went out to face the Burgundians, all of whom were professional soldiers. The two armies lined up on an open plain, with a lake to the right, the city to the left and hills behind. It was dawn. The Captain General of the Burgundian army issued the order to wait until the sun was higher in the sky, since if they were to attack at that moment, they would find themselves with the sun in their eyes, and at a serious disadvantage.

Groups of minstrels in jesters' outfits took up position in front of the Bernese army. Some were on stilts, others astride pigs and donkeys kitted out with the colours of Burgundy. All together they proceeded to stage, with bloodcurling yells, a pantomime battle, making a great play of the conceit of the Burgundians and presenting them as cowards, cuckolds, puffed-up ponces and shitty-pants. For a time, the Burgundians, compelled to maintain their formation, had to put up with these jibes and insults, and had no option but to watch this obscene performance. When, however, the minstrels dropped their trousers, farted and made gestures of defecating in the enemy's face, and of wiping their bottoms with banners bearing the Burgundian coat of arms, the whole line broke. Some hundreds of soldiers set off in pursuit of those ranks of buffoons, who carried on clowning and skylarking, and leading them ever closer to the ranks of the Bernese army. The officers roared out, they sounded the signal to return to the lines, but it was too late . . . battle was joined, and Berne carried the day.

It was for this reason that the ancient Statute of the City, unique of its kind, ordained that minstrels were to have the right of hospitality on any day of the year, no matter where they came from. Further, it was laid down that they had the privilege of protection and applause during performance, and, of especial importance, they were exempted from the payment of all taxes.

History, Compartments and Categories

Before ending this day, I should like to add a few words on the dangers of the narrowly schematic view. I have come across several works in which the authors, desperate to give some form of historical-cum-cultural organisation to the huge mass of styles and forms existing in the various theatres of Renaissance Europe, have resolved the entire question by placing on one side the Italian sixteenth-seventeenth centuries with the Commedia dell'Arte, and on the other the French theatre before and during the life of Molière, then the Spanish theatre, and further on, completely apart from the rest, the English theatre. This last is supposedly marked by its preconceived, literary quality, and is considered to be bereft of the verve of improvisation.

Since this simplification has reached epidemic proportions, and brings us back yet again to the Aristotelian Academies, let me repeat that the vertical divisions in question have no substance: history is not made for compartments and cages, everything in order, everything in place! Just for a start, whoever told these people that Molière's plays are never resolved with a burst of improvisation, or that English actors in the Elizabethan period never acted off the cuff? Shakespeare's and Molière's performers had no hesitation in launching themselves into improvisation. They made adjustments in the presence of the audience. To dispel any doubts on the subject, we have a version of *Hamlet* where we discover the actor Richard Burbage happily taking it on himself to rewrite more than one speech, stealing whole sentences from other tragedies, whether by Shakespeare or not.*

As to the other viewpoint, every bit as drastic, which sees the Commedia dell'Arte as the only form of theatre in Italy, I would like to remind you that among the active authors of the same period can be listed such men as Della Casa, Della Porta, Aretino, Giordano Bruno, Buonarroti the Younger – to mention only a few. I could run through at least another dozen writers who had no connection with Commedia dell'Arte in the strict sense.

However, the most outrageous of these tightly schematic approaches was one I heard articulated recently by a retired university professor. I quote: 'Commedia dell'Arte dies when it is formalised, in other words when set texts with fixed dialogue, whose characters are given established roles in the plots, replace outline sketches. When the taste for the printed, definitive work is stronger than the pleasure of the imponderable, at that point Commedia dell'Arte is dead!'

God knows how long they have been saying that when Goldoni decided to give rounded structure to the scripts, when he reformed theatre and stamped on improvisation, he slammed the lid on the coffin of Commedia. Nevertheless, I have a warning: I would go easy before tolling the funeral march. Don't rush to summon the grave-diggers just yet. I could never bring myself to intone: 'Commedia was born in such and such a spot, it took poorly in such another place, recovered a little elsewhere, but finally breathed its last in . . .' As far as I am concerned, Commedia has never died. I am still aware of its presence, and I know that in saying that I am speaking for a host of theatre people from today, yesterday, the day before yesterday. Sketches, variety theatre, comedy theatre of the whole of the century past, including figures such as Totò, did no more than hook themselves on to the great oxygen pipe of Commedia. They took up and developed endless themes and cues. The same could be said of Eduardo De Filippo.† The Neapolitan theatre of the last fifty years shows the impact of the inexhaustible inventiveness of Commedia.

So, to anyone anxious to raise a headstone bearing the words 'Here Lies', I would say – Go right ahead! As for me, I have always found the old girl in excellent health, boozing, carousing, making love and having a whale of a time with appetites undiminished. The same lush old whore as ever!

---

* A reference to the Bad Quarto *Hamlet*, a corrupt text which in parts is a reconstruction from memory by one or more actors of scenes from the play.

† A Neapolitan actor and dramatist (1900–84) writer of many comedies which portray harsh realities in a grotesque comic spirit.

Third Day

Pinning the Audience to their Seats: the Situation

Sartre wrote an essay entitled *Popular Theatre, Theatre of Situation*. In theatrical terms, what is situation? It is the basic structure which allows the progress of the narrative to be constructed in such a way as to involve the audience in the tension and to make it participate fully in the unfolding of the plot. That may seem a little bombastic, so it may be simpler to say that the situation is the mechanism that grabs the attention of the audience and keeps them on the edge of their seats. Blasetti* used a more colourful expression when he said; 'It is the nail sticking out of the stool which keeps the spectator's bottom in the right place.' In *Hamlet* there are at least fifteen situations, one after the other. Let us examine them.

The first is the ghost with a throaty voice which appears and starts to nag Hamlet: 'I am the enraged spirit of your father. Someone has killed me, and, as if that were not enough, they have run off with my wife! That someone is your uncle!' Can he be believed? As everyone knows, the dead get hopelessly confused, so Hamlet decides to make further enquiries. Next situation: the brother of Ophelia, who is herself in love with Hamlet, sets off for Paris to continue his studies. Polonius, the father of Ophelia, takes advantage of the farewells to present the overall situation of the tragedy. In this way we too are updated on the situation regarding the attachment of the young prince to Ophelia. At that juncture a new situation arises: Hamlet decides to have the strolling players enact, in the presence of the king, the story of a similar crime. His plan is to create, through the actors, a situation of tension worthy of 'psychodrama', so as to blow the murderer's mind. Perhaps the fratricide will not withstand such Machiavellian dealings.

A new situation: the uncle strongly suspects Hamlet of suspecting him, and Hamlet is aware of this, so, to avoid discovery, he decides to act mad. He acts the part of a babbling demon, he attacks his mother, he insults and kicks Ophelia who – further pregnant situation – begins to lose her mind, but this time for real. In fact she is the only one to have no understanding of the kind

---

* Alessandro Blasetti – Italian film director of comedies and spectaculars.

of situation she finds herself in. And so it continues in a satanic crescendo: corpses, sudden shifts in direction and situation right up to the final slaughter, which represents the point of conciliation of all the co-ordinates and of all the twists and turns of the situations. From these the closing catharsis is released.

It is a proof of the sheer genius of the complex of situations which is *Hamlet* that I once sat through a performance of this tragedy given by a bunch of the worst kind of hams, and yet I realised that I was still gripped by the story. Even though I knew the script by heart, the situations held me and were more than enough to overcome the vexation of that amateurism.

Juliet the Madwoman!

It has been said that without the basic situation in which Romeo and Juliet find themselves, no dialogue between the two lovers and no single speech would have any sense. For instance, take Juliet's soliloquy beginning:

> Oh Romeo, Romeo, wherefore art thou Romeo?
> Deny the father and refuse thy name . . .
> What's Montague? It is not hand, nor foot,
> Nor arm, nor face, nor any other part
> Belonging to a man. O, be some other name!

Just try and imagine that speech being delivered straight off by a girl of whom we know nothing. Picture the curtain opening and a young actress coming forward and declaiming: 'Oh Romeo, Romeo, wherefore art thou Romeo? O, be some other name!' Can you see the audience turning blankly to each other and shaking their heads: 'This one's mad!'

It is only because the situation has been set out in advance that we accept that paradox and find it poetical and even moving. The fact of knowing that there are two lovers kept apart because their respective families are locked in a feud to the death alters our perspective. A relative of Juliet's has just been killed by Romeo himself; the death of Mercutio, a close friend of Romeo, is at the forefront of our mind; and all this criss-cross of traps, misunderstandings and plots going wrong, in other words, this whole interplay of situations, determines the value and interpretation of the dialogue and brings out the meaning and the ethic underlying it all.

To pick up a line from Sartre, I would say that 'there is no theatre without situation'. There is no need to go any further than the Greek tragedies. *Medea* is based on a quite incredible sequence of situations: for love of an Argonaut, she abandons her father, betrays him, kills her brother, marries Jason – notorious thief of golden fleeces – who proceeds to leave her for another woman; thoroughly humiliated, Medea seeks vengeance by wiping out her rival, burns the other woman's father alive, and, just to end on a high note, slaughters her own children.

Philoctetes, too, develops on the basis of a fast-moving series of situations: a snake – a thoroughly nasty piece of work – bites him on the leg, which turns gangrenous and this leads to his companions deserting him on an island; Ulysses steals his bow and the son of Achilles goes berserk. All other tragedies, from *Phaedra* to *The Trojan Women*, could be looked at in the same way. In Roman comic theatre, there is a downright excess of situations – disguise, mistaken identity, role-swapping, misunderstanding and general topsy-turveydom. The comedy, as is evident, rests on such situations.

Under the Wheels of a Car with de Filippo

When dramatists discuss a new script or a play they have just seen, the first thing they explain is the situation. I remember once I was in Trieste in the company of Eduardo de Filippo, and as we walked the streets of the city, we were so taken up with telling each other theatre stories that it was only by pure good fortune that we avoided ending up under a car. Italian theatre would have been enriched by one piquant situation had we not managed to get out of the way in the nick of time with a leap that was a marvel of agility. De Filippo shouted after the driver, who must have a grudge against theatres: 'Trying to hit the headlines?'

Do you know what caused us to be so engrossed? We were trying to recall one of the most memorable situations in Neapolitan theatre. You may know of the 'Shepherds' cantata', a genre of theatre, closely linked to Commedia dell'Arte and to popular theatre, which appeared in the second half of the seventeenth century. The underlying situation is the furore created by the devils in their efforts to catch out the Madonna and the saints, but the decisive characters are two rogues, a couple of picaresque tramps, by name Razzullo and Sarchiapone. This pair, without a penny to their names, live on their wits. They pretend to be porters and offer their services to help a peasant woman transport baskets of farm produce to the market for sale, but when they try to make off with the goods, they find themselves hotly pursued by the woman's husband, intent on throttling them. Nothing ever turns out quite right for them.

Later, while rummaging through a dustbin near an inn, they pretend to themselves they are savouring a gargantuan meal. They suck a few fishbones, listing all the delicate flavours of those invisible lumps of fishmeat and, berating the cook for showing insufficient care and delicacy, they discuss the various techniques of high cuisine. Sometime later, they take a stroll along the Vomero* and there they happen to bump into the Madonna. The Madonna, dressed exactly as she is in the representations of the Virgin of Pompeii, is a stock character in the 'Shepherds' cantata'. In the popular tradition, there can be no other Madonna than that figure bedecked in necklaces and jewels, with trinkets, ex-voto offerings and bank notes attached to her dress by ornate pins.

She moves somewhat uncertainly, as though a bit lost, goes up to Razzullo and Sarchiapone and says to them: 'Excuse me, I'd like to go to Palestine.' The two stare at each other: where on earth is Palestine? They conclude that it must be somewhere in the Bay of Naples, and offer their assistance. 'Let's help this lovely lady on her way.' They steal a boat, help the Madonna aboard and find themselves in the middle of the gulf, when a wind gets up. The seas rise higher and higher and the two of them, although they had tried to pass themselves off as sailors, have no idea how to row and come within an inch of capsizing the boat. The wind gets stronger, the waves higher and Razzullo and Sarchiapone in stark terror throw themselves on their knees and implore the Madonna to come to their aid. The Madonna is there, but they turn their backs on her and cry out 'Holy Mother of God, help us'. The Madonna is moved by the prayers of these two wretches and works a miracle. What is it to her? A simple matter of stretching out her veil, which is swelled out with the wind, carrying the boat in mid-air, over the crest of the waves. 'Thank you, Madonna, for this miracle.' It never crosses either of their minds that the 'stranger' could have anything to do with the Madonna. All three continue on their way, still in the boat, on a peaceful sea.

All of a sudden, on the horizon, they espy a full-rigged ship, packed with pirates, who promptly take them prisoner. The two rogues try to sell the Madonna: 'She's ours, our property, but you can have her. All we are after is a slice of the ransom and our lives.' The pirates, however, captivated by her disarming gentleness, decide to let the Madonna go, and to chop off the heads of the other two. They are forced on to their knees, crying out all the while 'Holy Virgin Mary, Madonna help us!' but at that moment their heads are sent rolling. Both of them, even if decapitated, chase after their heads, grab hold of them and stick them back on, except that something goes wrong. They manage to pick up each other's head. Big-bellied Razzullo ends up with a thin, drawn face while Sarchiapone has a fat, round face on an emaciated body.

Finally they fetch up in Palestine, and the three go their separate ways, Razzullo and Sarchiapone on the lookout for someone to fleece. They hear

* A hill that dominates the bay of Naples.

tell of a stable where some redeemer has been born, and see crowds of people making their way in that direction, all carrying gifts for the Holy Family. The two of them exchange glances and then with one voice declare: 'There must be something in this for us, what do you say? There's a stable just up the road, so why don't we make a little crib of our own?'

'Right,' says Razzullo, 'I'll be the mother and you can be the father of this redeemer and we'll say this is the very place where he was born.' One dresses as a woman and the other as St Joseph, complete with false beard. They steal a lamb, wrap it in cloth ripped into strips and call out as the shepherds go by: 'The redeemers are us! This way. The crib's right here!' Some people fall for it and leave their gifts.

Now something unexpected happens. A group of heavily armed men, soldiers in the service of King Herod, who has given orders for the holy child to be beheaded, burst into the stable. They drag the disguised lamb from the cradle, cut off its head, and, just as quickly, go on their way. The two disguised rogues let out an almighty wail: 'Our one hope gone! These bastards of guards, they've even gone off with the baskets of gifts!' At that very moment, St Joseph and Mary, fleeing to Egypt with the child and ass, happen to pass in front of the stable. The two go up to her: 'How are you getting on, Ma'am? If only you knew what has just happened to us!' They do not even recognise her, but the Madonna is moved by their story and hands over most of the gifts piled on the donkey. 'Nice lady that, and no mistake! Wonder who she was. Pity we didn't think to ask her. Oh well, we'll have to say a little prayer to the Madonna for her.' Never once did these blind idiots have the slightest idea of the marvellous events they were witnessing.

Lazarus Taken Apart

To demonstrate how in the theatre situations are knitted together by montage, I would like to perform a well-known piece, the *Resurrection of Lazarus*, taking it apart and putting it together again before the audience. The play, even if it is a one-man piece, is crammed with characters and is clearly founded on a situation.

A huge crowd of curious onlookers gathers round the tomb where Lazarus was buried to witness the miracle of his resurrection. The atmosphere is like a village fair, with no sense of an impending mystical happening or of ritual tension. The people have turned up in the graveyard, without putting on their Sunday best, solely to enjoy the show. This is the underlying situation – the miracle seen as a conjuring trick and not as some victory of the spirit over death in the tragic and generous schemes of God. This approach is proclaimed from the very outset with the arrival of one of the characters in the graveyard. He asks the attendant if this is the place where the resurrection of Lazarus will take place and when it is likely to be. There and then the attendant fixes an admission charge for those who intend to spectate, and you can almost see him punching the tickets!

The action gets under way when people begin to crowd round. The spectator who got there first stares around to see where the miracle will take place, and his only concern is to find a place as close to the grave as possible, so as not to miss anything of the 'show'.

Along the way, I will stop to point out two essential elements: firstly, the summary of the story and then the situations which are being developed.

(*He assumes the pose of someone talking to another person.*)

'Excuse me. Would this be the graveyard where they are about to do the resurrection of Lazarus, him that was buried two or three days ago? In a wee while a saint, called Jesus Christ or something, is due to arrive and make two signs and call down a ray of light from heaven, and everybody will be screaming "God bless" and "Well done" and that kind of thing, and we'll all go off for a drink. Is this the right place?' (*He moves slightly, making way for himself.*) 'Yes, this is the place all right. That'll be twopence if you want to go any further.' (*He breaks off, turning to the audience.*)

Did you notice one detail? I hardly moved at all. It is sufficient just to sway your body slightly – one, two, three to create the illusion of a second person. From my entry, I have been addressing a hypothetical person standing in front of me, who does not remain fixed in this position but moves across the whole of the stage. And you, to a greater or lesser extent, are right now recording in your minds that the first character I was playing really exists and that he is introducing the second character. Let's have another go! First, turn one way, 'Excuse me,' then the other. (*He makes as though following someone moving from right to left.*)

'Excuse me. Would this be the graveyard where they are going to do the resurrection of Lazarus, the one who was buried two or three days ago?' The movement of the character asking the question was a result of these sweeping gestures. It is something which must be communicated by allusion, not by being battered into the audience's brain.

The passage from one character to the other – and this is something that you would not notice unless I pointed it out to you – takes place with the intervention of the following speaker, who is still standing with his back turned. In other words, I have not yet moved, I did not wait to take up a particular position before uttering the opening words in the role of the attendant. The reply, picking up the question, comes hard on its heels, so as not to leave any dead time. In cinema it is known as a 'crossed sequence'.

(*Starts again.*) 'Is this the right place? Yes, this is the right place, all right.' It is as though the voice came from outside and went back. 'Yes, this is the right place. Twopence, if you want to come in and see the miracle.' (*Points out the movement again.*)

'Twopence to you. What for?' (*He gives a slight twist of the head and shoulders.*) 'Because I . . .' (*These are two distinct phases, but revert immediately to the second.*) 'Because I am the graveyard attendant, and I have to be paid for all the trouble you people cause me. You come in here, you trample the grass, you knock over the hedges, you clamber all over the arms of the cross, break the arms and steal all the candles.' (*Imitates someone carrying off candles from a tomb.*) 'Twopence if you want to see the miracle.' (*Change of attitude as, extremely pleased with himself, he walks towards the right of the stage.*) 'Otherwise, just go and find yourself another graveyard, ha! ha! ha!. . . and see if you can get another saint like ours ha! ha! ha! who can raise the dead as though they were mushrooms! Ha! Ha!' (*Crosses the stage.*) 'You too, madam.'

The first speaker has now disappeared, and I have brought on another, a woman with a baby in her arms. It is the attendant who makes this known.

'You too, madam, and don't let us forget the baby.' (*Pretends to wave aside the protests of the woman.*) 'I don't care whether he can follow it or not. A halfpenny! When he's big, what are you going to say to him? A pity you'd such a tiny brain that you couldn't understand a thing. I paid a whole halfpenny, and just as it was coming to the crunch, you went and peed all over me! Dear God!'

(*Interrupts himself.*) You see, even before he finishes the sentence, another action crosses with it. He signals the arrival of a new character, a boy who is, in all probability, clambering across the perimeter wall to dodge paying the entrance money. So watch, as I go back a little. 'When he's bigger, what are you going to say to him? Pity you were so tiny you couldn't make out a thing. Just when it was about to happen, you went and peed all over me. Oh dear God!'

You see? I start to swing round at this point, to indicate the presence of the boy, even before I refer to him. While saying 'Dear God' I bend down to pick up a stone, and this action introduces the next line – 'Get off that wall!' (*Throws the stone, and turns to address the audience directly.*) 'Sneaky rat! Wants to get in to see the miracle and not pay.'

I have already suggested the action of the boy clambering over a wall: line/action. In this case the gesture is non-descriptive; it merely supports an action already under way, as happens with cartoons. The 'bubble' with the words is off stage, but it is enough to bring before us the boy clambering over the wall. At the very moment when the attendant performs the movement and comments 'Sneaky rat! Wants to get in without paying,' the boy disappears and the character of the first spectator, whom we had abandoned, reappears. It is important to master the technique of eliminating and reintroducing characters in the overall mechanism of sequences and situations. Let us continue.

'You rascal. Off that wall!' (*Comments to the audience.*) 'Sneaky rat! Wanted to get in to see the miracle free.' I have now introduced another character, cutting across the one already there. You have already remarked a new attitude, with its change of rhythm and behaviour; the new attitude is one of wonder, of amazement, and wants to take in, with a glance, everything in the field of vision. (*Comes forward towards the front of the stage.*) 'Dear God!' There is a silence. I draw a breath, then pick up the same words. 'Dear God, it's not half big, this graveyard.' We guess that this comment cannot come from the attendant, who sees the graveyard every day. Obviously another character has made his appearance. The sense of the line itself is sufficient to indicate the change, without further stage directions or any forced actions or gestures. The spectator with the desperate desire for miracles goes on: 'My God, what a huge graveyard! What a lot of people, what a lot of crosses!'

This is an anachronism, since it is obvious that at the time of Jesus Christ there were no crosses in graveyards. The ploy is deliberate. 'What a lot of crosses, what a lot of dead folk. I wonder where they buried Lazarus. (*A comment to the audience. Leans over towards the spectators.*) I like coming early when there is a miracle on. That way you get the best place, right in front of the grave . . . because there are some people . . .' I turn to the audience in the pose of someone who is about to confide something of extreme delicacy. First we had a reflection the character was making to himself, when he said – What a huge graveyard, what a lot of crosses, what a lot of people die! Who knows where they could have put – this is barely whispered, as he looks around in bewilderment – Lazarus's tomb. Then he destroys the image of the graveyard by addressing the audience directly. The fourth wall is torn down totally to allow for the introduction of direct address.

The Wheedling Tone

'Personally, I prefer . . . he says – I came along early because I wanted to be sure of a good place, right in front of the tomb.' The comment comes hard on its heels: 'Because there are some sly devils . . .' and saying these words, he should look over his shoulder surreptitiously. This style of wheedling comment has deep origins, from the Commedia dell'Arte by way of the clowns. It is a means of soft-soaping the public by making out that there are foreigners, outsiders who might be eavesdropping on the confidences I wish to make to you alone, because you are the only ones worthy of it. 'You keep it to yourselves, just you and me, OK?' So the actor gives a nod and wink that represent a touch of flattery to an audience who are being invited to enter a private conspiracy.

'Here's the secret I am sharing with you,' he seems to be saying. 'I prefer to come along first thing in the morning to get a good place.' (*Lowering his voice and glancing over his shoulder.*) 'Because there are certain holy men I could name who are up to all kinds of tricks. They put the dead man on top and underneath they stick someone who is still alive, and then along they come, make two signs in the air: "Come forth, Come forth!" the coffin turns upside down, the dead man ends up on the bottom and the living man walks out. . . ! Just leave it to me, there'll be no monkey business this time!' (*In a different tone, still addressing the audience.*) 'The last time I turned up bright and early, found a place right in front of the grave, spent half the day hanging about and they went and did the miracle somewhere else. I ended up miles away, hardly seeing a thing.' (*Deep sigh.*) 'This time I have gone and asked and they told me the man they have just buried was called Lazarus, so all I have to do is find a grave with the name Lazarus written on it, and stand there until . . .' (*Stops, looks puzzled, slaps his hand against his forehead.*) 'but even if I do find it, how am I going to understand, since I can't read or write! Oh God!' (*After another deep sigh, cheers up.*) 'Oh well, it didn't go too well the other time, so it's bound to go better this time. I'll just stand here . . .' (*Stops, pretends to lose his footing.*) 'Quit pushing!'

The situation has to change instantly. In this case, the switch is announced by the two or three glances I gave in all directions before complaining about the shove. That was done to convey the presence of something moving close to me . . . of other spectators arriving and joining the crush at my back. Then someone gives a push. Observe how, once I pretend to stumble, the frame widens. From being focused entirely on my face, the image widens to embrace the entire stage, and it is me who imposes this shift. Bear that in mind, for it is important.

Audience Video-dependent . . . on the Actor

I have already said that the actor or director must be able to alter focus for the audience as often as he feels necessary. We are frequently, often without being aware of it, able to zoom in on a subject, pick out a detail, widen the field of vision, range over a vast panorama, increase the depth and focus on a texture of colours or on background shades. In other words, we all carry inside our skulls a machine which no technical mechanism can equal. Our brain is a highly sophisticated camera. When an actor, or a group of actors, know their business, they can force the spectators to obey the commands they send with their acting.

Don't Fall into the Tomb

To return to the case in point. If I lower my voice and make the gestures smaller, I impose a heightened level of attention and concentration. I almost compel you to lean forward to catch my consciously miniaturised playing. The very next moment I give a wide gesture, throwing out both my arms, and project myself towards you. I turn round shouting: 'Who's pushing? Can't you see there's a tomb here!' and in so doing I make you imagine that the scene is packed with people shoving.

I'll do the scene straight through, without interruption. 'The last time, after I had been hanging around half the day, they did the miracle over there, and I ended up here, a right fool and no mistake.' (*Gives a wink, leans forward.*) 'But this time, I have made it my business to find out everything. They tell me he was called Lazarus, this corpse, so the moment I see a tomb with Lazarus written on it, I'll plonk myself right in front of it . . .' (*Slaps his forehead in consternation.*) 'Oh God! And just how am I going to understand what's written on it since I can't read a word?' (*Sigh, change tone.*) 'Oh well, it went badly the last time, so it can't go any worse this time . . .' (*Makes a gesture to indicate that he will stay where he is; at the same moment, he puts out his arms to counter-balance the shove he has received.*) 'Quit shoving! My God, what a mob. Don't push!' (*Turns one way, then the other.*) 'Can't you see there's a grave there?' (*Points to the tomb.*) 'I'm going to end up in there, and the holy man'll come along, make three signs and say: "Return to life, return to life" and here's me alive all the time!'

The tone of resentment is heightened not only to let people see that the character is afraid of being jostled into the tomb, but, more importantly, to communicate to the audience the fact that he is in contact with many others who are spread all around and pressing close in against him. Raising the voice and projecting it has the effect of widening the space and of involving the audience almost physically, so that they become like a chorus, or like full on-stage participants. This is typical of the approach of epic theatre. The spectator must be given the role of public bystander, fully aware of his own position, which is not that of someone lounging in his seat, whose only interest is in not having his digestion disturbed.

Complicity and Playing to the Gallery

However, efforts to establish this connivance can take a more ambiguous twist, and fall into near racism. Consider this approach. I shall go back a bit:

'Quit pushing, or I'm going to end up in there, etc. etc., then the holy man comes along, says "Come forth! Return to life," and I had been alive all along.' (*Moves his head as though looking around.*) 'What a lot of folk!' (*Changing tone.*) 'Eh, you quite fancy coming along to see the nice miracles, eh!' (*To the audience.*) 'This lot, they've nothing to do, ha! ha!' (*Looks towards a precise spot at the back of the stage.*) 'What have we here? They're spilling down from the hills now.' (*Raises his tone and projects his voice.*) 'Hey you, peasants! Never seen a miracle, eh?' (*Conspiratorial comment to the audience.*) 'Foreigners!' (*Stops acting.*)

This appeal to connivance is stronger than the other, because it contains an element of racist jeering against 'peasants', people, into the bargain, from the hills, therefore 'foreigners'. It is a well-known fact that they are a bunch of cretinous, gormless, open-mouthed idiots, while we are members of a superior class who see miracles all the time. Every other day we go along to spectacles of that kind, and now we can simply take it or leave it. The plan to play to the gallery could not be more obvious. It is a kind of nudge intended to win over the audience to your side. 'You're among your own kind here.'

Let us proceed. 'Foreigners.' (*He stumbles forward once again.*) 'No pushing!' From the resistance to the fresh push, a new character, standing beside me is created. The slightest of twists and there he is: one, two, three: 'Shorty!' Look at the size of that. 'Ow!' (*He draws in the air, with a few brief movements, the presence of a figure of minute proportions. He constructs with his hands, almost caressing the head as he does so, his tiny shoulders, then rests his elbow on them.*) 'Ha! Ha! Ha!' (*Takes a step back.*) 'What are you pushing for? I don't care if you are knee high to a grasshopper. Midgets should have been here first thing in the morning, to get a place up front.' (*Laughs, winking to the audience. Pretends to lean on his elbows to make a fool of the other.*) 'You think you're in heaven already? Where the little ones will be first and the big ones last?' (*Opens his mouth, miming a silent guffaw.*) 'God help us all!' (*All of a sudden, turning the other way.*) 'What do I care if you're a woman?' (*New character briefly indicated. Turns to his right in amazement. The movement of pushing the figure back is sufficient.*) 'What's it got to do with me if you're a woman?' (*Forcefully.*) 'In the face of death we're all equal!' (*Laughs wildly, but without making a sound. Winks again to the audience.*) 'God help us all!'

It is vital to link the laugh to the action of a wider glance, so as to convey the impression that over there, beyond the stage, there is something which interests me. My eyes must make the audience understand that I am waiting for someone of some importance, so that they feel involved in my wait.

So when is Christ going to Arrive?

The sequence is important. 'God help us!' Silent guffaw. Turn the head. 'Is this holy man coming or is he not?' (*Turning anxiously.*) 'He's not coming?' (*Directly to the audience.*) 'Do any of you. . . ?' It is you I am talking to. You are being transformed into acting spectators. 'Do any of you happen to know where he lives? Couldn't one of you run along and fetch him, because we're all here waiting.' The suggestion is that you, in your turn, are all ready to watch the miracle. 'We can't hang about here all day; we're all busy people, aren't we? If you fix a time for these miracles, you've got to stick to it!' (*Looks round about, leaning out over the footlights.*) 'No sign of him?' (*Without warning, goes over to the left.*) 'Chairs, chairs for hire . . .'

A new character arrives on the scene, someone offering chairs for hire. He has a pile of them on his back, and targets the women, so that they can enjoy the spectacle in peace. The chairs are available at twopence a time. When saying the words 'if you fix a time for these miracles, you've got to stick to it', I end up with my head turned to the right, and start crying the wares at once, as though the voice of the pedlar came from off stage. There is no need to go right over to the wings to accompany the chair dealer on stage.

Suggest, not Describe

The best policy is to reduce the entrance to a simple movement, miming someone with a chair in their hands. In this way, I introduce the idea of a chair and of the person who will be hiring them out. The performance expresses in summary form the passage itself, and has allowed me to cut to the bone the entire sequence. Had I been acting naturalistically, how would I have gone about it? In the first place, I would have had to abandon the character who was awaiting the arrival of the holy man. (*Moves across.*) One, two, three; having eliminated that character, I would have crossed over to the wings, and would have pretended to re-enter, would have mimed the pile of chairs and would have lifted the lot up to offer them to the spectators. The result would have been a mish-mash and a loss of tension and rhythm. The more summary treatment is a device which demands imagination and intuition from the audience. It is a style typical of the grand epic popular tradition; it eliminates all that is superfluous and all that smacks of mawkish descriptiveness.

Let us take up from where we left off. 'We're all busy people.' (*Abrupt movement, turning head and shoulders round, arms outstretched to show the chairs.*) 'Chairs! Stools! Twopence a chair! Now then, ladies, a chair for each of you. It's dangerous to watch a miracle standing up . . .' (*Makes as though to sit down.*) '. . . because when the holy man comes, if you are not seated . . .' (*Stands upright.*) '. . . and he makes his three signs and all of a sudden the dead man comes out, with his eyes sparkling . . .' (*Mimes the stiff movements of the dead man brought back to life.*) '. . . you'll get such a shock that your heart'll stop ticking. Just like that! (*Falls to the ground.*) 'Suppose you were to faint away and your head were to bang against a rock. Then what? Dead, that's what. Stone dead! (*Gulps of breath. Turns and makes off, shouting more loudly.*) 'And the holy man only does one miracle a day!' (*Going towards the left exit.*) 'Ladies! Last chance.' (*Fresh change of rhythm and gesture.*) 'Oh! Shorty!'

Did you get that passage? He speaks, raises a chair, goes off – 'Ladies, the holy man only does one miracle a day.' (*Rapid change of attitude, pause.*) 'Oh! Shorty!' Here we have another character coming back in. We already know him to be the small man we saw in front of the tomb. For my part, from being the man hiring out the chairs, I have returned to the role of the bluff individual we had seen before. I mime helping the little fellow on to a chair. 'Well then, shorty, need a chair?' (*He takes hold of the imaginary chair.*) 'Pretty useful, eh, for climbing up on.' (*Pretends to help him up.*) 'Come on, up you get. Ooh, what a big lad you are now. Ha! Ha! Ha! Don't lean there.' (*Indicates his own shoulder.*) 'Don't lean there, or else I'll give you a shove.' (*Mimes heaving the little man off his back.*) 'and you'll end in the grave, with a coffin lid on top of you. Bang! Bang! Eternum.' (*Mimes someone knocking from inside.*)

Sardines but no Miracle

(*Leaning out over the lights, searching for something.*) 'Any sign of him? Is he coming? Damnation, we can't wait here for ever; it'll be dark soon, they'll light the candles, his reverence'll turn up, he'll go to the wrong tomb, resurrect a different dead man, the first dead man's mother'll come along, she'll burst into tears, they'll have to kill the man they've just resurrected . . .' (*Pause, looks around.*) 'Still no sign?' (*Dashes off towards the right.*) 'Sardines.' (*Stops in front of the audience.*) A new street-seller. The gesture is important. A slight twist in the body while returning to the centre conveys the idea of carrying a basket. 'Fresh fish! Sardines! Twopence a packet of sardines, anchovies. Tasty sardines, lovely sardines, freshly grilled . . . good enough to raise the dead!' Note the passage – 'to raise the dead!' In the closing gesture, he tosses away the packet and disappears. The other character who calls after him is one of the onlookers: 'Sardines! Hey sardines, give one to Lazarus to prepare his stomach!' Someone else butts in: 'Cut out the blasphemy!' There's no need to change position; the angle of the body is adequate to suggest a switch of character; 'Cut out the blasphemy! Where's your respect? Swine!' Push the head and shoulders forward. 'The holy man is on his way! Where? That's him over there! Come on!' There are two separate figures involved in the exchange: 'Look at all those people round him! The apostles, the saints.' (*Change.*) 'I know that one. That's Paul, him with the beard and the bald head . . . the one next to him must be Peter . . . what a head of hair . . . Do you think he ever cuts that beard?'

Mark! Old Friend!

All of a sudden, another character enters, shouting in a loud voice: 'Mark!' The way is prepared for the arrival of Mark by the almost mechanical description, in near-identical terms, of the two saints who arrive on the scene first. Everyone knows the conventions and stereotypes by heart from having seen them exemplified countless times in paintings and frescoes. St Paul is bald, with a neatly trimmed beard, whereas St Peter, as anyone who has seen the film, *Ben Hur*, is aware, has a flowing beard and a shock of curly hair. The other one needs no description since absolutely everyone knows who he is; he is none other than Mark! Who doesn't know Mark? So: 'MARK!!' (*Waving madly.*) Shouting in a falsetto. 'Mark!' (*Chuckles to himself.*) The gestures in Mark's direction carry a sort of message, as though to say: 'God Almighty, fancy seeing you here . . . what do you say we meet up afterwards . . . and go for a drink together!'

At this stage, Mark's friend becomes aware that he is being observed with envy and jealousy by the people standing round him. This passage is vital. From the moment he becomes aware that he is being watched, his attitude changes, his movements slow down, he preens himself a little and turns to his neighbours with a touch of conceit: 'I know him. He's been at my house.' (*New change of tone. Abrupt turn of the head to stare over to the right.*) 'Goodness me! Look . . . There's Jesus! Look how young he is. Doesn't even have a beard! Just a boy. Looks very nice. He's quite small, and very young.' (*Breath.*) 'I expected him to be much bigger, with long hair!' (*Describes with a rapid series of gestures.*) 'I thought he'd have had piercing eyes, big teeth and hands so that when he gave a blessing . . .' (*As though wielding a sword.*) 'Whack! Whack! he'd have cut the faithful in two.' (*Further change of tone.*) 'This one's too small, too gentle.' (*Loud roar, almost on the verge of hysteria.*) 'JESUS!! JESUS!! How about repeating the miracle of the loaves and fishes? They were great.' (*Waving his arms in the air.*) What a feast we had that day!' (*Leans on the other leg, and glances over his shoulder.*) 'Do you think of nothing except stuffing your belly? Blasphemous pig!' (*Change of tone and attitude.*) 'Look at him! What a wonderful man he is!'

This alternation of brief silences with moments of high tension is very important. These pauses are deliberate, and they give everyone the chance to draw breath, because the basic aim is to make the audience breath in unison with you. If you overwhelm them, or fail to give them the opportunity to calm down after the peaks, or simply to get their breath back at the end of a laugh, or if you throw one thing after another at them, you finish up exhausting them and they are incapable of entering into the right measure of participation with you; in other words they are incapable of enjoyment.

The breathing is important. 'What a feast we had that day!' Then a glance over your shoulder: 'What a wonderful person!' He points at someone else; who can he be? Judas. Out of undue zeal for summary, I have cut out some pieces and the correct progression is different. 'What a wonderful person! What do you mean, who? Him! Him with the big smile, the bright eyes – he's a marvellous person! Who is he?' (*As though talking to a child.*) 'Judas!' (*Brief pause.*) 'Just marvellous.' (*Breath.*) 'What?' (*Another breath.*) 'His reverence has knelt down; so have the apostles. They are saying a prayer; all of you, say your prayers.' (*Turning to one individual.*) 'Say your prayers! Otherwise there'll be no miracle today!'

The character just addressed replies: 'You won't find me going on my knees. I don't believe a word of all this.' Reply: 'Blasphemer! May you be struck down on the spot! I'd like to see a great big stroke of lightning descending from the skies and sending you into eternity! And you needn't expect Jesus to be miracling you!' The two fall silent. 'Quietly, quickly, quickly . . . he's given the order to raise the stone.' (Pay attention to that jump.) He says: 'Christ has given the order to raise the tombstone,' and at that very moment someone appears to communicate the movements of the stone being raised and to organise the work. The transposition is more vocal than physical; the character in question gives the news, and it is he who makes the sounds and mimes the acts.

'Quickly, quickly, quickly, he has given the order to raise the stone. Oooooooh! Come on . . . up you go . . . all together . . . ooooh . . . watch your feet . . .' (*Leans forward but immediately jumps back, holding his nose.*) 'What a stink! That's a right nasty musty smell!' So the tomb has been prised open, as you can guess from my gesture immediately after going over to the tomb. I jump back, but only after repeating the line. If you speak the line too early, the entire effect is lost. Let me repeat the gestures one after the other: One, two, three, four, 'Damnation, what a stink!' The rhythm is internal, as with music. One, two: 'Damnation, what a stink!' three, four: 'That's a right nasty, musty smell!' one, two: 'What on earth have they buried down there, a dead cat?'

A second character comes along. He is someone else who enters the conversation, so it is essential to convey the whole exchange.

'No, no, it's him; it's him, that Lazarus that was buried. God Almighty! He's covered with worms; they're crawling out of his ears . . . there's maggots coming out of the eyes ... it's horrible!' (*Change of tone, turning round.*) 'They've played a right joke on him!'

'On whom?'

'On Jesus; they told him that Lazarus had been there for only three days, but in fact he was buried a month ago! The miracle's never going to work.'

(*Modification of tone.*) 'Why not?'

'Because this one's rotten through and through.'

(*Breath, then with emphasis.*) 'I still say he'll manage just the same, because this holy man is so good at his job that even if they only put four bones inside the tomb, all he has to do is make two signs and turn his eyes up to his father, God in heaven, and the bones could be covered with flesh and the person would come out bursting with life and make off down the street like greased lightning!'

'No, he'll never make it.'

'Want a bet?'

'Twopence says he'll not do it. Four! I'll go banker. Seven to five against, all right?' (*Waves his arms about, putting up different numbers of fingers.*) 'One, two, three, four; one here, two there, anybody for four?'

By now the bargaining has the whole place by the ears, but just then a cry rings out which freezes them all: 'God damn you! Blasphemer! Putting on bets while his reverence is over there praying ... it's an outrage! You should be struck down as well! Blasphemer!' (*So saying, he starts kneeling down, turning to the man collecting the bets.*) 'Fivepence for!' I remained in the same position to make everyone aware of the switch from the tension of the betting cries to the climate of the impending miracle. Therefore, 'Fivepence for!' with one hand still in mid-air and the face turned in the opposite direction. 'He's given the order to rise up; he's told him: – Come forth, Lazarus!' Another character comes on to contradict what has just been said.

'Come forth, Lazarus!' (*Sniggers.*) 'Wait till you see all the worms crawling out!'

(*Enraged.*) 'Blasphemer!'

(*Deep sigh. Speaking with difficulty, as though in a state of ecstasy.*) 'It's him! He's coming forth! Lazarus! Goodness me! He's raised him up before our very eyes! My Lord and God! Miracle!' (*Raises his arms to heaven.*) 'He's coming up, up.' (*Mimes someone having difficulty standing, staggering a little.*) 'He's on his feet, he's fallen, he's down, he's fallen; there, he's up again, he's coming out of the tomb – he's like a dog coming out of the water, shaking himself all over. The worms are falling off.' (*Mimes receiving a shower of worms.*) 'Oh hey! Did you see that? A bit of care, if you don't mind!' (*Interrupts.*)

This passage is perfectly clear. Description: one, two, three. (*Repeats the action.*) I take up position and that is enough to alter the images. Perhaps it would be better to say that our private camera has changed angle, swinging round to capture the person who is speaking.

Let us complete the sequence: 'He's coming forth.' (*Shakes himself.*) '. . . like a dog . . . all the worms are falling off! Oh hey! A bit of care! Damnation. Worms all over me!' (*Pretends to pick worms off himself, then abandons that action to throw himself forward.*) 'Miracle! He's alive! He's in tears!' (*On his knees.*) 'Oh, Jesus thank you, God . . . well done Jesus, well done . . .' (*Puts his hand to his back pocket.*) 'My wallet! Stop thief!' (*Points off stage, then turns back to the spot where the miracle had occurred.*) 'Well done, Jesus! Stop thief!' (*Gets up and runs towards the right, chasing the thief.*) 'Stop thief! . . . Well done Jesus! Thief!'

At this point, before considering any other examples, permit me a brief diversion to consider the position of actors who, if they wish to rediscover their own cultural roots, must go back to the origins. No one needs to tell me how hard it is nowadays to achieve this in the midst of the general levelling off, or levelling down, caused by the mass media, but that is the climate in which we have now to live and work. There is no denying that something has changed from the days when I started to work in the theatre. In the first place, the war had just ended and we had the inestimable advantage of being able to write on a blank sheet of paper. There was a widespread desire to sweep away the old and stale, and a willingness to face every subject afresh.

We knew nothing, or next to nothing, of the ideas and experiences which had been developed by actors, painters and writers in other countries over the previous twenty years, so we had a powerful impulse to research, to know, to discover. We were ignorant, but we were aware of it. Today we are just as ignorant, and nobody cares. There is a great deal of talk about research, but what is being researched? As I look round me, all this chatter about research seems to be no more than a bluff – quite apart from the fact that, for me, the term 'research' summons up the image of people examining their own navels. They scarcely ever manage to break free from the usual mannered clichés. In addition, they lock themselves away in tiny groups or gangs, each supported by some favourite critic or Arts Council official. Their talk is almost totally abstract and divorced from the genuine problems of day-to-day living.

When I was talking about the need to widen research, it was not only popular theatre I had in mind. Real research involves breaking clear of your own self-serving circle of interests. Personally, to prevent myself dozing off with my nose stuck up my own navel, I have taken to reading all the theatre I can lay my hands on, from eighteenth-century theatre to the theatre of the

East – in translation, obviously – stopping continually, obsessively almost, at the theatre of the Greeks. And I don't just dip into these scripts. Each time I find myself seized and repelled . . . every author both fascinates and disturbs me. It is much more convenient to live quietly with your own space, rhythm and familiar language, and not let yourself be disturbed. But I have come to the conclusion that to have your mind turned upside down is no bad thing. It is important to keep a hold of all the elements of the dialectical system. As they say in physics: 'if you have no knowledge of the opposites, you cannot know the effects of equals, of dynamic contrasts or of the fixed values'.

Developing your knowledge to the limit is essential for grasping the splendid maxims of contradiction. How often have I heard people say: 'That author is bourgeois, conformist and reactionary . . . he doesn't interest me.' Just like that, with no more ado! A nice little label, and end of story. Unconvinced, I went off to read him up and found there evidence of open-mindedness, as well as of boldness of the first order on both the formal and ideological planes. For how many centuries did gangs of agnostic-literary intellectuals snub clowns, acrobats, puppets, just as they refused to consider seriously the religious theatre of different peoples, including their own. I have found some outstanding things in that theatre. And how many so-called Marxists have sniggered at the very idea of examining the popular theatre of the rites, and especially that of the so-called 'Maggi'.

The Radiant Maggio

I discovered that nineteenth-century anarchists performed and sang the 'Maggi' and it is still performed in certain places today in the Apennines at the border with Tuscany and Emilia. I have attended performances given by groups in the Garfagnana, Prato and Pistoia. What was especially striking was the presence of one man in modern-day dress – all the others were in costume – who wandered about the stage with a script in his hand. He had the function of prompter-director, and came up behind the various actors in turn, following them step by step in all that they did. Everything took place in the full view of everyone present, so it could be considered epic theatre in its purest form. The tragedy of the 'Maggio' was in rhymed chant, in traditional octosyllables, to the accompaniment of an unchanging melody, repeated over and over.

At first blush, it was all rather irritating. It is generally the case that forms of expression and styles which go beyond our established categories or habits of mind are not to our liking, and I had little time for that style of gesticulation which was, to my mind, too spare and repetitive. There were certain fine passages, such as the one featuring a duel, choreographed like a genuine dance, with the cut and thrust, the blows, the gestures and the intricate steps all executed with considerable skill, but what left me dumbfounded was how the duellers managed to leap about, to grapple with each other and move with their whole body while all the time continuing to sing without so much as losing their breath.

The most charming item was, beyond all doubt, the costumes. It was clear that they were home-made: there were crests manufactured from the helmets of nineteenth-century cavalrymen, with the addition of sallets, figures of lions and eagles as well as feathers and ribbons. The armour was made of cloth, with pieces of metal stuck here and there. They wore boots and hunters' leggings, and the fustian trousers were decorated with red, blue and gold bands. In addition, every knight appeared in a cloak embellished with authentic works of embroidery, reminiscent of the copes donned by priests on special feast days. There were also costumes for kings, queens and ladies-in-waiting . . . all characters of some substance.

The one false note was the complete lack of any ironic counterpoint or any comic relief. The unrelenting seriousness gave rise to an imprecise sensation of mawkishness, so, at the end of the performance, I went up to the man in charge of the group, who turned out to be a university professor who had done a lot of research on the subject. He had produced a couple of weighty tomes and was considered the leading expert in the field of popular theatre in Tuscany and Emilia. I asked him why there were neither comic characters nor comic situations. He replied, with a smile of pity: 'Why? Are there any comic situations in Greek tragedy?' I remained for a moment open-mouthed, then pulling myself together, found the courage to ask: 'Are there at least any comic "Maggi"?' He replied: 'Not to the best of my knowledge. The Maggio is a tragic genre.' He was too sure of himself, and I felt that he was lying, so I began research of my own. I spoke to other 'leading authorities' attending a conference in Prato, and one researcher assured me that, until a hundred years ago, there had been one comic character onstage for the entire duration of the performance, whose role was to act as the comic-satirical foil to the speeches of the lords and ladies. This character had been revived by the early anarcho-syndicalists, who had inserted direct political references.

Nevertheless, that device had deep roots. Immediately the *sottises** from medieval French theatre came to mind, where a *sot*, that is a madman, had a part in the morality plays, which was to come on to deliver sarcastic comments in every action or dialogue. Shakespeare too had the same character, the

* A satirical farce in which the actors always wore fool's costume and parodied manners and political events.

Fool, in his *King Lear*. Continuing with my studies, I discovered that there was a place for this comic character in every work in the 'Maggi' tradition, and that, far from having the task of providing light relief, his role – and in this he was an exact equivalent of the Fool in *King Lear* – was to turn the progress of the plot upside-down and to provide a point of dialectical clash which allowed for the presence of contradictory values inside the characters and story. In other words, I discovered counterpoint in the 'Maggi'.

It was from the songs and mimes of the peasants around Pistoia that I picked up a version of *Medea* which I later used as the basis for a script that Franca Rame performed. The counterpoint is provided by a group of women (an anti-chorus) who in their complete subjection to men provoke grotesquely, violently ironic situations, sneeringly sent up by Medea.

A Devil with a Soul

The most startling, grotesque inversion of expectations I have come across was in a story dealing with a saint, St Olive, a woman who married a Roman Emperor and became a Christian. When her husband set off for war, Olive was besieged by all kinds of suitors who gave her no peace. The Empress was a woman of considerable charm and in every scene met up with some man who lost his head over her, attempted to seduce her and carry her off to bed. She, however, being a lady of high standards and very much in love with her Emperor husband, who is not exactly a nobody, will have none of it. They blackmail her, they tell her he has been killed, they slander her and even put her on trial, but all to no avail. At the end they send her into exile in a forest.

The foil is the devil, or, to be more precise, an impish, zany demon, a kind of Harlequin, up to all sorts of nasty tricks. In fact he turns out to be the only one in the entire story who takes the woman's part, the only one who shows human feelings or displays any pity or concern. In the early stages, however, he is a more traditional satanic figure, goading the men, both young and old, to make advances. He plays the part of the pander: 'Go for it, you fool! Isn't she beautiful? Look at the way she walks! Come on, she does it all the time!' He makes suggestive remarks to the halfwitted knight and feeds him with passionate, seductive phrases, but like the poor devil that he is, always after the good time and permanently short of food, his poetic imagery is continually drawn from the more succulent cuts of pork, from refined cuisine, from toothsome delicacies and from quality vintages. The comic impact is guaranteed, especially since, by the end, we become aware that he too has fallen for Olive and would give his soul for the love of her. However, in the version I saw in Prato, the devil character was no longer there. I wondered what considerations had led to the excision of that counterpoint from the 'Maggio'.

The Jesuits' Purge

The truth came out in a subsequent debate in the presence of many experts. It was the Jesuits who, in the seventeenth century, after the Reformation, had been responsible for this drastic piece of censorship. In other words, through orders from on high, the comic, the devil, the drunk, the meddling female, any character likely to cause controversy or to provide a dialectical foil, all disappeared. The professor from the Garfagnana, a typical example of Catholic conformism, ended up out on a limb, although he still managed to create a fuss, initially by trying to play the whole thing down and then by raising his voice in increasingly hysterical outbursts.

From this debate-cum-fracas, two clear, irrefutable conclusions emerged: first, authorities, any authorities, fear above all other things laughter, derision or even the smile, because laughter denotes a critical awareness; it signifies imagination, intelligence and a rejection of all fanaticism. In the scale of human evolution, we have first *Homo faber*, then *Homo sapiens* and finally *Homo ridens*, and this last is always the most difficult to subdue or make conform. Second observation: in their self-expression, always and invariably, ordinary people cannot resist, even in their representations of the most tragic of tales, finding a place for humour, sarcasm and comical paradox.

Carnival Dispel-fear

When I was a boy in the Valtravaglia, on Lake Maggiore, it was the custom at carnival time 'to go after the Malpagas'. The Malpagas were five brothers who, in the sixteenth century, had constructed a series of fortified structures, each with four towers, on rocks jutting out of the water a few hundred yards from the village of Cannero. From there their gangs set off to cause mayhem in the surrounding villages. They were the Turks of Upper Lombardy, and so deeply was the memory of those gangs of pirates rooted in the memory of the local people that even today, centuries later, they exorcise all recollection of the raids of the Malpagas by community performances, featuring clashes with the armed population, the capture of the gangs and their eventual execution. The whole thing is presented in burlesque style, complete with scurrilous chants and obscene gestures.

The memory of the Turkish hordes who swept down, centuries ago, to pillage and rape, is the impulse behind this satirical representation, and that is the horror they feel the need to exorcise by attaining, in performance, a moment of catharsis. The target is no longer those Turks of other times, but the Turks of today – power with all its deceits, its injustices, its insolence and its arrogance. There is a need to destroy it, strike it down, wipe it out and jeer at it in performance. Because of my own passion for popular plays, I have travelled around to see dozens of carnivals, such as the one in Asti, where they put a turkey on trial, the one near Trento, featuring the capture and trial of the tyrant Biagio, and others in Irpinia and around Sorrento.

Back to the Zanni, or rather the Zannone

I must confess that very rarely have I come across a festival as complex or as carefully structured as the carnival of the 'Zannone', big brother of the *zanni* of Commedia dell'Arte. The sheer number of people who take part in these celebrations, and the range of varied masks and differentiated, opposing characters is astonishing. They include the Pulcinella-Zannone, with all his routines on hunger and fear; the grand Turk, grotesque and pompous; the warrior, all solemnity and bombast; the savage, the bear, the hunter, the devil, the gypsy girl, the priest, the hermit, the queen, the Christian soldiers, the police officers and finally the wizard Merlin and the engineer. Everyone, as with the 'maggi', has to make their own costumes in their own way. I found one family who each year make, from grains of maize, the costume, breast-plate and all, of an infidel tyrant. Another digs out weapons from the armoury of knights of Savoy from the early part of the century. Anachronisms are wilfully and provocatively brought in: gendarmes, policemen, nurses, friars, doctors and perhaps, as happens in the 'Saw the old woman' festival in Perugia, ministers, bishops and lawyers.

The *zanni* carry noisy bells round their waists, like the *mammuttones* in Orgosolo in Sardinia or like the Selenes in Thessalia at the rite of the departure of Dionysus. All this goes back a long way, yet at the same time it is all very near. The Zannone has a cockerel on his head, like the Pulcinella of Antrodoco in the festival of the months, but he is a repulsive fowl with a phallus dangling from between his legs. Once again the obscene, thrown like a gesture of scorn in the face of all those right-thinking, hypocritical folk who harp on about sin, plays a decisive part. These festivals have lasted, with their ups and downs, across the centuries. They have disappeared, only to re-emerge at a later date; they underwent variations and transformations, sometimes colourful, but not always the most appropriate for improving their entertainment value.

What is the point of reviving such festivals today? Ours is a time in which the mass media have the effect of steamrollers or bulldozers; with their fusillade of big money games, of laser shows, of glittering lights and blaring sounds, they stun people, leaving them shell-shocked. The impact is of a flurry of movement with no harmony. The imagination which orchestrates the steps of dance is replaced by an unco-ordinated, obsessive epilepsy. In the words of a poet friend of mine, 'the young men and women seem like blossoms budding on a stem with no roots'. To celebrate a feast is an art, and the inclination to celebrate is not of itself enough. To ensure that it does not all degenerate into a formless bedlam, it is essential to have a feeling for the sorts of despair, fear or anger on which mockery, paradox and satire can be based. At the risk of seeming obsessive, it is in this context that the importance of connecting with tradition reappears. I can testify that nothing summons up avant-garde images like the observation of our carnival festivities.

I once had occasion to give a talk in one of our drama colleges. I was discussing Greek theatre, the political events which lay behind certain comedies of the fifth and sixth centuries BC and the satirical treatment of the idea of democracy governed by women in at least three comedies of Aristophanes. After a time, I glanced into the hall and saw rows of blank expressions on the faces of the young people who, with a fair gamut of Mediterranean gestures, were asking each other what on earth I was going on about. The professor in charge threw out his arms in despair, but this was hardly an isolated case. The lack of knowledge of any theatre, ancient or modern, in all schools is enormous, and it is better not to talk about the complete absence of training and cultivation that is now the order of the day, especially among the newest of recruits to our theatre.

Educating the Audiences

This discussion on cultural research leads me to the subject of so-called market research into the supposed needs and interests of the audience. In this regard, I am more than ever convinced that it is as important to educate audiences as to educate actors, so that audiences show willingness to attend bold works dealing with new and disturbing ideas, and giving rise to debate and possibly action. Regrettably, theatre today in Italy is overwhelmingly commercial, which means that producers, both public and private, have no desire to run risks that might affect box office returns or upset the paymasters. They prefer to play safe, and stick to a repertoire of the tried and tested.

For some thirty years, I have struggled to foster theatre that puts forward new ideas and is willing to renew itself not only in style but also, more importantly, in content. I have clashed with official boards, with public and private organisations and I have been in my turn insulted: a fair response. In my view, what we have around us is a dead theatre for dead people. Supply alternates with demand, and every culture has the theatre it deserves. In Italy, no one is more dead than the authors, incapable of producing anything other than literary texts, with grand speeches full of elaborately patterned phrases chasing and devouring each other. They deal with themes outside all time-scales, all treated with a lushness that is both antiquated and senseless. They present our times as though they were mythical and ancient times, as though they had never been alive. The important things are to secure advances and rebates, not to upset the bureaucrats at the ministry or the politicians, to get a fat grant for production costs, not to stir things up, and to ensure that the received wisdom is that you are not one of those theatre types who cause bother. Amen.

The Plight of the Unperformed Author

I recently took part in a conference in the town of Stresa with writers and critics from all over Europe. The speeches followed a ritual now established by centuries of unvaried repetition. On the one hand, there was a denunciation of the excessive power of directors, on the other a lament over the scarce or non-existent power of the author. This weeping and lamentation over the position of the theatre writer has become, in my honest opinion, grotesque.

For years and years in Italy, there have been countless initiatives. To assist playwrights, prizes were invented, special subsidies were offered to directors of private or public organisations prepared to put on works by writers who were both alive and Italian. The tax authorities came up with various incentives for directors producing Italian authors, reducing the burden of direct taxes by one third, and even rebating at the end of the fiscal year the entire amount of tax deductions, but all to no avail. With every year that passed, the presence of the living Italian author on the hoardings outside theatres became more and more ephemeral ... like the amphetamine-inspired vision of some junkie high on an overdose. The illusion of seeing Italian authors appear on the posters outside our theatres is the real 'theatre of the ephemeral'.

Authors go for Gold

The most recent suggestion I heard being made, in all seriousness, is this: 'The State should assign a certain sum of money, running to hundreds of thousands of pounds, to us authors. Not to all of us, no, no, not at all, but to a group of upright individuals of the highest standing and of proven artistic talent. A committee elected by us would proceed to choose a couple of meritorious works, and then a company or two would be set up and financed to put on the works selected by us. In other words, the author sets himself up as State.'

All nice and neat. We might have cause to deplore the weekly pillorying of some author or other in the course of the lengthy academic discussions that would inevitably ensue in the committee charged with choosing the works of merit, but nothing to cause alarm. The number of unperformed authors is infinite.

Undoubtedly the problem of unearthing and making known new authors is a serious one, but what is to be done? What is the best method to follow? For a start, there are no schools.

Who Teaches the Trade?
There are schools for actors, for mimes, for designers, for directors, for technicians and theatre administrators but not for theatre-writers. There exist faculties of ancient and modern literature, where anyone who is interested could learn to write stories, essays, belles-lettres, or novels, but there is no faculty that teaches the composition of drama, with all that it entails in the way of imagining a scenic space, writing moves and tones as well as words, devising lines to be projected over distances as much as those to be spoken at close range or even thrown away, contriving a balance between actions and words, knowing how to fashion a script for performance at the front or back of the stage while walking, sitting, lying down or swinging on a see-saw. The aspiring author has to know what it means to act in a wash of light, in side or back lighting, he must understand recitation with a cadenced rhythm as distinct from speech without peaks and troughs, he must grasp the need to flatten tonalities, to eliminate droning or, alternatively, to invent a musical delivery. Somebody who aims to write must know what a rake or a ground-plan is, what flies are, how a turntable works, what is meant by battens. Is this cultural terrorism? I know the reply. 'These are matters for the director and the technicians', and that is frankly wrong.

It is like claiming to design a house and then leaving the door frames, the stairs, the ceilings, the roof – in other words the whole superstructure – to the building firm to attend to. What nonsense! Did nobody ever tell them that the superstructure is the house?

A Kick in the Teeth for the Idiot Spectator
There is another notion that I would like to discuss, whether from the perspective of the actor, author, director or even stage designer – forgive the intrusion of this last, but it is the only profession for which I possess a professional qualification. The problem concerns the relation with the

audience, the product user. I recall that during a discussion in the notorious conference in Stresa, the director of a prestigious theatre, the Staten Theater from Hamburg, got to his feet to declare: 'The real king is the audience.' This simple utterance had a colossal impact.

All my life, I have been saying that the audience is important, indeed crucial for the development and growth of a work. In these present talks, nothing I have said is of greater moment; for an author, actor or director, the audience represents the litmus test, the proof, the quality control as well as the possibility of valuable assistance. Never descend to playing to the gallery, however, because often the audience will turn out to be a disaster. Not all audiences participate with delight, and in many cases they can be passive and doltish. It can happen that the audience before you is not in the slightest open to innovation, and that what you have in the stalls is a mass of reactionaries. An audience is frequently given to adulation or is blinkered in its adoration. It can often come to the theatre foolishly preconditioned or brimful of prejudice and all too often accepts bizarre styles or has it own fixed ideas which it can be difficult to dislodge with one performance. Audiences, even if made up of different individuals, often fuse into one and impose their rhythms on you.

How do you go about determining the character of an audience? I have a method of my own, tried and tested in my own blood. I have on my side the good fortune of being an actor as well as an author and of having with me an actress-wife of – let me say this in the utmost modesty – extra strong qualities. Together we learned to employ mechanical elements right from the introduction of our plays. At curtain up, it is our practice to give and improvise a prologue – we have revived this excellent custom of the best of old-style Italian theatre – and this serves as sounding-board, as warm-up and as bond with the audience. There is even an anti-prologue. On each occasion, we make it our business to help people find their seats; we throw about a few barbs, and deliberately put the spectators at their ease, or unease.

Let me give an example: there's always one person wandering up and down the aisles looking for an empty seat, and he always causes arguments. At this stage, I would step in and address him directly: 'Excuse me, is there some problem? I see, because the seat is occupied by an overcoat, you want to claim it for yourself. What if I tell you that it was taken by a lady who had the most urgent personal reasons for momentarily absenting herself? What do you mean? I was not aware of the rule:

> Anyone feeling nature's call
> Should hold it in and not move at all,
> For anyone called to the WC
> Gives up all right to his seat, you see.

Everyone bursts out laughing and I carry on from where I left off.

In other words, the rule is this: keep your eye on certain forceful and prominent individuals in the stalls so as to understand exactly what kind of audience you will be dealing with in a few moments, and, above all, do all you can to help people relax. We sprinkle a kind of acid solution, perfumed with jasmine, to act as air freshener, and this allows people to take off their shoes and let their feet breathe.

The aim is to induce the spectators to familiarise themselves with, and grow to love, the space in which we are about to perform. In acting, it is often necessary to begin slowly or at a precise rhythm, or alternatively, quite the contrary, it may be vital to begin with your foot on the accelerator because you guess, or feel, that the audience, like some masochistic beast, requires a no-holds-barred assault. Sometimes, you will feel compelled to shoot the lines straight at them, even at the cost of squandering them. You won't wait for them to absorb the dialogue in its entirety, but you force them to crane their necks if they are to hear what you are saying, because, like the right bastard you are, you knowingly lower your voice only to yell in their faces when they are least expecting it. The theatre is a struggle where punches and kisses alternate, where the Queensberry rules don't run, where the referee is blindfold and where to secure victory just about anything goes. The very meanest, the most son-of-a-bitch of ruses and wiles are permissible, and these are only a few of the devices we employ to understand the mood and seize the attention of the audience so that we can coax them inside terms and rhythms that are ours, inside a dimension that can be controlled and managed by us and where they are in our complete power. 'Now's the time, now's the time, power to the trickster; play low and see the audience in the palm of your hand.'

The method set out here with, perhaps, a touch of the grotesque, imposes on us, as authors and directors, the obligation of adapting text to differing situations and of making it match the deepest and most imaginative needs the audience requests and requires. This method of preliminary investigation, with the audience contact that goes with it, has allowed me on many occasions to identify even quite serious mistakes and imbalances in the script, and to spot lifeless, wordy or obscure sections in the work as a whole. An ordinary author, to whom this special means of verification is not available, would have found himself facing an irreparable disaster, and would have had no option but to withdraw the play and trot home cursing that gaggle of hams who had destroyed him. 'A masterpiece down the drain!'

The Trick: Pull it all Apart

I am referring to the experiences we had with one of our plays, a kind of updated Atellan farce dealing with the imaginary kidnapping of Fiat boss Agnelli, whose title in English was *Trumpets and Raspberries*. I have to confess that at the first readings before a live audience we received a blank response; there was a certain unease due, we believed, to the hesitancy of the initial run-through. We took refuge in the illusion that the response was the result of a lack of fluency in the performances, but when we had the script off by heart and stood up on stage for a week of previews, we discovered that it still did not work. There were gaps, sections that jarred, slithered about all over the place and lacked all sense of direction; the rhythms were all wrong, the situations could not be brought out with any clarity, and, above all, there was no way of grasping from the discussions with the audience that followed each performance the reasons why the play was not taking off.

During a break, Franca delivered her verdict without fear or favour: we were making no headway because we were performing a script with a format from other times. It needed to be more firmly rooted in present-day reality and to deal with the burning, awkward issues that really mattered to us and to the public at large, but which we were, cunningly and conveniently, tending to edge out or overlook. We had to meet the requirements of the audience and avoid resolving problems with mechanical solutions, such as sticking in sequences of jibes against the same old politicians or jokes taken from the usual run of stories from the daily press. We spent two months cutting, filing and rewriting whole scenes before we succeeded in raising the tone of the work satisfactorily. The third act was completely redone, as was a large part of the first. We had also to restructure the general progression of the story.

Tripping up the Critics

Here I must admit that we played a dirty trick on the critics, because we put them in a position where they wrote about a play which, some months later, was completely transformed. People turned up at the theatre after the reworking was completed, and after reading in the papers an account of the work, and said: 'What the hell were that lot on about? Where were they?'

We were, every so often, relatively generous and let the public know: 'Look, it's not really their fault, poor souls, it's ours for changing the text.' It happened more than once that the official critic of some newspaper did not bother to return to check the fresh version of the play, as he should have done, and simply reproduced the earlier review from the first night in Milan, never imagining that in the meantime we had gutted the work completely. To be fair, it was not always the case and there are certain critics who do their job with great honesty.

Trumpets and Raspberries was produced again the following year, once again in a modified version. A year after the last performance, matters of great importance had taken place, and this compelled us to vary the action and the situation. Reality always seems to be lying in ambush, to jump on top of us or to trip us up, as we had done with the critics!

News more Fantastic than Fantasy

In the interval the headlines were dominated by the story of the kidnapping of the Neapolitan Councillor, Ciro Cirillo, and of how his liberation was negotiated by the *camorra*, the Neapolitan organised crime syndicate, and by the Christian Democratic Party, with the P2 Masonic lodge* and the police special forces looking on. It was an absurd table, worth no more than a sketch in variety theatre, but behind it lay a real tragedy. Cirillo was captured by the terrorists, bundled off to the so-called people's prison – although, strangely enough, while the people had no idea where it was, the *camorra* did. You may have noticed how, all of a sudden all talk about terrorism and the Cirillo kidnapping vanished from the newspapers. It became a taboo subject. In Naples, however, the comments of Neapolitans themselves were ferocious, displaying an unthinkable cynicism: 'What's keeping those red bastards? They should flay him alive; he was a thief, a gangster . . .' This was the brutality, at once grotesque and tragic, of day-to-day events and it was this that we had to reflect in our theatre.

Everything that crops up daily in reality itself has to be taken as an example in thinking and working out a text. It is always disastrous to fail to take this into account, because all of a sudden you will notice that the play just does not stand up any more, for the reason that news bulletins, as they vary from day to day, have swept you aside and overtaken you.

The News undoes Fiction

In one of the closing speeches at a critics' conference, a well-known professor of theatre history in the University of Urbino, who is also a critic and an author, introduced the tragic theme of the impossibility of producing nowadays works of drama linked to current events. Said the professor-critic-author: 'Take the assassination attempt on the Pope, a spectacular event which many of us saw almost live. We only missed by a hair's breadth seeing

---

* A Masonic lodge which in the nineteen-seventies was suspected of being a meeting-place for political, financial and military figures conspiring against the Italian Republic.

the sequence in which the terrorist stretched out his hand and fired. The effect of broadcasting more or less simultaneously a tragic event of such overwhelming power is that an audience for any subsequent film or theatrical reconstruction of the same facts will be left completely cold. The live programme sets out the facts without mediation; everything, down to the tiniest details, is shot and recorded with cool brutality. The great, small and intermediate anxieties make every nerve of the sensory mechanism tingle. It is the great show in a showbiz society!'

So, in the view of those who would have everything 'live' (served up still reeking and blood red), there is no point in the attempt to deal with current topics or with daily life through the medium of imagination, since all such topics are already dated an hour after they occur.

In other words, ever since the advent of television, civil theatre can be consigned to the rubbish bin. Allow me to state that in my view this mode of thought coincides perfectly with the interests of established authorities and achieves the great ambitions of those who hold power, be it of the economic, political, institutional, multinational or religious variety. Power bends over backwards to ensure that people's native imagination atrophies, that they eschew the effort involved in developing alternative ideas on what is occurring around them from those purveyed by the mass media, that they cease to experience the thrill of opposition, abandon the vicious habit of searching a reasoned detachment from immediate things, foreswear the tendency to sum them up, reconsider them and above all to portray the essence of them in styles that are different.

I watched the live broadcast of the assassination attempt, having by chance switched on the television two seconds before the shot was fired. (I have my own reasons for following the Pope in his travels, since he helps to freshen up my personal performance repertoire!) I literally jumped out of my seat when I saw what was happening, and followed the story with some anxiety and concern, hopping from one channel to the next in an effort to come to terms with the motives and timescale of the whole thing. Then, quite suddenly, I found myself projected into the realm of tragi-comedy, or more precisely of the grotesque, as I found myself identifying with the character of the television director, who at that precise moment was doing his level best to co-ordinate the news and the pictures as they came in: he had to transmit some, jam others, set some up, block out others; there he was bawling out orders and counter-orders to an assortment of reporters and cameramen, while all the time replying to the calls of the network director.

The Sacred Duct!

At one point, some fool of a reporter had the temerity to talk about the Pope's sphincter. My God! Does the Pope have a sphincter? The Pope has a sacred duct! How dare this imbecile permit himself to discourse about transplants of sphincters made of plastic or borrowed from some common animal, like a goat or a baboon? Another reporter butted in to add that for the moment they had inserted a waste canal, a kind of provisional anus, level with his navel. Just to enrich the suspense of the unfolding drama, a third reporter made his appearance on the screen to add an especially gratifying detail: 'The bullet that struck the Pope exited through the navel. From which point was the bullet fired? Through which part of the body did it enter?'

'Through the buttocks?'

'No.'

'What was that? Through the buttocks?'

Meanwhile the co-ordinating director on the other end of the line in the studio was reduced to screaming 'Shut up, that's enough! The Pope doesn't have buttocks, you bastard. No more about the sphincter.' At the same time, the voices of the directors could be heard down the line: 'Pull the plug on him, get him off there! Who in God's name is that fool? Sack him! Blow his brains out! Tear his sphincter to pieces!'

Biblical curses of the first order were ringing down the wires, and at this stage it was no longer possible to talk about the grotesque. This was the other face of tragedy in close-up for anyone with eyes to see, in all its brutality, its spectacular crassness, its hypocrisy, its need to offer a reverent presentation of events which, in their details, and precisely because of the coyness with which they were commentated, were becoming obscene.

For this reason, I insist that staging the tragedy of the programme director, of the continuity director or of the director general, and of their efforts to give shape to a story that continually slithers from their grip is more important and more alive than any live broadcast. I can just imagine the chit-chat between the directors of the programme as the news comes in. 'Bloody hell, let's hope it's someone from the Red Brigades that's behind this . . . It is the Red Brigades? Foreigner . . . well, let's at least hope it's one of those Baader-Meinhof people from Germany. What do you mean Turkish! What in the name of God have the Turks got to do with it? What the hell are these Turks doing around here? He's what . . . right-wing . . . a fascist? That's blown it!'

That improvised exchange must have been very like the desperate anxiety of the TV directors to square the assassination attempt with the atmosphere of the run-up to the abortion referendum. How nice it would have been to announce that the suspect who fired the shot was pro-abortion! But, damn it all, it just wouldn't work. Along comes our bold commentator with

Minotaur-like eyes, statement at the ready linking the outrage with the climate of violence created by the Radicals and Communists, and on hearing that the would-be assassin was a Turkish fascist, nearly fainting – 'What in God's name have you made me say? I was given that information by the Vatican Secret Service.'

In Theatre, Trust Only Lies
In other words, a more detached and deeper reading of what lies behind the information already in the public domain will enable us to develop a grotesque, a tragic or an ironic approach in areas where live communications will never reach. It is our duty, or, if you prefer, our professional task as writers, as directors and as theatre practitioners to devise a way of talking about reality that permits us, with the chemistry of imagination, with the cynicism of reason and with irony, to smash standardised schemes. In this way, we can encounter the programme and the strategies which the powers-that-be bring forward, and that is to teach people never to use their critical sense; brain dead, imagination zero.

As you may have guessed, I have no love for a certain category of academic nor for the greater part of critics. I recall once being invited to speak at a conference bursting at the seams with intellectuals of that class. My speech was along these lines: I want to address that colleague who spoke of the delight of writing, and told us of the pleasure that constructing a story and putting together written words afforded him. I, on the contrary, find that when I write I feel myself assailed by a sense of anxiety mixed with a feeling of transgression, as though I were committing an illegal or sinful act. (The audience of writers looked at me in bewilderment.) The reason is that many – especially fellow authors – have managed to convince me of a truth I have striven in vain to deny.

Why Don't You Love Me?
For years they have done everything in their power, with articles, essays and massive tomes to persuade me, to make me see that I manage to get along in theatre not thanks to my ability as a writer of plays but thanks to my extraordinary gifts as an actor. I resisted, but at the end of the day was compelled to see reason and give way. Yes, I am now convinced; you have before you one of the most prestigious actors in the world. (Someone in the stalls has already begun to cough.) Indeed, I have come to the conclusion that the greater the success of one of my works, the easier it is to demonstrate that my qualities as an actor have soared to the level of the divine, while the qualities of the play have sunk to the depths beneath contempt. My writing is

rubbish, but I know how to package the rubbish with such skill and talent that I can overturn that disadvantage. I am a monster, indeed I am God Almighty. To be more precise, I am the father of God Almighty! – but only in the role of comic actor, you understand! (I hear a subdued groan from the front rows.)

Obviously, my amazement and stupefaction know no bounds when I notice that abroad – mad fools – they translate and produce plays of mine and of Franca's. Good Lord, these megalomaniacs in places like Paris, London, New York and even Japan manage to find a spot on their programmes for the works of a woman, an actress no less, and keep them there for years on end. At this point, I am forced to admit that abroad they are all a bunch of idiots, with no understanding of theatre; plainly these are the troglodytes of the entertainment business. Toss any old thing in their direction, even the most outlandish piece with the academic imprimatur – that means almost ignored by critics here – and they seem to relish it. The reason is that they have no authors of their own. We, on the contrary, have writers by the score but these benighted foreigners are ignorant of them and will not take the trouble to come here and find them. (Thunderous applause from solitary, elderly and slightly deaf author.)

Pause, then I fearlessly carried on: Fifteen years ago, there was living and working in Rome an elite association of theatre writers of established repute, all buzzing round the minister in office, a certain Giulio Andreotti.* They were delighted to be in his pocket and he, in return, made available some rooms with kitchen and bedroom facilities in the very building used by the Ministry of Culture. This association lived in conditions of the most appalling misery; they were sick to their back teeth of having to put up with two of the most outrageous illiterates who had ever disgraced the profession of author.

As luck would have it, one of these hoodlums was myself, and the other could have been my father – a certain Eduardo de Filippo. By chance I found myself following the same path as him. We had the cheek to continue to produce plays, and, as if that were not enough, year after year headed the charts both in terms of box office returns and of attendances. Further, we, mere actors, had the unheard-of impudence to write the plays and also do the staging ourselves. Two entertainer-performers! Italian actors who had the gall to set themselves up as authors and directors! Who had ever heard of such a thing!

The upshot was that these authors of established repute – unperformed –

* A Christian Democratic politician who has filled a series of important government posts, including that of Prime Minister.

subsidised by the ministry (I absentmindedly pointed a finger at a group of veteran writers) intrigued together until they managed to persuade the minister to pass a very curious law, whose terms forebade the payment of fiscal rebates (the restitution of the total of taxes paid in the course of a season) to those authors who were simultaneously actors and directors. It worked for a year, then was withdrawn. De Filippo and I had threatened to exchange plays; he would have staged mine and I his.

Let us come back to ourselves. In many speeches, I have heard the old lament on the crisis facing living authors, and on how only the works of dead writers are performed, but I wonder how sure we are that these living authors are really alive. (From the stalls, a murmur of indignant protest.) Undaunted, I continued apace. Rooting about in theatre history of all times, I notice that where authors were genuinely tied to the history of their own age, they invariably found an audience to support and encourage them. The *hypocrites* for the Greeks was the performer who had the task not only of replying to the chorus but also of retelling the stories of the myths by translating them into an idiom, and transposing them into a dimension, accessible to the living audience who came to hear them. His task was by no means to lull or gratify those spectators. I have emphasised 'living audience' to stress the presence of people who reacted, participated, applauded, jeered and lost their temper. It was no accident that between the stage and the stalls there was a deep pit, just as in modern football stadia.

Jeer at the Audience – They Love It!

In Greek satirical theatre the author, backed up by the whole chorus, came on stage himself to hurl insults at the audience. The greater his ability to provoke them and get under their skin, the greater was the esteem in which he was held and the applause he would receive – and the greater too his risk of ending up battered and bruised.

It was very much to the author's advantage if the topics of his satire were based on real events, if the comedy was not an end in itself and if he pushed himself beyond mere clownish display into the realms of political affairs, touching on brainless behaviour, heightened by marks of general inertia in the face of authorities, *vis-à-vis* the city rhetoricians. Nor could the classics expect any respect. It was a bit of luck for them that Aeschylus, Sophocles and Euripides had not as yet received the academic treatment. There was no hesitation over discussing famous authors with the same lack of reverence shown for run-of-the-mill chorus members or for supposedly glorious generals. They were not yet sculpted in marble and were not in the habit of going around with myrtle or laurel on their skulls. It is well known that the life

Fo as Harlequin

Fo miming the monster phallus in the prologue to *Harlequin*

Fo scaling the ladder to mend the curtain

Fo and the lion

of a classical author was not always a bed of roses – arrest, prison and death were as likely as applause and triumphs.

Toss Them in Jail

The thirty years of the reign of Elizabeth I saw a proliferation of awkward writers. There were around 250 dramatists who not only wrote but produced and directed their own work. It is true that the runs were not lengthy; on average, a play could expect seven or eight performances, but the important thing was that during the English Renaissance theatrical works were turned out at a great rate. These people had a somewhat tense relationship with established powers, and, if truth be told, were responsible for many of their own difficulties. They were mad enough to persevere with direct references to what was going on around them, and in every work, on every opportunity, instead of conducting themselves like classics, they mixed in references to real facts and real people, at times veiled by allegory but at others made quite explicit by the use of christian and family names.

Allow me, then, to give a piece of advice. Friends, fellow-authors, do you wish to be performed and regarded as genuinely alive? All you have to do is attempt to write scripts that run the risk of upsetting entrenched power. In other words, get yourself thrown into jail every so often! Better still, very often.

I have to confess that that time the applause I received from my colleagues was not such as to indicate enjoyment. Indeed, there was an almost total silence, with, in the background, the gnashing of teeth and the clamour of dropped jaws. Only one imprecation rang out with any clarity, from an elderly author: 'Oh God, my false teeth!'

To make you understand more clearly the condition of modern-day playwriting, just imagine what would happen if a selection of comedies and dramas from recent seasons were gathered together and placed, undated, in a special steel capsule and fired out into the stratosphere. Suppose that some five centuries were to go by before they were discovered by some astronauts, who brought them back to earth and handed them over to a group of scholars for study and analysis in an effort to establish by whom and at what period of history they were written. Do you imagine they would succeed? Where would they find references to current events, to social conflicts, to the tragic affairs of our own era? On the contrary, they would find nothing but a stream of grand concepts and of words playing blind man's bluff without ever finding each other; there would be nothing but characters out of time and bereft of all sense of reality. Nobody would ever manage to guess when or by whom those works had been written. Days, nights, months, eras – all without context.

The Question of Commitment

On the subject of the commitment to write about topical subjects, there is one objection continually put to me, and it runs like this: 'It's all right for you, you have a growing following among the young . . . and the not so young . . . no one can deny that you have a vast audience . . . but at the end of the day, is that a good thing? I mean, do you not run the risk of being sucked into the system? All this work you do – social, political and religious satire – it all goes out on television, and is seen by millions of viewers, so is there not the chance of it being distorted and of you being manipulated?'

There is undoubtedly a problem about avoiding mystification and ensuring that there is no twisting of your work when it is broadcast. Perhaps it is especially vital to have an open door at your back, so that you can make your escape the moment you realise they are trying to box you in. It is also essential to be on the alert with yourself, to keep probing your own conscience. You must keep asking yourself: 'What am I doing? Am I being taken for a ride? Where have I got to?'

Personally I have Franca at my side, and if I were to be less attentive than necessary, she would not be slow to sound an alarm that would awaken the dead.

Dangers of Having Your Own Theatre

We have also the immense advantage of having external assistance. Time and again we had no sooner sat down than someone made it his business to haul us back to our feet. For instance, we once had a perfectly suitable theatre when . . . *bang*! they took it away from us. I am referring to the Palazzina Liberty in Milan, where we were extremely comfortable for five years until the Milan City Council, generous and open to a fault, desperate to house needy companies as best it can, evicted us so as to restore the building to the state in which we found it – that is, a derelict ruin, infested by sewer and house rats of a colossal size. So we found ourselves compelled to move with extraordinary agility from a theatre to a cinema, then on to a sports complex and finally to a deconsecrated church. A settled, cosy theatre would have lulled us to sleep and enfeebled our spirits. The City Council was good enough to see that we remained on our toes and in a rage!

As to any dangers deriving from being seen or listened to by too large an audience . . . by the masses, in other words, there's no need for any beating about the bush. That is exactly what we have been after for ages! I have a personal distaste for small, carefully selected audiences of the great and good. I relish the prospect of playing before crowds of hundreds of thousands or millions, if possible. Forgive me if I am showing signs of a Pope John Paul syndrome!

The Clown Auguste

There is one other point I wish to make about actors, a point little understood by people who are not members of the acting profession and often ignored by those who are. It is the question of listening and responding to dialogue. It frequently occurs that when I distribute the parts of a new play to members of a company, the first thing they all do, men and women alike, is to thumb through the script to see how many lines they have to speak. Very few pay heed to the importance of their character independently of the role or of the number of speeches and lines they have. Here I need to say something about the importance of the supporting actor and of listening in a play, and about the ability to deliver snappy replies.

In clown-shows, there is always a fast-talking clown who fires words ten-a-penny at the audience and at other clowns, and there is one who remains almost silent throughout, listening, nodding slightly, disagreeing with elaborate politeness, looking round with an air of wonderment, showing amazement at every little thing, however ordinary it may be. The first is the white clown or the Louis and the other is the Auguste. In spite of what may seem to be the case, the silent partner is the principal actor, while the Louis has the supporting role.

I remember a sketch in which the white clown recounted an astonishing adventure, and the comments of Auguste were always brief and disconcerting. The Louis declared: 'I play the violin.'

The Auguste: 'Why?'

'Because I like it.'

'And does the violin like it?'

'Like what?'

'The way you play it.'

'I have no idea. What can it matter?'

'It certainly does matter. If it is a good violin, it has a soul.'

'So what?'

'You are the classical musician who destroys the soul. I'm going to call the cello and have you arrested.'

Enter a clown dressed as a cello. With this device the absurd spiralled towards the impossible.

To help you grasp the importance of crossfire – as the interplay between the two is called – I would like to give a little demonstration with the assistance of two young actors whom I have known for some time.

Let us try it off the cuff. How about using a joke as the basis, and seeing if we can retell it in an amusing manner? There is a Neapolitan joke about an octopus which I find very funny. Two friends go into a restaurant to have octopus with pummarola. One of the two sings the praises of the way they cook octopus in that restaurant. And what is the secret? asks his friend.

'Simple, in this place it is always fresh. They slaughter it on the table before your very eyes. Just you wait. Let's call the waiter.'

The table has a marble top, and remember that these details are important, because you have to recount them to the audience. The waiter comes over.

'What can I do for you?'

'Octopus for two, but we'd like to see it killed here on the marble table.'

'Right away, sir.' The waiter goes into the back shop, picks out of a tank an octopus which curls its tentacles round his hand, and he goes back to the table. He raises up the table cloth and Whack! Whack! Whack! The octopus flops on the table, its tentacles growing rigid. 'One fresh octopus.'

The waiter goes back to the kitchen, but once he is on the other side of the curtain, he tosses the battered octopus back into the tank. He then opens the fridge door and takes out an ancient octopus, covered with ice, which he throws into the pot, shouting 'Octopus for two!' The octopus in the water tank comes round slowly, and lying flat out on the bottom of the tank sends up a stream of half-hearted bubbles. Then it starts to slither up the side of the tank, sticks its head over the edge and groans, 'What a way to make a living!'

Obviously the joke is no more than a pretext for a demonstration of the value of the feedman. Our friend will take the part of a great teller of jokes, and I'll be one of his fans and I'll twist his arm to make him tell the one about the octopus. He doesn't want to know anything about it, but at the end, just to get rid of me, he tells it with something like disgust. It's the twentieth time I have made you tell the same story, but for me you are ace; there's no one like you in the world. With a display of nonchalance and detachment I'll praise your abilities to the high heavens before the audience. Let's have a go.

Dario: Ha, ha, ha! Am I glad to see you! Please, Carlo, do me a favour. I need a good laugh. Tell me the one about the octopus.

Carlo: No, for God's sake . . . not again.

Dario: Oh yes, come on, nobody can tell it like you. It kills me. (*To the audience.*) Wait till you hear the way he tells them! Ha, Ha, Ha . . . watch you don't die laughing! Just listen to this!

Carlo: No, please, I'm not in the mood.

Dario: Look, I'll give you a present. Wait a minute, I'll make a collection for you. I'll go round the audience, and I promise you a thousand pounds. Will a thousand do?

Carlo: Don't talk daft. Who's going to give you a thousand for one joke?

Dario: All right, then. Do it for free. Come on, get started. (*Jumps up and down excitedly.*)

Carlo: You'd drive a saint to drink. All right, then, I'll tell you it, but very quickly.

Dario: No, why quickly? Draw it out . . . bit by bit. Please. Slowly, very slowly. Knock me down dead. Silence now! If anybody as much as breathes . . . Quiet there! Let's hear it. (*Prepares to listen, in rapt attention.*)

Carlo: OK. There were these two friends who went into a restaurant . . .

Dario: Ha, ha . . . magnificent! Have you ever heard anyone like him!

Carlo: The first one says: 'Do you like octopus?' The other one replies 'It all depends on what kind of octopus and how they do it.' 'Alive,' says the first man. 'You can eat live octopus!'

Dario: Ha, ha, ha! Live octopus! The very idea! (*Suddenly doubles over.*) Would make you sick, ha, ha, ha.

Carlo: 'No, they cook the octopus, but when it is still fresh. They slaughter it there on the table, in front of your very eyes.' And the other one says: 'Why have they no tables in the kitchen?'

Dario: Ha, ha, ha! that's a new bit. He's just made it up on the spot. What a man! (*Gives him a smack on the back of the head.*)

Carlo: 'No,' says the first man, 'it's just so that you know that it is not deep frozen.' 'Oh, I see,' says the other one. 'Waiter, octopus for two.'

Dario: He's coming to the good bit now. Ha, ha, ha! (*He gets excited and slaps Carlo on the back.*)

Carlo: The waiter goes behind the curtain where there is a tank with only one octopus, and goes over to the tank.

Dario: Ha, ha, ha! Goes over to the tank . . . ha, ha . . . metaphysical, eh? Ha, ha . . . you're really great!

Carlo: The waiter pulls up one sleeve . . .

Dario: And then sticks in the wrong arm, isn't that it? The one with the sleeve still down, watch and all?

Carlo: Yes, the watch ends up under . . .

Dario: Ha, ha . . . and he says – it's time I was buying a wet suit. Ha, ha, ha!

Carlo: Ha, ha . . . right again! Must get a wet suit, he says.

Dario: Sure he's great . . . what imagination . . . glug, glug . . . all those bubbles coming up from the watch. Ha, ha, ha . . . you're going to make me die laughing.

Carlo: The waiter grabs hold of the octopus and comes back into the

127

restaurant with the testicles . . . I'm sorry, the tentacles wrapped round his arm.

Dario: Ha, ha . . . how does he manage it . . . how can he dream up all those things! Obscene but awfully good. Ha, ha . . .

Carlo: He raises the table cloth . . . and batters the octopus . . .

Dario: The octopus! Ha, ha, ha . . . and bang, bang he whacks himself on the hand and smashes it to bits. Oh you're very good right enough! (*Interrupts.*)

Stop! That'll do. It's clear that my part, which on paper was meant to be the support role, has become the principal role. Antonio, let's give you a go, and we'll reverse the situation, with you trying to tell the story and me showing not the slightest interest. You persevere and I grow more and more bored and desperate at the mere idea of having to endure another of your stories. Watch how the supporting role is developed this time.

Antonio: Hey, Dario. I've got this fantastic story I'm dying to tell you . . . one of the best jokes you've heard in your life.

Dario: Oh please, if you don't mind, I've got a sore stomach . . . a joke's the last thing I need.

Antonio: This one'll cheer you up no end. It'll settle your indigestion. It's not one of your usual jokes.

Dario: It's an alka-seltzer!

Antonio: No, I mean it's got a moral . . . it's nearly a parable.

Dario: I bet you've taken it from the Bible.

Antonio: Well, yes, the two friends could be apostles, Saints Peter and Paul, maybe.

Dario: Listen, I don't like jokes about saints.

Antonio: All right, no apostles, just two ordinary friends.

Dario: God, what next? These jokes about the same old two friends make me sick!

Antonio: Nooo, they're not really very good friends, in fact they hardly know each other at all. That's why they decide to go and have a meal of boiled octopus.

Dario: Give us a break! Two people who hardly know each other go and eat an octopus together.

Antonio: What's supposed to be the matter with that?

Dario: It may seem all right to you, but it's the first time I've heard of boiled octopus cementing a friendship!

Antonio: What's that got to do with it? The joke's got a different point. Ha, ha . . . just you wait . . . you're going to love it. Well, these two friends go into a restaurant: 'Waiter, octopus for two,' and the waiter says, 'Coming up,' and the other man says: 'Yes, but we want you to slaughter it right here, in front of our eyes.'

Dario: Why all this sadism? What satisfaction can it give you to watch a poor creature who has never done you the slightest harm stretched out on a table . . . groaning . . . then . . . Wham! What is the octopus supposed to have done?

Antonio: What do you mean? Are you going to tell me that you'll have octopus for your dinner only if it's done something to upset you? OK . . . have it your way. The octopus shouted out, 'Down with Reagan and up with Ghadaffi!' I get annoyed and I'm going to eat it. Is that OK now?

Dario: Ha, ha . . . what a scream! Do me a favour. Take the octopus away. I can't stand the idea. Couldn't you put chicken in its place? Let's have chicken on the marble surface, eh?

Antonio: A chicken in a water tank?

Dario: Why not? A tank they're using as a battery unit. All glass.

Antonio: No, it's got to be water, otherwise the joke falls flat.

Dario: All right . . . but at least make it boiling hot . . . a chicken done in water, with three carrots, one potato and two onions.

Antonio: No, no . . . there's nothing funny about a chicken . . . it's just got to be an octopus.

Dario: Nonsense. I think a boiled chicken's much funnier than a boiled octopus. Look, I'm splitting my sides . . .

That's enough! I have to say that Antonio was quite excellent because even though he had the role of Louis, in other words the straight man, he managed on a couple of occasions to give a commanding comic perfomance . . . without overdoing it. We'll change the approach once again. This time I'll tell the story with you listening and relishing it as much as me. Both of us experience the same wild delight in the telling and in the listening.

Dario: Ha, unbelievable . . . I've got to tell you . . . ha, ha, ha.

Carlo: Hold it, I'm not ready yet . . . ha, ha, ha . . . I can hardly stand up and I've not heard it yet.

Dario: Ha, ha, ha . . . neither can I. Ready? Here goes, an octopus . . .

Carlo: Don't tell me . . . what did you say? An octopus?

Dario: These two friends . . . what a carry-on . . . they go into this restaurant and one says . . . (*Trying hard to stop himself laughing.*) I'm sorry, I just can't go on . . . anyway, he says: 'In here you can get live octopus,' ha, ha, ha.

Carlo: A live octopus . . . that's good, that is. They eat live octopus! (*Handshakes, slaps on the back, embraces.*)

Dario: He sticks his sleeve right in, right into the water . . . (*Gives Carlo a kick on the shin.*)

Antonio: The whole sleeve . . . ha, ha, ha . . . without taking off his watch! (*The two shove each other around a bit.*)

Dario: That's right! Ha, ha . . . what a chicken! In the tank, there's a chicken with a watch on its tentacles, a chicken that doesn't know how to swim! And it goes and smashes the watch to pieces. Wham! Wham! The chicken slaps the waiter on the table top. Ha, ha, ha . . . the waiter . . .

Carlo: Ha, ha, he tosses him on to the table . . . and then shouts out . . . a boiled waiter for two . . . with a large watch! (*They punch each other.*)

Dario: No, no . . . the chicken with the tentacles goes to the fridge. (*They both end up on the ground.*) He pulls out a frozen waiter . . . here's two fresh French waiters for you! And the one in the tank drags itself up to the top, and goes glug, glug, glug . . . what sort of way is that to make a living?

In this final case, there was neither supporting role nor Auguste, because each one was simultaneously lead and support. No, this last version did not really serve to prove anything at all, but we did enjoy ourselves. There was one entertaining and original innovation – the fact that in the excitement we ended up pushing, punching and kicking each other all over the place, and by the end came close to killing each other. In spite of that, in the context of the absurd, the whole thing appeared quite plausible.

Mad Actor, Mad Spectator

Before closing this talk on the actor, I would like to read out a question handed to me on a slip of paper by a young man who has a special job.

'Dario, for some time I have been employed in my home town as theatre worker in the Mental Health Service, together with psychiatrists, sociologists, social workers and so on. At one stage, we decided to put on, with mentally ill people as actors, a play along the lines of Commedia dell'Arte. We had no great pretensions, but the patients enjoyed themselves and so did the people who came to see it. We made our own masks, with clay models, plaster casts and papier mâché. What happened was that after this experience the rate of admissions declined, in the sense that there were a number of mentally ill people who would very frequently sign themselves into hospital, but who now, having this outlet either in the craft of maskmaking or in performing, no longer felt the need to do so. I would like to ask you: I am aware that you have performed in mental hospitals, but have you ever had any mentally ill people act in your plays? I would also like to know what you think in general of this matter and if you have any advice to give.'

Reply:

Yes, I have had a certain amount of experience inside mental hospitals, and that was by design. It came about as a result of my friendship with Franco Basaglia, the psychiatrist who was responsible for opening the mental hospitals. He has always attempted to keep a dialogue alive inside these jails, to involve people in the problem and to ensure that it was a question for all society and not an inconvenient problem left to a few doctors transformed into jailers. In keeping with this approach of his, I have performed in all the hospitals run by him. I have worked in Trieste, in Parma and in Gorizia and even in Turin, in an institution called 'The Fifteen'.

Anyone from Turin will tell you what 'The Fifteen' is. It is the name given to the section for the untreatable cases, those who are normally held tied to their beds or to their chairs. In this case, they had been released shortly before from that modern version of the pillory, and I went to perform for them. The nurses were on tenterhooks in case those men and women threw a fit or started behaving wildly during the performance. In the event, nothing at all happened but instead, after an initial moment of mutual tension – for I have to admit to being tense myself – we all unfroze. I gave a relaxed performance and they enjoyed themselves and laughed at the right times. They made some quite witty remarks, considering that they were supposed to be a bunch of dangerous madmen.

There was one moment in the course of the dialogue between the drunk and the angel, which is part of *Mistero Buffo*, when a woman got to her feet to start shouting. She was getting annoyed with the angel who would not let the drunk get on with his story, and yelled: 'Let him talk, you bastard! Otherwise, I'll come up there and give you a kick in the halo.' The amazing thing was that she was raging at the character whom I had sketched out in the air; she was pointing at the spot where I had left him. Another patient got up and shouted out: 'Nurse, will you stop it?' The angel had been transformed into the day-to-day authority they had to deal with.

There was a debate afterwards, or more precisely, an inquiry by me and by the doctors. The medical people were taken aback by one totally unexpected fact; all the inmates spoke. Indeed, they pressed insistently to be allowed to speak, and at one point all shouted together. It required a lot of patience to persuade them to speak one at a time. Most of them recounted the effect that those tales had had on them, and almost all of them had experienced the desire to get up on the stage and perform on their own behalf. What would the subject have been? Their own lives, or rather tragedies and bizarre episodes in their lives. We made some of them recount these episodes. They were weird stories, with certain lucid passages, which then trailed off into the impossible. A row broke out between two patients. One accused the other of having stolen his story (copyright does not exist inside an asylum). Several told of their lives inside 'The Fifteen', of the violence, the criminal treatment, the monstrosities they had endured.

Ship of Fools

In this way, I really did manage to understand exactly the nature of the organisation of mental health. And to think that there are people who want nothing more than to go back to that vile system! These people's dearest wish is to resolve all problems by consigning to a ghetto undesirables or individuals who are useless to society and something of a nuisance. For many people who boast of their impeccable liberal credentials, the only way forward is to return to the Ship of Fools, that famous vessel, familiar from Bosch's painting, dreamed up by the Flemings and Germans of the Hanseatic League, and still in use in the sixteenth century. Once a year, they got hold of some hulk of a ship that was no longer in service and packed on board all demented, witless or odd individuals – in other words, any unbalanced person who could not contrive to act in perfect harmony with the rules and regulations of society. Many of them were anything but mad, but they created a nuisance with their endless criticism and mockery of the sacred clichés of respectability, of the relationship with the Divine, and with public authorities. The ship, provided with neither pilot nor rudder, was towed out and left to drift on the currents of the North Sea. The hulk inevitably finished up among the ice floes . . . and that was the end of that.

It may be that the Hanseatics of the Middle Ages were simply more honest and courageous when compared with what is being done today in the asylums of Italy, where there has been a return to segregation, to the total annulment of the patient and to the administration of drugs that tranquillise and kill. All the labours of Franco Basaglia for a more humane and civil school of psychiatry look likely to go for naught.

Coming back to the question of theatre for the mentally ill, I have made various attempts. I once spent five days in Turin with other actors of the La Commune Company putting on brief sketches with patients. The results were not startling, because we plainly needed more time, at least a month, if we were to achieve anything worthwhile. That would have been true even with a normal professional theatre company. Regrettably, our group is not capable of undertaking work of this type in addition to our day-to-day work.

The note does not finish there. There is a second question. 'I read in an interview that you cannot stand people who have no doubts, who express themselves in fixed stereotypes. I can assure you that I have no shortage of doubts, especially regarding the activity I am engaged in, so I trust that I come into the category that you have some time for. I would like to know one thing: among the mentally ill, I have persuaded certain people who take themselves seriously, indeed extremely seriously, to go on the stage. Obviously I got them to attempt elementary types of gesture and mime, and this they managed, even if with some clumsiness. In all honesty I am not even sure that they were aware of what they were doing, but the fact is that one of these very serious-minded patients, who previously did not talk at all, by the end, as happened to you in The Fifteen in Turin, began to mutter a few words. So some form of progress had been made.

However, there are now some people in the world of psychiatric medicine who go about accusing people like me of immorality and of cynicism, because, they say, what we are doing could lead to the abuse of a defenceless subject. What we are attempting, they continue, is a form of manipulation of the alienated being, and they charge us with being at best no more than self-deluders who for reasons that are in no way therapeutic are using these people as puppets; puppets, moreover, who are liable to find themselves, once the game is over, with deeper disturbances and anxiety symptoms than those they possessed at the outset.'

Reply:

We're back to the Ship of Fools. It is now well established that the use of drama has given and continues to give astonishing results in the treatment of mental illness. Only an idiot or someone acting in bad faith could sustain the contrary. People of this type would be happy to face the problem of asylums by closing them down all right – but only with the patients inside, walled up and perhaps with a few canisters of nerve gas to keep them company.

Who is Sane?

On the subject of dialogue with mentally ill patients, an odd and amusing thing once happened to me in Trento. We put on a play in the mental hospital before an audience which was a mix of ordinary spectators from the city – the so-called normal people – and of patients in the hospital. Often it was not possible to distinguish the one from the other. With some anxiety, I kept my eye on one unfortunate individual with wide rolling eyes and a nervous twitch, only to discover that he was the consultant in charge of the ward! His job was to look after the patients! On more than one occasion, several members of the audience jumped excitedly to their feet and yelled at each other as though on the very brink of hysteria. These must be inmates, I thought to myself, but it turned out that the most hysterical of them all was the local police sergeant – the representative of law and order. In other words it was no easy matter to tell those who were subject to restrictions from those who were free to circulate as they wished.

At one point, a friendly, jovial young man of about thirty, with a long beard, came to sit beside me. We had just finished the first half – a scene from *Mistero Buffo* – and were preparing the stage for the second half, when he said to me: 'I saw you in the Marriage Feast at Cana and you were very good, but I thought you went over the top a bit. You came over a bit heavy, but don't, for goodness sake, get the idea that I was upset.'

'Why, what did I say?'

'Listen, you are much too bright not to be aware that some jokes which come dangerously close to blasphemy can, with certain people . . . but I enjoyed it myself . . . there is nothing wrong with my sense of humour . . . as you ought to know.'

'Have we met?'

'You don't know who I am! You've been talking about me all night, and you don't know who I am!'

'Who are you?'

'Jesus Christ.'

I sat there with my heart in my mouth. I could not laugh. Undoubtedly, it is funny, but if I had as much as smiled, he might have split my head open. I tried to be witty.

'How is Peter doing?'

He glared at me for a moment, then said: 'Are you trying to make a fool of me?' Then he went on: 'I am not a shitbag like him, who goes around blabbing every time a cock crows!' Pause: 'I know how to keep my mouth shut! If only it had been some dumb duck!' Another pause, then, with a sigh: 'I must have been off my head to make him head of the church . . . he could hardly run a farmyard, that one!'

I swear that I have not invented a word.

The Objective Object-lens

I would like to widen out the discussion on theatre montage and link it to two related topics; firstly, to the question of acting objectively to the camera's object lens, and secondly, as previously discussed, to the possibility open to the actor or director of pressing into service the camera which each member of the audience unconsciously carries inside his own head. This phenomenon is all the more amazing when we consider that long before the invention of cinema with all its up-to-date equipment every actor worth his salt managed to compel every spectator with any sensitivity or culture to employ the identical camera, the identical fields and counter-fields of vision, identical universal focus, identical wide-angle lens – all long before the Lumière brothers had even been born. So it is only a question of convenience for us, in choosing our examples, to turn to cinema and its language.

There can be no getting away from the fact that as a result of watching films, cartoons and television shows, today's audiences have acquired a code for reading images and sounds which is immensely different from what people a century or so ago possessed. Therefore those directors who, when putting on a play from another age, stage it in the form they find it, without attempting to bring out the subject, or without doing that work of mediation and translation which is essential to render the language comprehensible to today's audience, are quite simply mad. They have a conviction – and this is the real paranoiac stupidity – that only a reprehensible meddler would touch them at all: 'The classics are sacred!'

I am the (obscure) Wolf-cat

As part of a conference on medieval studies, I once attended a performance of *Lu Gatto Lupesco* (The Wolf-cat), one of the earliest minstrel pieces, featured in any good anthology of Italian poetry. The monologue was written around the year 1100, and provides the approach to the *Divine Comedy*.

In it, the performer comes on in a half-cat, half-wolf mask, reciting the words:

> I am the wolf-cat
> Laying bait for anyone
> Who does not tell the truth.

That is, I prepare traps to catch hypocrites red-handed. The wolf-cat has been lost in the forest – hence the connection with Dante – and meets up with a leopard and other terrifying animals. He encounters an old man, a hermit, who will become his guide (the prototype of Virgil: it becomes clear that Dante did not invent anything at all!). Later the two go underground to hell, to re-emerge at Jerusalem, the promised land.

The little that is extant of the tale is full of life and creates its own tension. It moves at an urgent pace. Little of this was apparent from that production, so much so that I who knew the text by heart could hardly follow it. The director did not even bother to introduce the play with a prologue. The performer jumped all over the place like a dervish, never attempting to harmonise his gestures with what he was saying, and sailed blithely on declaiming in a language which for the people there could as well have been Double Dutch or Swiss German; it would have made no difference. This refusal to assist the audience to follow you is at heart an attitude of pure snobbishness practised by imbeciles; it conceals an insuperable inability – an inability to communicate.

A few months previously, I had performed the identical work before an audience of students in Turin. It was not that they were experts on the subject, since they were engineering students, but the thing worked perfectly. I took the trouble to explain the text beforehand and to set out the links with Dante and with the Provençal Troubadours. I went out of my way to translate the whole script sentence by sentence before launching into the performance. To ensure greater clarity, I deliberately signposted some of the words and backed them all up with appropriate gestures, while, obviously, being careful to avoid being unduly descriptive. In other words, the important thing is never to forget that even if you are one of the geniuses of the stage, you are, as it happens, alive today and that your task is to communicate with the men and women of today: the 'if you understand, good for you, if not, go to hell' mentality is only fit for second-rate aristocrats.

So then; let us learn to make ourselves clearly understood at all times, using every available means (always bearing in mind the overriding need for a certain style); therefore, method, rationality and an emotional force, but one kept under control; further, a concern for the spectator and an effort to discover on every occasion exactly what kind of camera he carries in his head.

Fourth Day

Make-up and Tricks of the Trade

Today's theme is connected with the discussion on masks, but also takes in the question of costume and the use of various accessories for disguise and dressing up, including make-up and wigs. It is a subject that embraces not only Commedia dell'Arte but also more ancient theatre. The use of costume, whether with or without masks, has often been considered secondary in theatre, but in my view this is a serious error of judgement. At the beginning, we saw how Tristano Martinelli, the first Harlequin, did not wear a mask but painted his face with black grease, leaving spaces on which he dabbed red and white squiggles. Similarly, other Commedia characters, like Pulcinella, Razzullo and Sarchiapone, in the early days used no other make-up than coloured paints.

It was not particularly easy to match a wig with the mask. The head was covered with a helmet pulled over the skull and passed under the chin, whereas the Greeks and Romans as well as, in many cases, the Indians, employed a one-piece mask-cum-wig. Undoubtedly the most prominent of the accessories with the Greeks and Romans was the 'buskin', or more properly the 'buskins', since they were generally used in pairs (if you exclude the unusual case of one-legged characters!). The Greeks maliciously tagged many politicians 'buskins', that is, shoes which could be worn on either foot, as the need arose. In Naples, there is a painting from Pompeii of an actor putting on a buskin with a sole about thirty centimetres high. The device raised the stature of the actor considerably. To conceal this stilt-like apparatus, it was the custom to wear a tunic which reached down to the ground.

Actors often had to widen their shoulders by as much as twenty centimetres on each side. At times, the shoulders had to be raised by thick padding to bring them up to the level of the ears, causing the neck virtually to disappear. These were the very limits of artifice, and such devices were necessary when someone had to appear as a divinity or as a hero like Hercules. In such a case the head began from the actor's forehead, that is to say, a mask was placed on his head as though it were a gigantic hat, and the actor's mouth ended up inside the neck of the mask, forcing him to speak in muffled tones.

There was one further trick. Once the body had been made taller, the arms, which stuck out from the mantle or toga, appeared short and clumsy and needed to be stretched out to reach a reasonable size, so the actor would hold the wrists of a dummy hand, resembling a puppet's or an artist's model's, in his own, and when he moved the arms from inside the sleeves, the resultant movement had a reasonable resemblance to the real thing. With these devices, they could raise their height to between two metres and two metres fifty, when the average height of a Greek man or woman was of the order of one metre fifty. It seems that they suffered no loss of agility. I have myself seen actors at the Odin* walk on stilts some two metres in height, wearing masks and dummy arms, and still perform leaps, twists and turns and even somersaults.

The Greeks, the Reflector and the Foreshortening Effect
This extraordinary enlargement effect was disconcerting for an audience, but Greek actors, not satisfied with the results obtained by the use of prostheses, pushed the effect to its limits by bringing the foreshortening effect into play. It is worth recalling that in a Greek theatre, the stalls, the position a modern audience would expect to occupy, simply did not exist. Everyone was placed on an extremely steep gradient which, using the terms of a contemporary theatre, would reach all the way to the top circle. Some of you will have visited Greek theatres which are not to be confused with the theatres adapted, widened and therefore levelled, by the Romans. I am talking of those that were not tampered with, like the one at Epidaurus. The incline is truly staggering, and the staircase so steep as to cause dizziness. Anyone who trips is liable to roll all the way down to the foot without being able to stop himself. The stage is laid out on a circular plan, with a diameter of around twelve metres, scarcly any bigger than today's normal proscenium. Immediately beyond stood the flight of steps, which rose almost perpendicularly. This meant that the spectators were looking down on the actors from a height, and the foreshortening effect came into play. The actors' shoulders were widened precisely to exploit this effect.

To increase the illusion of size of the characters, it became customary to throw shadows projected by enormous mirrors. It appears that the term 'reflector' (*anaclatoras* in Greek) derives from the stage directions for this

* The Odin Theatre is an important experimental theatre founded in Oslo in 1964 by Eugenio Barba, and now in Denmark.

system: 'apparatuses to reflect light'. Sheets of reflecting mica were glued to giant wooden disks or large shields. The mirrors were movable, so it was possible to follow the progress of the sun, catch the rays and project them on to the performance area. The stage was kept in darkness, so the reflected light could be manoeuvred like a present-day spotlight.

I have performed at Epidaurus, and found it a very moving experience. I was able to observe this effect at first hand. Contrary to what people believe, the plays were put on in winter, when the arc of the sun is low. Thanks to the lie of the theatre, the stage was already in complete darkness by late afternoon, but with the aid of the reflector mirrors it was possible to project the light in precise diagonal rays on to the actors. They even managed to convey the beam of light in two phases, one mirror positioned on the hill caught the sun and projected its rays on to another mirror lower down, which in its turn cast an almost piercing light on to the stage. The result thus achieved exaggerated the foreshortening effect. In fact, if I lengthen the shadow thrown by an object, I give the impression that the object itself has grown taller. With the actors lighted in this way and the shadow stretched out, the enlargement effect was guaranteed.

Let me repeat, this distortion of the image was reserved for the gods and for the great heroes. The actors who played parts which, however weighty, were human avoided all such tricks, not least because of the clumsiness and lack of credibility occasioned to both character and actor.

The Greeks at Theatre
The inventiveness and ingenuity of the Greeks did not stop at stilts, lighting or foreshortening effects. It could be said that virtually everything in use in a modern theatre was invented by them: the stage equipment, machines, towers, cranes, mobile bridges, trolleys, sound effects and fireworks. Nevertheless, before going any further, it is essential to emphasise that the theatres of the Greeks and Romans did not look the way they do to a modern visitor.

We are familiar with the rows of seats of bare stone, with the stage and rear arches similarly fashioned from marble or granite. In reality, what remains is no more than a basic structure, which was then almost entirely covered with wood. The stage was wooden, and the steps were wood-covered, and this is hardly surprising, since, apart from any advantages for the actors from performing on an elastic surface such as a wood flooring, there are other advantages deriving from the acoustic resonance which a set-up of that kind can offer. It must be once again repeated that the season for drama fell in winter, with the last performance being given from 20 to 24 March. However mild the climate of the Mediterranean countries may be, nobody needs to be reminded how unpleasant it is to sit outside, on a stone bench, exposed to the elements, from December to March, be it in Syracuse or Sparta. However, on a wooden bench, with an earthenware pot filled with smouldering embers under your bottom (the famous Attic vases), your feet resting on a warm stone, wrapped in a stout woollen rug (it even had a specific name), the prospect could become more bearable. If it seems that I am going over the score in tossing aside the facile, but false, notions we have of ancient theatre, think of the efforts made by the theatre organisers to reduce the force of the wind which cut across the spectating area. To this end, they planted rows of cypresses close together along the top of the stairway to create an artificial windbreak. The stage was not fixed but ran on trolleys. There were different storeys placed one on top of the other, mounted on little wheels that ran on tracks.

The scenery too was mobile. The façade of the palace in which Phaedra, for example, resided would open out in the final scene to allow the retractable flooring, the *ekkylema*, on which the prone body of the dying Phaedra was lying, to emerge. It was a kind of cinematic 'dolly shot' in reverse. The author required the audience to follow both the action and the character from close-up during her final speech, and, being unable to move the whole gallery forward – No problem, sir! – landed the character in the audience's lap. Further, there is equipment capable of bringing up from below (from beneath the stage) imposing pieces of scenery like the vertical section of a temple complete with oracle and priests' chorus, structures with boats which float in the space above the mystical gulf, towers crowded with soldiers which are hauled, skidding and slipping, across the length of the forward stage and, if that were not enough, machines to make the characters take flight.

In Aristophanes' *The Birds*, the two Athenians who have fled from the city find themselves performing suspended in mid-air, in the company of other actors playing the parts of the owl, the crow and the hoopoe bird. In *Peace*, also by Aristophanes, the hero sits astride an enormous beetle and goes flying about some thirty metres above the heads of the spectators. To attain these effects, the Greek technicians used high towers, cranes with outstretched arms of enormous proportions, winches and pulleys with huge lengths of cable and tackle. With practice, these theatrical craftsmen developed such skills that they were able to transport, suspended above the stage, winged horses, burning chariots and even full-size ships carrying up to ten gods, as happens in the closing scene of *Philoctetes*, when, out of nowhere, a god makes an appearance on a machine. The expression 'deus ex machina' derives from this closing twist, which gives a satisfactory resolution to the plot.

Out You Come, Euripides!

It seems that Euripides went over the score with his use of machines. Hardly a soul made an entry on his own two feet. Both the hero and the lesser characters had to come in transported by some device or other. Aristophanes was not the man to let an opportunity of that kind slip, so in *Parliament of Women*, who should turn up but Euripides himself? The leading comic actor, in a very pointed quip, invites Euripides to come down to the public square, and positions himself in front of a mock-up of the façade of the great dramatist's own residence. 'Come down, Euripides,' he says. 'I'm waiting for you! Can you manage by yourself, or do you need someone to drop by with a carriage?'

The Protagonist, Actor of Talent

Another unknown detail of Greek theatre was the switching of roles: in a tragedy such as *Hippolytus* by Euripides, there are six characters, plus Aphrodite (who speaks the prologue) and Artemis. The complete cast consists of Phaedra, Hippolytus, Phaedra's nurse, Theseus – father of Hippolytus and husband of Phaedra – a servant and a messenger. In addition, there are two choruses with their respective chorus-leaders. Nevertheless, there were only three actors involved. In the whole of Greek theatre, that number was never exceeded. The chorus had an independent structure all its own. The first actor was known as the protagonist, the second the deuteragonist and the third the tritagonist.

If I were to ask one of today's actors how the Greek actors divided the parts in, for example, *Hippolytus*, I would receive an answer along these lines: 'The principal actor would take the part of Phaedra (Greek actors played both male and female roles, since women were barred from the stage, as they are in Kabuki theatre to this day), the deuteragonist would take the part of Hippolytus and the third actor would play the nurse.' What roles were left for the others, in that case? 'Ah, yes, there were three other actors, but they had no lines to say. They had walk-on parts.' No matter how obvious it may seem today, that answer is wrong. The parts were divided up according to an entirely different system. In the first place, each of these three actors possessed a complete outfit of at least four masks with appropriate tragic costumes. In the case of Hippolytus and Phaedra, to kit out eight characters a minimum of three outfit sets were required.

In the opening scene, the principal part is undoubtedly Hippolytus, so the protagonist comes on dressed as a prince, in conversation with his servant, a lesser but still important part. The nurse, played by the deuteragonist who consequently has to dress as a mature woman, makes her entrance immediately afterwards. After a passage involving the chorus, Phaedra enters to tell of her encounter with Hippolytus, and once again the part is taken by the protagonist, who had to make full use of the verses recited by the chorus to slip off and get out of the mask and costume of Hippolytus and come back on in a new guise. There are two non-speaking characters on stage and these were in fact walk-on parts.

After the Scene, the Intermezzo

The biggest part in the second scene is the one taken by the nurse, so, during a recitation by the chorus, the protagonist races into the wings, pulls off the wig and clothes of Phaedra, hands the queen's part over to the deuteragonist, the two of them carry out a rapid switch of the various essentials of the roles and back on stage they go. At the same time, the tritagonist has stripped off the dress and mask of the servant and has assumed the part of Hippolytus. And so on, scene by scene; each time one of the characters has an important speech to make, the protagonist will stake his claim. The best parts in the tragedy are all his property. The other two actors, in a descending scale, will take the supporting roles or deliver the additional dialogue. At the end, if you notice, everything is, more or less, resolved in one great closing monologue, delivered under a variety of guises.

It is also true that the protagonist was by far the best of the group. As a superstar his pay was one talent per performance, enough to enable a whole family to live in some style for a year. Today no actor, no matter how important he may be, will ever earn a similar amount.

Anecdotes apart, what interests me is the enormous conceptual gulf which divides Greek theatre from us. First of all, the script was written, in its general outlines, with the constant purpose of arranging dialogues, entrances and soliloquies so as to favour absolutely the protagonist, so it is almost impossible to find in either tragedies or comedies a conflict in which the two sides are given an equal say. The part played by the protagonist is always by far the most important, so his opponent will have to keep his powder dry, since his passionate reply can only be delivered in the following scene, that is, once the protagonist has had time to switch costume and reappear in the role of his erstwhile antagonist.

I must confess that I laughed till the tears were running down my cheeks when I discovered that lines were drawn along the stage beyond which no one except the protagonist was allowed to advance; in other words, the protagonist alone had the opportunity of moving freely about the stage and of going as far as the footlights, or where the footlights would be today. Indeed, when he mounted specially made trolleys, he could have himself carried further out beyond the mystical gulf to end up suspended above the audience. On the other hand, this privilege was not extended to the deuteragonist. Under no circumstances was he to venture beyond the line drawn approximately three metres from the mystical gulf; the third actor had to remain a good six metres from the proscenium, while the bit players were kept even further back. The audience were thus able to tell from the positions the performers took up on the stage which actor was concealed under the masks and finery of which character.

The *Hypocrites* and the *Ethopios*

There is one question continually asked about Greek acting. Did the acors take the trouble to imitate the various voices, male and female, of the roles they played? Certainly, even if in the early days (the sixth and seventh centuries) identification with the character was no more than hinted at. In fact, custom required a constant epic alienation from the characters.* Even if wearing costume, the actor was never to forget his role as narrator, and indeed it was considered improper, if not downright vulgar, for him to actually identify with the character. It is said that Solon, listening in a theatre in Athens to an actor – it may have been Thespis – with an unusual ability to put on male and female voices, young and old, rose to his feet in a fury and yelled out: 'Stop! He's no actor [*Ethopios*]. He's a rascal of an *Hypocrites*!' Oddly enough the two terms re-emerged in Commedia dell'Arte to indicate a role and particular character. Ethopios is the one who can alter the morals of men.

On Mime and Pantomime

I would like to pass on to the language of gesture. Conventionally, the verb 'to mime' is used to indicate a series of gestures employed to convey an idea or tell a story without the use of words. In fact, as I suggested on the first day, the correct term for this is pantomime. For the Greeks and the Romans, to mime meant to narrate with body, voice and masks, to perform tricks on stilts, to dance, perform acrobatics, to act and sing. In other words, every available means were pressed into service. Mime in ancient times was considered an inferior, dubious and scurrilous genre, and was censured, as has been everything which the authorities have been unable to control and manipulate for their own ends. Only when the people themselves began to display an overwhelming interest in mime did it attain a level of public acceptability. To

* A reference to Brecht's 'epic theatre', which aimed at alienation of the audience.

avoid ambiguity, let us adopt the modern convention, and call mime that style of acting which does not employ language.

Mime is not a sign language for the dumb. Mime is effective when, with the use of gesture, effects can be attained and a clearer, more efficient, more advantageous style of communication established than would be possible with words alone. There are, however, subjects that can be very clearly conveyed by the use of the voice, so what is the point of overdoing things, gesticulating like a madman? The art of mime is the art of communication by synthesis; it does not aim to imitate natural gestures slavishly, but to hint, to indicate, to imply, to goad the imagination. Theatre is the pretence of reality, not its imitation.

Generous and Petty Gestures

There are thousands of conventional gestures which in day-to-day speech are used to facilitate communication. To rub your hand on your stomach, as everyone knows, indicates anticipation of a delicious meal. In Italy, these signs are more numerous, so that running your thumb down the cheek indicates someone who is sharp and a bit sly, whereas pulling down the skin under the eye means open your eyes, smarten up! Resting the cheek against one hand and leaning your head slightly conveys the information that you are tired, and so on. The mime must completely ignore signs of this sort, precisely because they are banal, well-worn stereotypes and do not indicate the presence of intelligent imagination. Any actor who made use of them to express sleep or hunger would be the poorest of performers, because in theatre it is as essential to re-invent gestures as it is to re-invent words.

It is important to begin from reality and not from the conventions of reality, and this categorical imperative is every bit as true for women mime artists. I have seen actresses who, asked to play a working-class woman, stand with their hands on their hips, rub the backs of their necks and cup their breasts, and when asked to play a prostitute, sway their hips and bawl left and right, all the while dishing out great smacks on the belly and the bottom. By the same token, I have seen others play a noblewoman by pronouncing their R in the French manner, standing with their neck erect, moving their hands in little butterfly gestures, fluttering their eyelashes and walking as though they had a feather up their backside. Any woman who behaves in that way show herself an actress of very little talent and imagination.

To become a good mime, several things are essential: to learn the skills of an acrobat, to develop physical agility and suppleness, to learn to do leaps and multiple jumps, to know how to arch your back, to execute dead-falls and to walk on your hands; secondly, to learn how to breathe in time with the movement, because it is important to avoid gasping; thirdly, to master the use of the hands, to know how to manufacture things out of nothing with a few gestures, how to pick them up, move them around and put them down again. For example: if I want to pick up a bottle by the neck or by the base, I have to stretch out my fingers to grip it, and carry out the gesture of lifting it with both hands. In this way, obviously, I manage to give a more precise sketch of the bottle. With the left hand clenched in a tight grip, I draw the neck, and with the other I suggest the shape of the bottle itself. With the same gesture, I can imply that the bottle is light or, feigning exertion, that it is a dead weight.

Disarticulation and Distortion

In mime, it is a good rule to publicise gestures and articulations, in other words to move muscles and limbs which, for ordinary exertions, would not be employed at all. This 'over-gesturing' serves to give clarity, to establish the style of the action, to make it less banal and to give it a certain spaciousness. For example, I lift the bottle with the hand, with the other pick up and raise a glass – it makes no difference whether I wish to indicate a wine glass or a tumbler – and then make a pouring action. It is important to use sizes which make the dimensions of the objects look credible. If, while pouring, the two objects are held at an excessive distance apart, the impression given is of holding in your hand a bottle with a gigantic neck, whereas if they are brought too close together, both the neck and the bottle disappear. The audience gets the impression that the actor is pouring from the bottom of the bottle.

The answer is to put it down on a surface, but not too heavily, otherwise I will be compelled to mime the bottle breaking into pieces, blood flowing from the hand and splinters of glass being extracted from the fingers and palm of the same hand. If you remove your hands without opening out your fingers, you only give the impression of eliminating the bottle. When you open out the hand, everyone understands that you have let go of the bottle.

Let us take the matter one step further. If I have here a real bottle and glass and make to pick up the glass, it is clear that I have no need to open my fingers wide or draw imaginary pictures in the air. When I pour, no one is going to be watching my every act, since there is nothing interesting about it. On the other hand, when I mime an act, it is the pretence that arouses attention and interest. Now if in those circumstances I limit myself to repeating the natural gesture of lifting and pouring, and keep to the normal sizes of real objects, the whole thing becomes banal, tedious, petty and above all not credible. Truth applied to the imaginary is false, and irritating into the bargain. To obtain a credible impact, it is necessary to manipulate reality.

The same is true for the action of opening and closing a non-existent door.

The problem is always to find a means of presenting an object without destroying it. A worthwhile exercise for anyone who wishes to gain familiarity with the techniques of sketching spaces and shapes and keeping them firmly in the audience's mind, is to practise with so-called 'fixed points'. A mime artist can describe a wall by placing the palms of his hands fully on it, as though they were resting against glass; then he must move them gently, feeling his way along the imaginary glass, until he wants to suggest a corner. It has to be presented, and the angle can be implied by putting one palm on each side. Marcel Marceau is splendid at this move. Raising the hands above the head and stretching out the arms is enough to give the impression of a ceiling, and if I wish to imply that it is falling and crushing me, I keep the palms fixed and move my body, shoulders, pelvis and legs. If I move the hands even slightly, the illusion is shattered.

A similar exercise involves rope-pulling. I take hold of a real piece of rope and pull; there is no need to lean forward unduly, since the maximum effect can be obtained with the tiniest movements of the body. If, however, I wish to perform the identical act, but this time with a non-existent line, I have to loosen up completely to have any success in producing a sufficient illusion. The movement of the shoulder, drawing it forward towards the rope and simultaneously moving the forearm, must be emphasised. The whole arm and wrist must swing into action at the same time. First I stretch out the muscles of the wrist, then relax them, I bend over, move the neck forward, then back. Then the pelvis is moved forward, the right leg bent, the left leg pointed then stretched. The impression given is of a strong tugging effort. All the moves have to be repeated; take the rope, stretch and pull, then the reverse; I move my back upright, push on the hips, lean the neck forward, then push on the hips again, pull back the pelvis, straighten out the left leg, bend the right, stretch and bend the arms, in alternating movements. This sudden switch gives the impression of a superhuman effort, although if I were to act in that way in reality, I would hardly succeed in shifting a pound weight. Once again, an arbitrary but effective re-invention of reality.

Promenade sur Place

To end up – walking on the spot. I drag the left foot while leaning alternately on the heel and toe of the right. Then I drag the right, putting the weight on the left, and so on. It is a very complicated step, invented by Etienne Decroux; it requires a bit of application to learn it, but it is not difficult. There is a different step used to go up and down stairs, which is executed by bending the knee slightly at each step. In all of these movements, there is no attempt at imitation. Each one of these steps is totally false in itself, but more than probable in performance.

This is no more than the briefest outline of the skills that are worth acquiring, but always bear in mind that the day all the techniques of mime have been fully mastered, the next step is to learn how, when and where to apply them – and above all when to do without them. We all know mime artists of the highest calibre who are incapable of jettisoning anything at all, who have not, in other words, learned how to use sounds, words and gestures sparingly. This view about the need to jettison aspects of the art has the same sense as Louis Jouvet's* advice, which I quoted earlier, about not acting up to the hilt in every situation. The mime who insists on describing every single detail soon begins to pall and to annoy. The good mime will have learned to jettison all that is superfluous, and that means economy and, once again, synthesis and style.

I went to see a German actor last year in Frankfurt doing my *Story of a Tiger*. He went over the top with his descriptions. Every act in his repertoire – struts, gesticulations, acrobatic somersaults, whether relevant or not, was on display. The more he threw himself about, the less the audience enjoyed themselves.

A Sense of Measure, Please
I find myself repeating one thing, almost obsessively: there is no need to display the whole gamut of your technical knowledge on each and every occasion to convince the audience of your mastery of the business. People grasp this instantly, just from the way you come on, walk, sit down, or pick your nose. To show that you are in high spirits, there is no need to do a one-legged backward somersault. Anyone in possession of adequate training and a reasonable gift as a storyteller will have no problem in conveying their talents to all and sundry by their every movement and gesture.

How do you decide when, rather than gliding over it or giving the merest hints at its sense, it is appropriate to perform every detail of a vocal or gestural passage? At this stage, there arises what is, in my view, the crucial problem regarding the quality, and approach, that one decides to give to a production. From the very outset of our collaboration, dating back some thirty years, I have always disagreed with Lecoq on the ideological, as well as dramatic, weight to be given to the use of mime.

* Louis Jouvet (1887–1951), gifted actor and successful actor-manager.

Preamble to a Morality Tale

At this point, in order to introduce the next theme, permit me a brief digression. It is well known that almost all medieval plays use the term 'morality' in their title. *The Morality of the Blind Man and the Cripple*, or *The Morality of the Birth of the Minstrel*, and so on. What is the meaning of the word 'morality'? It means that in the text a moral subject is under discussion, in the sense that the work sets out the indication of a concept of life, of behaviour, of the idea of being and becoming in relation to God and his teaching, but also in relation to the society of men with all their laws and conventions. In other words, the plays contain, in addition to teaching regarding Divine Law, a viewpoint on the proper rules of social life, and a condemnation of injustice and wickedness. Morality, then, also takes in politics. There does not exist in ancient theatre, be it religious or secular, a drama which does not set out to include as a fundamental presupposition the teaching of a principle held to be moral and civil.

I mentioned a while back the occasionally heated debate I have been conducting over a period of years with Jacques Lecoq. These clashes have taken place within a context of complete mutual respect, and any time I am in Paris I never fail to go along to his school, and he always invites me to give a demonstration for his pupils. Jacques is in complete agreement with me that mime must not be allowed to degenerate into the art of deaf-mutes. But he adds: 'In my school, I offer the pupils the entire repertoire needed for physical and gestural expression. It is then up to each individual to apply it as he sees fit.'

'No,' I reply, 'it is a grave mistake to separate technique from its ideological, moral and dramatic context.' It is beyond doubt that all Lecoq's mimes, be they Japanese, Filipinos, Romans or Americans from the state of Massachusetts are all carbon copies of each other, and they never manage to rid themselves of the mechanical, gestural stereotypes they have been taught.

An Exceptional Master with whom I Disagree

Lecoq, as he often says himself, requires his pupils to search inside their own bellies to uncover their individual expressive identities. But what about the audience? How can anyone learn without real practice, which means addressing a live audience? It is a bit like learning to play on a guitar that does not produce sounds, made with strings that were taken from the day's mail. At the end of the day, the Jacques Lecoq school gives more weight to technique than to any other aspect of the art. Pupils are taught how to breathe, how to develop body language, including the language of the emotions, but they overlook the word, its sound and its impact. Not one of them knows how to pitch the voice, how to breathe, with the result that, theatrically speaking, they have become deaf-mutes. Moreover, nobody bothers to explain to the pupils exactly why they ought to choose one particular gesture rather than another, and the consequence is the absence of a specific style.

In a famous work of kabuki theatre, the actor who plays the character of the fox mimes the animal – its prowl, its tail wagging, its crouch – all without ever actually stretching out on the ground. He never goes down on all fours and never even needs to bend his back. It is sufficient for him to wave his arm in a certain way to make you aware that that is his tail. He turns his head to one side, swings round the other, darts his eyes and holds them in the one spot, and you have a fox to a T, even for someone who has never seen a fox in his life. The act portrays all the wiles and cunning, and when he speaks, the voice is that of a hypocritical and unreliable being. Behind this display there lies a choice, a moral choice. I might almost say that in addition a certain political value is given. An ideological presupposition stands at the root of the whole story, and this choice conditions the manner of styling the gestures, the synthesis, the rhythms and the cadences.

It is dangerous to learn techniques unthinkingly when no prior care has been given to the moral context in which they are to be employed. It is like learning how to put up a house, walls and foundation, without taking the trouble to find out where the house is to be constructed and whether the site is swampy or rocky or hilly. Any school of architecture worth its salt always teaches the students first to examine the site and then to decide on the materials and type of construction that will be appropriate.

Proceeding on other principles will produce mime-actors who are empty robots bereft of all mental elasticity, of all authentic sensibility, and, worst of all, of any real personality. They can never be other than cardboard cut-outs of the master. Personally I have been godfather to hundreds of young actors, male and female, and have never set myself up as master, although in fact I believe I taught them some essential, perhaps decisive, matters. Some who possessed exceptional gifts have gone on to become outstanding actors, but I can boast of one thing: none of them is an imitation of me, none of them apes me and each one has preserved his own personality.

Fifth Day

The Voice: Declamations, Drawls and Sing-song

Having considered self-expression by gesture, it is time to turn to the problem of the voice and of breathing in acting. To train and develop vocal tone and power, as well as clarity of delivery, there is no one established method that is immediately applicable to all subjects. Each actor will simply have to experiment until he finds the technique best suited to his needs. There are certain basic techniques that can be used by the majority of speakers, and others that will be of assistance to very few. Each individual will have to arrive at a knowledge of how his own vocal apparatus is structured, and try out one by one the exercises and practices designed to develop power and resonance. It is essential for everyone to begin from their own natural attributes, so as to make the most of their strengths and their weaknesses, and turn both to best advantage. Not all great actors were blessed with great voices; Ricci, Ruggero Ruggeri, and, much more so, Petrolini all had nasal voices with very few low-pitched sounds. The acoustic registers of their speaking voices tended almost exclusively towards the middle-alto, but they were successful in projecting the voice and even if they had very limited tonal ranges, they exploited them to the full.

The most important thing is to learn to project the voice, to articulate and form words in the most intelligible way possible. The organ on which one has to push so as to produce crisp resonance is the abdomen. It is essential to stretch the solar plexus like a drum skin, and to undertake exercises to achieve this aim, so that sounds of the lowest possible tonality can be obtained. Acting with the chest voice or from the abdomen prevents the voice from going hoarse, because the vocal chords, which are a matching pair, produce a series of shorter, slower vibrations when creating deep tones and the risk of the so-called abrasive whip-effect (when the two rub one against the other, with disastrous consequences) is avoided. In addition, the lower tones of voice make a bigger impact on the listener. It is a common mistake to believe that raising the pitch or going into falsetto helps projection, when exactly the opposite is the case. Pressure on the abdomen with the emission of deeper sounds is the most effective means of throwing the voice furthest.

Sinking with the Basses

If I need to deliver a lengthy speech without drawing breath during the delivery, I draw in as much breath as possible at the beginning of the sentence, without overdoing it, as though I were taking a plunge under water, and I go on talking until I have used up every drop of air in my lungs, in the pit of my stomach, in my ear-holes, in my nostrils – until I am literally deflated and just cannot go on.

The key to success lies in letting the breath out very slowly, without undue pressure; in other words, no more than is needed to project the voice the required distance. Never believe that an almighty release of breath is required for an expression of great vocal power. This is one of the most common mistakes of amateur dramatic societies. Resonance is determined principally by the pressure that is brought to bear on the abdomen and on all the muscles of the vocal apparatus, that is, the muscles of the oesophagus, of the glottis and the epiglottis as well as those of the velum, the back-palatal zone.

It is control and not the quantity of air expelled, that determines power and produces efficient voice projection. Another essential trick of the trade is the method that allows the talker to take in rapid gulps of air while talking, without having to stop to open his mouth. To be more precise, I should correct the expression I have just used. Rather than a trick of the trade, it is a technique that must be acquired by practice, an exercise involving the use of the nose (assuming it is not blocked by a cold). It is important to use this technique sparingly, and often it will be better to breathe quite naturally, drawing attention to the fact rather than attempting to disguise it.

The Classical Drawl

I always advise actors to be alert at all times to what they are doing even when simply chatting to relatives or friends at home: take advantage of the opportunity to bring pressure to bear on the abdomen and to try out the lower registers, and even when reading the newspapers do it aloud and project the sounds. You may be taken as insane, but theatre needs its victims! Once your abdomen is in trim, you will find that the 'mask voice', the head voice or the falsetto comes more easily and with less effort. While acting, it is important to use as wide a range as possible, but always with a sense of measure and never just for effect.

At all costs, avoid the 'classical drawl', that style of mournful recitation, marked by drawn-mouthed, sickly, swooping up and down scales, so characteristic of many of the actors and actresses of refined theatre. When I was a young actor, taking my first steps in theatre, I met dozens of performers whose delivery was of this type. Their oily cadences clung to my ears like fly-paper. I was stupid enough to believe that the reason for that irritating affectation was a special technique imitated from opera singers – a technique and vocal style that entailed grimaces, little simpers and a great deal of mumbling, and so I refused point blank to apply myself to picking up the basics of correct delivery. My voice in all its untrained force roared out in theatres, it soared up in fluting falsettos that would have burst a hundred ear-drums, and the result was that my throat seized up and I went around producing such vast quantities of spit that, nowadays, by comparison, anyone would think my salivary glands were burned dry. And without fail, I would lose my voice.

Arrogant and pig-headed, I paid no heed, until once, while playing at the Mercadante Theatre in Naples, my voice went completely, and I could not produce even the semblance of a sound. I ended up puffing like an iguana with adenoids. The consultant who saw me at the hospital diagnosed 'severe aphonia' aggravated by the formation of polyps on the vocal chords. I was told to observe complete silence for a period of five days, and the company had to suspend its performance in Naples. The incident persuaded me to become a professional, and the first thing was to learn voice control. Today I can allow myself to yell, to do a squeaky falsetto, to entertain an audience for hours and I am no longer likely to have problems with my voice, unless I should happen to contract bronchitis and pharyngitis at the same time.

The Abdominal Pitch not natural to Women

Can the same technique of voice formation be recommended to aspiring actresses? The first point is that nature has not equipped women with the abdomen voice, and their instinct is to shun it, because nature herself was concerned to protect any children who might be carried in the womb. Pressure on the solar plexus or stretching of the muscles of the abdomen could create problems for babies in the womb, so nature has shifted the vocal apparatus higher up. For this reason, women by preference use the head or the 'mask' voice, whereas men find it easier to use the abdomen. Therefore, exercises to re-activate the solar plexus and to freshen up its use must proceed gradually, without force, and obviously it will be difficult to learn the technique.

Over-emphasis is a vice learned at school. Teachers tend to train us from the earliest years in the bad habits of 'sing-song' or 'over the top' delivery.

Some time ago I was invited to take part in a congress on the theatre of the sixteenth century. A procession of venerable professors ascended the rostrum and occasionally in their papers had to read extracts from the comedies of, for example, Aretino, Giordano Bruno, or Ruzzante. I thought I was going to split my sides laughing, because I have never witnessed such displays of snivelling or high-sounding grandiloquence as from those pompous academics. You might have expected such gentlemen to produce a spare and sober diction, but not a bit of it. They let rip with good old sing-song stuff, overloaded with grand emphasis.

Directors are a different kettle of fish. It is a well-known fact that virtually every director burns with the desire to get up on the stage and act, and if, in spite of the best efforts of friends and family, he succeeds, he can be relied on to create mayhem. I have heard of one who couldn't pass up the chance when an actor, who was also a close friend, ended up with a multiple fracture and had to be rushed to hospital.

No one, however, can out-do a poet. Have you ever heard a poet recite? Has anyone heard Montale, or, even worse, Ungaretti declaim his own poetry?* It is hard to imagine anything more outrageous or preposterous than that selection of basses, falsettos, squeaks and nasal tones. There they are puffing and panting, wheezing out a delirium tremens drawl, passing on to the old Shakespearean-actor nasal tones, voice aquiver all the while.

How can excesses of this sort be avoided? It is a matter of study, of the acquisition of the ability to recite the intentions present in a speech, rather than the words. Once again improvisation is of capital importance. There is a method I often use. When I am putting on a show and find I am working with actors who are tone deaf or have a sing-song voice with all kinds of artificial sounds, I invite them to retell the story they are about to perform in their own words, using their native dialect. I train them to think of the composition of the sentences and the rhythms in the language that comes most naturally to them, and I promise you it always works. They quite automatically jettison all those phoney phonetic mannerisms they have picked up either apeing certain famous actors or, at drama school, apeing master-apes.

So here is a piece of good advice for which, I have no doubt, all would-be actors will be eternally grateful to me: when you learn a text, always translate it first into your own words, and then into your own dialect, if you have one. I have known actors who did not have a dialect of their own. They ended up repeating lines of the most flat, ascetic phonemes, without a hint of musicality in their tones or in their cadences. I myself find that if, writing a script, I stumble over a sentence or dialogue, what I do is think the whole thing out in my own dialect, and then re-translate back into Italian. I make no claim to

* Eugenio Montale (1896–1981) and Giuseppe Ungaretti (1888–1970), two major Italian lyric poets.

have invented anything original. The first person to write through a dialect was none other than Dante – apart from the fact that, transforming the spoken speech, he invented a language straight off. And what a language! To succeed in his project, he searched far and wide collecting, in his *De Vulgari Eloquentia*, expressions, terms and idiomatic expressions from all over Italy and beyond, including Provence.

Someone else who invented a language of his own was Manzoni.* Few people are aware that the author of *I Promessi Sposi* (The Betrothed) very rarely spoke Italian. Normally he expressed himself in Milanese dialect, as did most of the aristocracy of Milan at that time. At home, he spoke French by preference, and conducted most of his correspondence in the same language. There is no doubt that when he sat down to write his novels or stories, the language structure he had in mind was that of his native Milanese. I have tried to translate sections of *I Promessi Sposi* into Milanese dialect, and it works perfectly, so much so that I have no doubt that if Manzoni had written directly in the dialect he thought in, he would have become a genuinely universal novelist, instead of being relegated to the status of Italian writer.

Finally there is Pirandello, the greatest theatre writer of this last century. He too writes in Italian while plainly thinking in dialect. The rhythms, the grammatical structure, the idiomatic phrasing, not to mention the innate feel for scenic description, the atmosphere of perennial conflict between the characters, the blending together of the tragic and the grotesque are all born from the language and culture of Sicily. In other words, if you do not have a dialect, find one!

Space and Resonance

I would like to return to the subject of the voice, particularly in relation to space and projection when using mechanical devices such as amplifiers and microphones.

The mechanical projection of the voice was a problem we had to face around fifteen years ago with the La Comune Theatre Company, when we began acting in huge spaces without resonance and, even worse, with quite appalling boom and echo effects, spaces like the recreation rooms of working men's clubs, the huge covered dance halls in Romagna and Emilia, industrial plants, sports halls and deconsecrated churches. Performing in such places using your natural voice was out of the question. Before we tried, no one had ever put on a show in something like the Palazzetto dello Sport in Turin,

* Alessandro Manzoni (1785–1837), poet and novelist, whose historical novel *I Promessi Sposi* was an outstanding achievement in nineteenth-century Italian literature.

which was 320 metres in diameter, or in the one in Bologna, which was 230. These halls could hold between ten and thirty thousand people.

Until a few years previously, in the official theatre, we had been accustomed to working on stages that were on average 9–10, and at most 12–13 metres square. Before tackling the problem of acoustics we had to deal with visual problems. In such a vast space, would it be possible to continue to use old-style scenery? We had just opened in Milan with *Accidental Death of an Anarchist*, and had put up the set in the premises in Via Colletta (an old factory which had closed down some months earlier). The space was some 20 metres wide and 35 long, with a playing area of around 15 square metres. In other words, it was already wider than normal, but in the Palazzetto dello Sport in Turin, in order to give the stage some prominence, it had to be extended to a good 30 metres. We scraped together some additional props to add to those we already had.

While putting up the actual scenery, we were worried sick. We unloaded all the backdrops we had brought along with us. The first thing was to forget the classical scene with the central focus. We arranged everything, the flats, the furniture, the fridge, the washing machine and the various bits and pieces like windows, doors, steps etc. on the horizontal, as though it were a craftware exhibition. The scene ended up looking like a squeezed bas-relief, with no depth, and we had to perform arranged in a horizontal line. In the early stages we must have seemed like a group of restless demons, as we moved ceaselessly from one side of the stage to the other, desperately trying to fill that immense area. Finally we got the measure of it. There was also the whole question of gestures, because we had to get the hang of those wider spaces. Therefore, less hurried and more expansive gestures were the order of the day. There was just no point in delicate side glances, in facial expressions, or in minute movements of the eyes, since, from thirty to forty yards, only gestures of the whole body, made with the aid of amplified voice, had any chance of being understood. And that brings us to the next point.

Rock and Amplifiers

Today we use the Sennheiser radio microphone, an astonishing machine which manages to reproduce even the subtlest of tones and to give the timbre of voice that comes closest to reality. In those days we were still using the earliest radio microphones, which had much lower power. Into the bargain, we had only two of them, so most of us were reduced to performing with a microphone round our necks, dragging the wires over the stage behind us. Every so often they got tangled up, with one or other of the company coming close to strangulation. With the familiarity that we now have with the

Sennheisers and with the Semprinis (another make of radio microphone), there is simply no point in using the natural voice. On those occasions when I am obliged to, even when I am familiar with the acoustics of the theatre, I must, so as to ensure that the words arrive clearly, make a different kind of pressure on the abdomen and produce the individual syllables with greater care. A falsetto produced with a microphone round your neck requires a completely different technique of breath release. Rock stars do not know, and have no interest in learning, how to make the best use of the voice when singing unaided. Remove their amplifiers and you have a corpse on your hands. Their style of singing is both improved and conditioned by the mechanical tools of their trade. Fortunately for me, I am often obliged to use the natural voice, so I never get out of practice, but I do not doubt that after an extended period of exposure to the microphone, I would be reduced to the status of the rock star.

In any case, to get the best out of a radio microphone, with its attendant high fidelity and high power amplification, it is essential, yet again, to exercise, to study and master all the various technical tricks of the new technology, so as to make full use of the extended vocal range it offers. These machines are now so highly sophisticated as to make possible tones and sounds of a depth and pitch simply inconceivable with the natural voice alone. You will still find groups of old-style nostalgics, hankering after the human voice pure and unadulterated, repeating to anyone who will listen that the amplifier has been the death of live theatre, but these people remind me of demented creatures propelling themselves along the motorway on a skateboard, screaming out to passers-by 'Watch me! Here's real speed for you!'

The Actors of the Volksbühne

On the subject of actors, it might be worthwhile to recall a conversation I had with Claudio Meldolesi.*

Meldolesi: I think it would be interesting if you were to speak about the productions of your work abroad. Müller, the German author you know well . . .

Dario: Which Müller do you have in mind?

Meldolesi: Heiner, the one who wrote *Philoctetes*.

Dario: Yes. A wonderful comedy, or rather tragedy.

Meldolesi: He told me he knew you.

* Claudio Meldolesi, Professor of Dramaturgy at the University of Bologna.

156

Dario: We met in Berlin at the Volksbühne for the first night of a satirical piece on the history of a struggle in a factory in East Germany. It was a comedy that the censors had blocked for God knows how long.

Meldolesi: Heiner told me a story about you.

Dario: Which one?

Meldolesi: About something that happened during the run of *Can't Pay? Won't Pay!*

Dario: I remember. He told me as well. It's a good story. On you go, tell it.

Meldolesi: It seems he found himself two years ago with the Volksbühne, but this time in West Berlin. They were doing the fiftieth production of your play, when about thirty young people turned up, demanding to be admitted free of charge, since it said on the poster that you did not have to pay. You must understand that the Volksbühne of West Berlin, even if the name means 'People's Theatre', has nothing at all popular about it, so the actors immediately sent for the director, who huffed and puffed and said that that was only the title of the play, nothing more. The young people, very wittily, and with that pragmatism which has made the Prussians famous, waved under the nose of the director and the assembled cast the poster that advertised the show, shouting, 'It says here that you don't have to pay. If that is meant as a joke, you should say clearly on the posters – WON'T PAY, but don't take it seriously, because you'll pay through the nose. We have had to travel a good 100 kilometres from outside the city, and you got us here under false pretences, so you owe us travel expenses, overnight stay, two meals a head because the whole day has gone for a burton! There are thirty of us, so what are you going to do about it?

Dario: So the director ended up with egg on his face.

Meldolesi: It gets worse. The police were called, and, to cap it all, they had no idea what to do, but since the young people played their part with such panache, the police ended up on their side.

Dario: And that is not all. The actors became aware of the hue and cry in the auditorium, and went to find out what was going on. They had a hurried confab, and then their leader (it was an actors' co-operative) went on stage to announce that if the trouble-makers were not thrown out, there would be no show that evening.

Meldolesi: Exactly. Things got out of hand. One part of the audience booed the actors; the rest howled at the group who had been responsible for the whole thing; the police had no idea where to look. I never did find out how it was resolved.

Dario: I understand they had to abandon the play, which says a great deal about the nature of the relationship these actors (especially since they were members of a co-operative) had with their audience and with the text they were performing. Not all of them seem to have entirely grasped the central thrust of the play, since it deals with solidarity among people ground down by profiteering, with the struggle against the arbitrary hiking up of prices, and since it also pillories selfishness and idiocy. This cast immediately revealed themselves for what they were: a group of opportunists and nothing more. They had selected that play exclusively because it guaranteed them a sure-fire success. People came along, had a good laugh at the comic scenes, and got caught up in the notions it was putting forward, which is more than can be said for these miserable hypocrites of the Volksbühne. Apart from which, nobody was asking a lot of them. If you are putting on something meant as provocative, you can hardly complain if somebody tries to put one over you. What is to stop you having a good laugh over it? If thirty people turn up with the clear intention of taking you on at your own game, the least you should do is go along with them, fool about a bit, accept the joke and have a giggle. Whereas this lot couldn't wait to get on their high horse and issue their proclamations: 'Anarchists out, or we down tools!' Unfortunately, I only got to hear about their behaviour too late, when they had already completed their run, otherwise, I assure you, I would have withdrawn the performing rights.

These, however, are not the only actors who go on stage without caring about the sense of the work they are putting on. Obviously I am not suggesting that each and every actor has to identify with the author and his ideology, but a minimum of coherence is indispensable. As it is, actors of great talent find themselves performing reactionary texts on Tuesday, escapist pieces on Thursday and revolutionary plays on Saturday. The main thing that interests them is to find a challenging part, a play that works and bums for seats. Art is above all ideology!

Unfortunately, all too often I see plays of mine or of Franca's put on exclusively because they rake in the cash. Directors, producers and leading actors never come and say: 'Look here, you know we are only doing this play because it works and it is funny, and we could not care less about the political or moral points that you are putting across.' To hear them speak, the only thing that counts is the message, the politics, and it is that that gives me a pain you know where. However, once a company has opened, how can you take the responsibility for throwing all those actors and technicians out on the street, even if there were no problems over the performing rights?

The Stage Italian

Thankfully, it is not always like that. There are some quite wonderful companies around, like the Berliner Ensemble, or Gavin Richard's troupe, who put on *Accidental Death* in London, or the Co-operative, directed by Echantillon in France, or the Mime Group of San Francisco, all of whom, even if with certain touches that were not always wholly convincing, have put on works of ours with great style and panache. All of them were, by and large, in sympathy with the spirit of the works they were presenting.

The main defect I note in the productions of our theatre abroad lies in a certain zeal for colour. They almost invariably overdo the effects, stick in a series of over-the-top gags, and rarely realise that with some plays, where the thrust of the situation is itself comic, you need nothing, or very little, to give sufficient entertainment. Further, they rarely display any sobriety or detachment in their style of delivering the lines. Here, as elsewhere, it is worth recalling the motto of Louis Jouvet. 'Ils jouent toutes les repliques.' At the same time, they plaster their faces with expressionistic make-up, in accord with the prevailing fashion, even when it has no connection with anything happening on stage. They twist their faces into bizarre contortions, and all the jokes end up sticky and syrupy. I am baffled as to why they manage to be successful all the same. Perhaps in our plays there is something miraculous that we have never noticed.

In all truth, I have to admit that audiences abroad have shown themselves to be highly appreciative. Beyond all doubt the Italian audience is the most demanding of all those I have had the fortune to play to, and by now I have tried them all, except the Bangladeshis and the aborigines of Tierra del Fuego. I must also add, without straying into excessive chauvinism, that Italian actors are by far the most able, sensitive and gifted that are known on this earth. As it happens, with a few honourable exceptions, they are also a gang of unprincipled scoundrels, but that is another story.

When theatre people in Europe or America decide to produce works by Italian authors, and this includes Pirandello, they simply cannot rid themselves of the notion that a couple of shady characters with yellow, or, even better, black and white striped shoes, pitch-black, well-oiled hair with sideburns down to their jaws, will be an indispensable element of the set. Babies in Italy, it is widely believed, are born with long sideburns and drooping moustaches. In addition, they are convinced that a real Italian, when he speaks, flaps his hands and arms wildly about, like a juggler tossing pancakes. I have noticed that when they actually watch me or Franca on stage they are struck speechless, and marvel that we neither wave our hands or feet, or even do the heavenwards roll of the eyes, and above all that we manage to talk on stage in calm, unexcited tones.

Who knows what they would have made of Eduardo de Filippo, had they been able to see him in *Saturday, Sunday, Monday*, standing quite motionless at the back of the stage, watching in complete silence the other actors running to and fro about the house. His mere presence in the half-light was enough to draw the attention of the audience, so that when he came forward, speaking quietly, making scarcely perceived gestures, you could feel the whole house hold its breath. There was never anything descriptive in his movements or his voice, nothing naturalistic; everything was invented with an extraordinary synthesis and economy. And it held you pinned to your seat.

Improvisation, Situation and Gags

It might be an idea to examine in greater depth the techniques of improvisation, with, where appropriate, the use of mime, of dialogue and even of props. Before launching into a piece of improvisation, it is as well to outline the subject under discussion, as well as the space in which the action, dramatic or comic, will occur. In other words, it is essential to state the situation and the approach that will be adopted.

For example: let us decide on a train compartment, and think about whether first or second class is more suitable. Perhaps a sleeping car would give more scope. Shall we go for second class? Characters: a boy, a girl and a ticket inspector. We will have the girl seated and reading. The boy comes in and attempts to start up a conversation, a perfectly normal situation. And, to keep it all equally straightforward, the girl keeps herself to herself, at least at the outset. Let us see how this situation would work out.

I need three young actors to volunteer, two males and a female. (*Dario and the three actors arrange two lines of facing seats in the centre of the stage.*) These seats indicate the structure of the compartment, and if we arrange them in a V formation, we allow the audience easier access. You (*indicating the girl*) will be the lead character. Find a book or a newspaper . Do you have a handbag? Good, hold on to it, and pretend to read. In the meantime, you (*taking one of the two men to the space behind the chairs*) stand here, imagine that this is the corridor of the train, and when I give the signal, you come on. Action! (*The boy dashes towards the spot designated and makes as if to enter the carriage.*) Stop! (*Dario stops the action.*) Not like that! You cannot enter with such violence! You're like a catapult. First of all, we must presume that there is a door, probably closed, so you must start by miming the act of opening it. So, here's the corridor, walk along it, go in. Try to pull the door along, glance inside, and remember that you're out to give the audience the impression that you're in search of a compartment where you'll find someone, preferably female, with whom you can pass the time enjoyably. So, walk along, pass the compartment, stop, look inside, turn back, pull open the door. At this point, you must have some idea of the character you are playing. Is he to be shy, brimful of confidence, an expert in chatting up? Perhaps he prefers the old-style approach, along the lines of 'Do you mind if I smoke?' Or maybe he's witty and debonair? Let's see.

(*The boy moves along the imaginary corridor, stops, opens the door, gives the most cursory of greetings and mimes putting his luggage on the rack.*)

Girl: Excuse me, would you mind closing the door?

Dario: Good! Just right. He had forgotten to pull the door shut, not from any sense of bad manners, but just because it had completely gone out of his mind, so it was smart of the girl to take advantage of the situation and draw it to the attention of the audience, without making his forgetfulness seem anything out the ordinary. Let's go on. Give us your line again.

Girl: Would you mind closing the door?

Boy: I'm sorry. I had my hands full.

Dario: Excellent. A good retort.

(*The boy sits down facing the girl, glances in her direction, then turns to stare out of the imaginary window. The girl in her turn looks over at the boy.*)

Boy: It's a bit hot in here. Do you mind if I pull down the window? (*Gets up.*)

Girl: No, I'm very sorry but I've got a cold. I'd get a draught right in my face.

Boy: Couldn't you move over to this side, and I'd go over there? I'd be quite glad of a bit of a breeze.

Girl: It's just that I'm never comfortable if I am not facing the way the train is going.

Boy: No problem. If you come to this side, you will be facing in the right direction. Look, the trees are going that way.

Girl: How amazing, when we left Rome, we were going the other way.

Boy: Yes, but when you arrive in Florence, they attach an engine at the back of the train.

(*Establishing the approach.*)

Dario: A right argumentative pair we have here! All right, but now we must establish the situation. Until now you have concentrated on drawing character, and that is very amusing, but let us take a step backwards. Concentrate on finding a specific approach, something that will get the story under way.

Girl: I am perfectly all right where I am, thank you. If you need to open a window, there are plenty of free compartments further along the corridor.

Boy: Why has it stopped? What's going on? The train has come to a halt. (*The girl makes no answer.*) There are people on the line. It looks like policemen with dogs. They must be on the look-out for someone. (*The girl hardly bothers to look. Dario gives a signal to continue with that line, which is proving promising.*) They couldn't have found a bomb?

Girl: A bomb! (*She gets to her feet in some consternation and looks out of the window.*) There are policemen everywhere. Maybe they are hunting terrorists. Forgive me, but it couldn't be you that sometimes . . .

Boy: Me that you sometimes what? What are you getting at? Me a terrorist! For your information, I am a graduate of the Conservatoire, in the violin . . . I'm doing a post-graduate course in the viola.

Girl: I was just asking. Don't get so annoyed.

Boy: It's easy for you to say – don't get annoyed . . . I'd like to see how you'd feel! That's just how it starts: you're on a train, minding your own business, trying to start up a conversation with a good-looking woman, for some reason she gets suspicious, reports you as a terrorist and before you know where you are you're inside, with nine years before your case even comes to trial. You can kiss your viola degree goodbye! And bang go all those years you spent learning the violin!

Girl: There's no need to go on that way! It's just that you had such a suspicious air when you came in . . .

Boy: Me, suspicious!

Girl: And there's something funny about that case!

Boy: Of course it's funny. It's my violin case. Have you ever seen one before?

Dario: Very good! You're real professionals, you two! Go on in the same style. Now you have to choose. Either the train starts off again and it was all a false alarm, or else you see through the window someone being led away in handcuffs. But your comments will have to be brief, otherwise we risk losing the tone. In any case, decide for yourselves, I don't want to interfere.

Girl: They've got him! (*Mimes lowering the window.*)

Boy: Who?

Girl: Somebody, I don't know who . . . There he is!

Boy: Is that a turban he's wearing? He must be an Arab.

Girl: No, it's a bandage round his head. He's wounded, can't you see? They're taking him to an ambulance.

Boy: To an ambulance, in handcuffs!

Girl: Marco! Oh my God! (*She makes as though to shout from the window, then stops herself.*)

Boy: You know him?

Girl: No, just for a moment . . . but it's not him.

Dario: Perfect. This is an excellent situation, and could be developed in all kinds of ways. On you go. You thought you knew him. Do not let the situation drop. Start from the last line.

Girl: I thought I knew him, but it wasn't him.

Boy: Then why have you turned so pale?

Girl: Pale! What do you mean?

Boy: Your face is all pale. Are you unwell? Look at how you're trembling. Is there anything I can do? (*He puts his arm round her waist.*) Take it easy. Lie down. Lean on my shoulder.

Girl: (*Pushing him away.*) Leave me alone. Don't try to take advantage!

Dario: (*To the girl.*) Go on, don't stop. Stare out of the window with the same intensity. (*To the boy.*) And you continue with the same suspicion.

Boy: (*Pretending in his turn to look out of the window.*) That man with the wound seemed to be looking this way, he's angry with you. He's obviously recognised you.

Girl: (*Drawing back.*) Me! Impossible. I've never seen him in my life. He must be mixing me up with someone else.

Dario: No, no. Stop at the word 'impossible'. If you go on the way you are going, the justification is too obvious, and the whole thing collapses. At this point the boy has to change direction. It would be better to leave the suspicion hanging, so that it is there over their heads, all the time. In fact, let's try something else. Why don't we cut to the arrival of the inspector? (*The second boy gets ready to make his entrance.*) Ask someone to lend you a shoulder bag. Let's go back a little.

Girl: (*Repeating.*) I've never seen him in my life before. Look, the ambulance is moving off. (*Rolls up the window.*) The train's moving off as well.

Second boy: (*Enters, miming the act of pulling back the door.*) Tickets, please, all tickets been inspected already?

Boy: Yes, someone has been round before.

Second boy: Makes no odds. I want to see them again, if you don't mind.

Girl: (*Searching in her handbag.*) I've got them right here, I'm sure I have.

Boy: Take your time; no hurry.

Second boy: That is my job! I'll just have a look at yours while we're waiting.

Boy: No problem. (*Goes over to the girl and puts his hand in her bag.*) Let me give you a hand. I know a thing or two about handbags. Allow me.

Girl: What do you think you're at? Get your paws out of there!

Boy: Only trying to help. You're in some state. (*To the inspector.*) It's all because of that individual with the bandage round the head – the one we saw being led away. Any idea who he was?

Second boy: They say he was a terrorist. The police grabbed him while he was trying to place a bomb.

Dario: No, you mustn't be so explicit. It lacks credibility! And be careful, because if you go in that direction you risk undermining the whole story, you destroy the situation. I think you'd do better to concentrate on doing your job as inspector, and to say as little as possible about the terrorist. 'Well, I dunno.' Everybody back to the previous line.

Boy: That man with the bandage round his head, do you know who he was?

Second boy: How should I know? Can I see your tickets, please?

Boy: What do you mean you don't know? They arrest somebody, break his head and he doesn't want to know. He could have been a criminal, a murderer.

Dario: (*To the girl.*) Come on, now. It's time for you to come in. You could come away with some defensive expression, like 'No, he was never a criminal!'

Girl: No, he was never a criminal!

Second boy: How come you know so much about it?

Boy: Oh . . . it's because she knows him. His name's Marco.

Second boy: Yes, that's right . . . Marco Ramberti. Did you really know him? (*Dario offers advice, coming up behind one or the other.*)

Girl: No, I don't know him at all . . . there was one moment . . . but . . .

Boy: You expect us to believe that? The moment you saw him, the colour drained from your face. And I saw him looking towards you, almost as if . . . what can I say . . . as if he was in love.

Girl: It's none of your business.

Second boy: It certainly is his business, it's all our business. I'm an official of the railway. Have you any form of identification? If not, I'll have no option . . .

Dario: (*Whispering into his ear.*) You'll have to call the police.

Second boy: You'll have to help me. (*To the other boy.*) You hold her here, don't let her escape. I'll go for the police. (*The inspector goes out.*)

Girl: I beg you, don't destroy my life.

Boy: Look, it's time to stop fooling with me. Tell me the truth and I swear I'll do all I can to help you.

Girl: Then, yes, I do know who he is. I am a terrorist.

Dario: No, no, not at all, you must develop this situation, not bury it. A final revelation of that kind might be merely banal or obvious. You've got to deny everything, and aim to be, at least in part, credible. You know him, but you've got nothing to do with the whole thing yourself. Start again from the second last line. (*Points to the girl.*)

Girl: Yes, I know who he is. He was my boyfriend until some years ago, then I lost touch with him. I swear to you that's the truth. I have no idea of anything he might have done. Help me. They'll never believe me. God knows how long I would be left to rot in prison before they even tried me.

Boy: I believe you, but what are you going to do? Where could you run to? Anyway they'd shoot you down if you tried to escape. There's only one thing for it. Pull the emergency cord and flee through the fields.

Girl: Yes, stop the train for me! I'll jump out the window.

Boy: All right. Hold on, here goes. (*He tugs the cord.*)

Dario: Go on! Mime the impact of the brakes, so that you are thrown into each other's arms. Love scene! The people in the auditorium could imitate the screech of the brakes and stamp their feet. (*Great din in the gallery. The two performers act as though being tossed about, but in an excess of realism they end up banging their heads.*) Come on, you're not dead. A goodbye kiss, just to please everybody. (*They do so, a bit awkwardly.*) Help her down from the window. (*The boy lifts the girl and assists her down.*) You forgot to roll down the window, but we'll put that down to the power of love. It doesn't matter.

Boy: Just let yourself fall. There you are there! Run for it!

Girl: Thank you! Goodbye!

Dario: Now it's the turn of the guard. (*To two men standing near the stage.*) Jump up and come here, please. Would you do the parts of the police? Just a moment. You must assume that he is responsible for her escape. Walk on.

Second boy: (*Walking ahead of the two policemen.*) She's right here. (*They enter. The other boy is seated, patting down his hair.*) Where is she?

Boy: Who?

Second boy: The girl who was here just now. Don't act the goat! She got away, right? It was you who stopped the train.

Boy: I didn't do a thing. She gave me a thump on the head; I must have passed out.

First policeman: A blow to the head with what?

Boy: With her own head . . . she stuck the head on me. She had a right thick skull, that one!

First policeman: May I see your documents, please?

Second policeman: (*Pretending to look out of the window.*) There she is! Stop! Stop or I'll fire! (*Mimes the act of aiming a gun.*)

Dario: Perfect. (*Pointing to the first boy.*) Now it's time for you to come on and create a diversion. Start by blocking the policeman.

Boy: No, don't shoot. She's got nothing to do with it. She's innocent. I helped her escape to put you off the track.

Second boy: I knew it . . . he's an accomplice.

165

First policeman: She's an accomplice, so he's an accomplice's accomplice.

Boy: No, she's nobody's accomplice. I'm an accomplice, but of the other one, of Marco. (*He has handed a document to the police.*)

First policeman: (*Leafing through the passport.*) Don't believe a word he says. He's lying in his teeth just to save the girl. Have you ever heard of a violinist robber? That's what it says here. (*Showing the document to his colleague.*) Get out your gun, let's at least get the girl . . . (*Mimes taking a gun from a holster and taking aim towards the girl.*)

Boy: No, you've got to believe me. I'm in league with Marco Ramberti. We did the job at the bank in Padua together.

First policeman: Indeed! A bank robbery and then a quick getaway by Italian Railway!

Second boy: Excuse me, have you got something against the Italian Railway?

Second policeman: Shut your mouth, you! (*To the first boy.*) Come on, out with it.

Boy: Hold it right there! We did the actual robbery in the right way, with a stolen getaway car. It's just that when we came rushing out with the cash, we discovered that they had hauled off the car. It was a no-parking area, and the traffic wardens are very strict. There happened to be a bus passing at that moment, so we hopped on, and it took us to the station where we got on the first train. It turned out to be one that stopped at every station. Somehow or other we got separated, and I ended up in one carriage and he in another.

Second boy: And what about your tickets? I assume you did get your tickets. Can I see your ticket, please?

Second policeman: Very clever, Mr inspector. Where is the booty?

Boy: I don't know. He had it.

First policeman: I'll tell you where it is. The girl's got it in her handbag. Get her. Open fire. Shoot.

Boy: No, stop. I'll tell you everything. You're right. I've got it.

Second policeman: Where?

Boy: There, in my violin case.

(*The first policeman climbs on to a chair and mimes reaching down the case.*)

Dario: Halt! At this point we require a further twist in the tale. We could have the girl coming back in to save the boy, with whom she is now in love. In that case she could re-enter, armed with a semi-automatic, Rambo style, with three ammunition belts over her shoulder, a red ribbon round her forehead and a machete knife between her teeth. Maybe that's right over the top. Who can suggest another solution? (*He discusses the matter with the three performers.*) All right, from the last line.

Boy: It's in the violin case.

(*The policeman pulls it down.*)

Second policeman: What's that ticking? Have you got a bomb in there?

First policeman: A time bomb?

Boy: (*Throws himself to the ground, tries to wriggle under the seat with his hands held tightly over his head, as though he were waiting for an explosion.*) We're done for! Get rid of it! Throw it out of the window. What are you waiting for? (*Dario makes a signal and the second policeman makes to hurl the case out of the window.*) Quickly. Before it goes off!

Second boy: Hold it right there! It's a con. You throw the case out of the window, the girl's hiding nearby, she picks it up, sets it off, and where does that leave you? How do you expect to get a guilty verdict with no body?

First policeman: (*To the boy.*) You, open the case and defuse the bomb. (*They aim their guns at him.*)

Boy: All right, but first, put away those guns. I'm a bit nervous as it is. It's a delicate job. (*He mimes opening the case. The policeman and the inspector move back.*) My only consolation is if anything goes wrong, we'll all go up together. (*He goes into the case and brings out something which he tosses at the police.*) Hold on to the cash for me, there's a good fellow. There's about a hundred thousand in each package. Just like winning the pools, eh? (*He mimes throwing package after package. The police grab them one by one. Some fall to the ground, others he hurls over their heads. He improvises a juggling act.*)

First policeman: Oh, God, now he's gone and tossed the bomb!

Boy: (*Continues juggling.*) One of these is a bomb. Any minute now we'll have a big bang.

First policeman: Stop! are you mad?

First boy: I can't stop! As soon as I stop we're all up in the air. If you want my advice, I'd say it was time to run for it! I can't go on much longer. (*The police and the guard get out.*) It's falling! I can't go on! Get out! Get off the train! (*He follows them along the corridor, the policemen and the inspector backing away all the time.*) Everybody off the train!

Second boy: It's starting off!

Boy: Right! Better jump before it gets up speed.

(*The two policemen and the guard mime opening the door and jumping on to the stage. They lose their balance, get up and, moving with their feet close together and legs held stiff, give the impression that the train really is moving away. The boy waves from the window.*)

Boy: Hard luck, policemen! Fixed you there! The bomb was a Japanese quartz alarm. Look after it for me, will you?

Dario: (*To the audience*.) Stamp your feet and give us the sounds of a train. (*The audience makes stamping and whistling noises*.)

Voice from audience: All we need is the happy ending.

Dario: Is that not enough for you? You mean the return of the girl? You want the two of them kissing and setting off together for a honeymoon in the Falklands? Well, who knows? Anyway, it has gone on long enough. Let's have another go with different people, and see what variations we have from the same starting point.

The Alternative Approach

(*Dario brings about ten young people up on to the stage. Once again a girl is sitting in the compartment and takes out her knitting. Once again a young man enters, but this time it is clear that he is particularly shy and has no intention of communicating. He sits in the far corner of the compartment and buries himself in a newspaper. The girl gets agitated, changes seat, rolls down the window, rolls it up again. She resumes her knitting, sighing deeply. Finally the boy peeps over his paper. The girl turns her face away, pressing it against the corner of the wall and window. The boy gets up and goes over to her*.)

Boy: What's wrong? Is something the matter?

(*The girl turns round, the boy puts his hand on her shoulder. The girl throws herself into his arms and devours him with kisses. Dario steps in to point out that with this rather paradoxical move the situation is closed, rather than opened out. The action takes up again with the girl approaching the boy more hesitantly, embracing him then drawing back and moving to the opposite corner. She continues weeping, and when the boy once again goes over to her, she rises to her feet and points a knitting needle at him as though it were a sword. The ticket inspector, a woman, enters and seizing hold of the young man strikes him on the face. The boy makes an effort to explain to the inspector what has happened, but she refuses to believe him, so finally the girl comes in on the boy's side. The woman inspector is convinced that the girl is lying for fear of being involved in some scandal, so the girl launches herself into an elaborate mime, grabbing hold of the boy and covering him once again with kisses, to show what had happened. The guard tries to keep the two apart but discovers that the two gang up on her, hugging and caressing all the while. The inspector herself bursts into tears and throws herself into the corner seat. The two, bewildered, ask what is wrong but the woman sobs more and more bitterly. The girl goes over to her and puts her arm round her waist, making a signal to the boy to go out and leave them alone. The woman explains that she has been reduced to a state of despair, because her boyfriend, a colleague at work, had announced half an hour previously that he planned to leave her. Seeing the obvious affection between the two had reduced her to tears. At this point, the boy, accompanied by another young man in company uniform, re-enters. It transpires that the second young man is the ex-boyfriend of the broken-hearted woman, and he begins immediately to shout at her. Apparently the two had split up after a jealous quarrel, with him accusing her of having an affair with the station master, something which she denies. He strikes her a blow, then throws his arms round her, begging forgiveness and bursting into tears in his turn. Everybody ends up in tears.)*

Dario: (*To the audience.*) I trust you all noted one exceptional thing, that they all managed to avoid any trace of sing-song intonation, and had no problem in breathing in the right places. It may be that there was not sufficient incisiveness and cleanness in voice production, and I heard someone in the audience complaining that they could not make out all the lines, but by and large everyone seemed able to hear without undue strain. Certainly there was no great inventiveness in voice or gesture, and the overall effect was unnecessarily naturalistic, but that is something that can be dealt with at a later stage. The important thing is to avoid the mournful wail produced by many learners, not to mention several seasoned professionals!

Improvisation at the Berliner Ensemble

The same method was used by Bertolt Brecht. Once, at the Berliner Ensemble, I had the good fortune to listen to tapes of some exercises in improvisation very similar to ours, even if along different lines, which Bertolt Brecht had his actors perform during rehearsals, in an attempt to rid them of that colourless routine, or that phoney, rhetorical exaggeration to which, it seems, German actors are more prone than their counterparts elsewhere.

Another device that Brecht was fond of was to compel his actors to go for a run round the courtyard behind the stage at the Berliner, and then have them act when they were still panting and out of breath. In this way, they were forced to flatten their tones to the greatest possible extent.

Exercises and Warm-up

The drawback of this method is that were it to be made compulsory for the bulk of our actors, they would resign in droves, but that's a pity because a pre-performance warm-up can add considerably to the quality of the performance. Frequently Italian companies, especially touring companies, are hampered by the sheer lack of time. They are compelled to accept openings one on top of the other, in theatres that are all too often unsuitable, and on stages that are frequently too cramped. On the other hand, I have seen groups beset by these very problems overcome them with astonishing imagination and resourcefulness, and succeed in carving out the time for themselves. I am still referring to Italian companies, because Eastern companies, as a matter of course, dedicate hours to preparation, to unwinding or to muscular relaxation, as well as to yoga and meditation, but only a fanatic would consider imitating them, since their rites are linked to their culture and special style of theatre.

At any rate, I have experienced the positive effects of a spell of warming-up. Two or three hours prior to a performance, especially if I am tense or worried, I go jogging for five or six kilometres, doing other exercises along the way. When I get back to the theatre, I lie down in a quiet spot on the stage wrapped in a thick blanket, sweating freely. A shower, and there you are, all ready to go! I have worked off all the nagging worries, and am ready to face anything.

Anyone going into this business should bear in mind a piece of advice that I got at my debut: to overcome stage fright, never take pills, gulps of whisky, brandy or anything like that before going on stage – just do a couple of press-ups. Get your head down, do a spot of yoga, if that is your style, have a sauna or a shower, and above all go on determined to have a good time yourself.

Genius and Unpredictability: First Rule

Since there are no rules in theatre, you will at times come across actors who will be up all night carousing, spend the afternoon in a studio dubbing some film, and there they are in the evening on stage, brilliant and unaffected, in stunning form.

In Paris a couple of years ago, I went to see Carmelo Bene during the interval of his *Macbeth*. He offered me a beer from a huge case he had on his table, saying 'This is my ration for the day.' There was an army of empty bottles, neatly lined up in threes, and I said that if I were to devour that amount of alcohol, I would fall flat on my face within the first five minutes of the performance. He had acted the first act with remarkable vehemence, and in the second part he leaped about like a frisky goat, snarled and snapped, spat out words at top speed, all the while maintaining perfect pace and co-ordination.

I know some British actors whom you have to handle with extreme care before they go on stage, because if anyone were to shake them, alcohol would come shooting out of their ears the way it does from a slightly heated champagne bottle. Yet on stage these walking pubs perform to perfection night after night. In other words, it all depends on the kind of theatre you are involved in, on your own particular cultural and psychic relationship with the stage, on your own physique, and, above all, on the kind of subject you are treating, that is, on whether it is rational, emotional or visceral. At the same time, I can assure you that there are just as many actors, including some of the best, who every so often, either to overcome the tedium of the 2000th performance or to give themselves Dutch courage for the opening night, knock back alcohol by the gallon. They have no doubt that it will make them give of their best, but they are fooling themselves. I have lost count of the number of times I have watched them, sodden with whisky, stumble, lose the pace, puff and pant, slow down or speed up for no reason at all. And at the final curtain, without fail, they strut about, preening themselves, 'Wasn't I in form tonight!' Never ever did one of their colleagues have the courage to tell them – 'You were hellish.'

Clowns

A clown's act is made up of a collection of elements from diverse, often conflicting, sources. His profession has much in common with that of the minstrel or the mime of Greek and Roman times, inasmuch as he employs the same means of expression: voice, acrobatic gesture, music, song and, very often, magic and numbers with animals. Almost all the great clowns are highly skilful jugglers and fire-eaters, and know how to use fireworks and to play one or more musical instruments.

While doing *La Signora è da Buttare* (Discard the Lady), a show in which we employed real clowns (The Colombaioni), I had to learn various daredevil tricks and acrobatics, like cartwheels, the trapeze act, walking on stilts or plunging headlong into small tanks. Obviously these presented no problems to the Colombaioni who could execute them all to perfection, and they taught us many others not in the original text. They taught me virtually all I know about clowns, including how to play the trombone. Franca learned how to swing on the flying trapeze, and how to hang upside down by the feet with crossed legs. Because of the complexity and the sheer number of different skills a clown must acquire, it is clear that any actor who masters the techniques will be much the better for it, and not only in the overtly comic parts. It may horrify the purists, but they will have advantage in the tragic roles as well.

All too often I have seen actors trying to imitate clowns by doing no more than sticking a red ball on the end of their nose, putting on an outsize pair of shoes and squeaking in a funny voice. At best this is an exercise in sheer naiveté, and the result is invariably cloying and irritating. The only way to become a real clown is by long, energetic and dedicated work, and, yet again, by years of practice. You do not make it as a clown by improvisation.

In our days, the clown has come to be a figure whose job is to keep the children happy. He is synonymous with puerile simple-mindedness, with picture-postcard ingenuousness, and with sheer sentimentality. Today's clown has lost both his ancient capacity to shock and his political-moral commitment. In other times the clown used satire as a vehicle against violence, cruelty, hypocrisy and injustice. Centuries ago, he was an obscene, diabolic figure; in the cathedrals of the Middle Ages, on the capitals and the friezes above the entrances, there can still be seen representations of comic buffoons in provocative couplings with animals, mermaids, harpies, grinning broadly as they show off their organs.

The clown's origins are very remote, and certainly clowns were already in existence before the advent of Commedia dell'Arte. It could be said that the characters of Commedia were born of an obscene marriage between female minstrels on the one hand, and storytellers and clowns on the other, and that, after an act of incest, Commedia spawned hosts of other clowns.

Power and the Clown

All the stories, the situations, and the types of show involving clowns rely on the grotesque deformation of the voice, on the use of funny expressions or grimaces as well as on the employment of unusually bright make-up. We have already seen how Harlequin, in the beginning, made use of the make-up associated with both the clown and with Pagliaccio, who is nothing else but a character of early Commedia (1572, company of Alberto Ganassa). In a later description by Salvator Rosa,* Pagliaccio appears with his face painted white, and at a later stage, he will be transformed into Gian-farina (Johnny-flour, in reference to the white face), and finally into Pierrot.

Clowns, like minstrels and 'comics', always deal with the same problem – hunger, be it hunger for food, for sex, or even for dignity, for identity, for power. The problem they invariably pose is – who's in command, who's the boss? In the world of clowns there are two alternatives: to be dominated, and then we have the eternal underdog, the victim, as in the Commedia dell'Arte, or else to dominate, which gives us the boss, the white clown or Louis, whom we already know. He is in charge of the game, he gives the orders, he issues the insults, he makes and unmakes at will, while the various Tonys, the Augustes, the Pagliaccios live on their wits, occasionally rebelling but generally getting by as best they can.

I remember one number by the Cavallini company. Auguste and Toni came on, sat down beside each other and began to play, one the trumpet, the other the saxophone, continually interrupting each other as they tried to agree on the tune. Auguste wrote out the notes on the mixture of sand and

* Salvator Rosa (1615–1673), Italian Baroque painter and comic actor.

sawdust that made up the ring. They had only just reached agreement on the notes when the white clown came along and sent them on their way. 'No music permitted here. Area of absolute silence. On your way!' Before going, the two clowns gather up in their hats the sand and sawdust on which they had scribbled the tune. They move over to another spot, fix out the seats and scatter the sand and sawdust in the space in front of them. They start playing again but as soon as they reach the first chorus, they hit a wrong note. There is obviously a note missing, one which they had not managed to pick up. At once they return to the original spot to search for the missing note and, when they find it, they gather a handful of sand and sawdust, go over and scatter it on the new place and continue playing their music, in total peace and harmony.

The Clown Pander
Inside this basic framework – of making the best of things – there exists the more ferocious notion of the struggle for survival itself, and in this very often can be detected an utter cynicism which undermines all the conventional values of the moral code – honesty, human respect, fidelity.

In this context, ancient farce is particularly significant because we can already detect there the figure of a clown who is the mirror of Pulcinella. The Pagliaccio-clown, as is normal, is constantly hungry. Offsetting him is a second clown, the 'country bumpkin', complete with a cart packed with every imaginable titbit. The starving clown does his best to persuade the peasant to part with some cheese, some salami or some eggs. The peasant insists on seeing the cash first, while the Pagliaccio-clown does his level best to get hold of something to fill his stomach. The peasant-clown is a bit more hard-headed than he might seem, and is having none of it. Pushing his cart, he makes his way down the street past the house where Pagliaccio's girlfriend is employed. She appears at the window, asks the price of the chicken, haggles a bit, then goes back in. As soon as the peasant-clown disappears, Pagliaccio calls his girlfriend to the window and begins to create a jealous scene. 'I saw everything,' he says, 'you are in love with that good-looking young peasant.' 'Me! I've never seen him in my life! I don't know what he's like.' The Pagliaccio draws an extravagant picture of the man, and tells her that the moment she came to the window, the blood drained from his face and he exclaimed: 'God! What a woman!' Not only that, but he nearly gave you the chicken for nothing. If you had carried on bargaining with him a moment more, he would have given you the cart as well. But I'm warning you, if I as much as see you talking to that so-and-so, I'll kill you!'

Pagliaccio's woman goes back into the house, flattered at the idea of this new conquest. Pagliaccio himself lies in wait for the peasant, and as soon as he approaches the woman's window on his way back, he attacks him with the words: 'Keep your hands off my woman! If I see you taking advantage of the fact that she has lost her head over you . . .'

'Who is this woman of yours? I don't even know her.'

'Ah, you don't even know her! The one who came to the window a short time ago, pretending to want to know the price of a chicken, that's who she is. She was all a-tremble as she spoke to you with her eyes sparkling, and the moment you moved away, she said out loud – 'My God, who is that fine-looking young man!'

The poor fellow's head is turned. Pagliaccio begins to shed tears and, crying fit to burst, pretends to pick up a card which he hands to the peasant. It read: 'To the Peasant-Adonis, Prince of Love.'

The peasant cannot read. In fact neither can the Pagliaccio, but, shameless as ever, he declaims aloud the contents of the letter. With extravagant flourishes, he sings of the irresistible passion which has seized the heart of his woman. He pretends to be in despair, grabs hold of a carrot from the cart and makes as if to stab himself. The peasant does his best to console him, and at that moment Pagliaccio's woman, still flattered but uncertain, comes to the window. Pagliaccio strikes the pose of the unsuccessful suitor – distraught, disconsolate but prepared to make way for the better man and to do anything that would secure the happiness of the two lovers. The peasant-clown is encouraged to make his way up to the woman's room, and she, although still unsure what is going on, consents. Pagliaccio, howling his heart out, proclaims his despair to the world as he locks the door on the two. The cart, still loaded with every kind of foodstuff, stands outside, and taking its handles he makes off singing: 'What a cruel destiny is mine! While others give themselves to the pleasures of the senses, I have to content myself with the pleasures of the belly.'

In the vast repertory of the clown, there are many seemingly puerile jokes. For instance, one clown says to the other: 'Let's play at bees making honey.' The first clown buzzes about the place, until the other says: 'Bee, bee, pretty little bee, give me your sweet yellow honey,' whereupon the clown playing the other bee squirts a mouthful of water in his face. The clown, soaking wet and looking foolish, insists on getting his turn at playing bee. He goes off, fills his mouth with water, comes on buzzing around the second clown, who looks blank and takes an age to give the order. 'Bee, bee, pretty little bee give me your sweet yellow honey.' The other splutters and spills the water all over himself. Off he goes again, fills his mouth with water, re-enters to find his colleague prancing about, joking and cavorting so as to make him laugh. He does his best to hold it in, but once again bursts out in giggles, soaking himself. The smart clown laughs uproariously, but the foolish clown produces from his baggy trousers the end of a hose which goes right down his trouser legs to a tap outside. He turns a sudden gush of water on the smart clown, all but drowning him.

Eat Me – but don't Mock

It often happens that the clown on the losing side manages to turn the tables on his partner, thanks to a kind of 'thus far and no farther', that is, a kind of desperate resolution to lose everything, but to go out with a final flourish.

In Paris some years ago, at the Medrano Circus, I witnessed an extraordinary display, the most spectacular routine with animals that I have ever had the good fortune to see. The lion-tamer asked if there was anyone who wished to go into the cage with the animals, and, as invariably happens, a little man at the back raised his hand. 'Excellent!' exclaimed the lion tamer. 'Here we have a courageous fellow.'

'Who, me? I was only wanting to go to the toilet.'

The lion-tamer tried to encourage him. 'Come on, you'll do fine. You can't disappoint all the ladies who were cheering you on.' He invited him into the cage.

The other man continued to insist that he needed the toilet, but there was nothing for it, and he was literally thrown into the cage. In stark terror, he grabbed hold of the bars and tried to climb up the sides of the cage. The lions gathered round, closer and closer, sniffing at him. In his efforts to get out, the clown – the supposed spectator – dug a hole in the sand. A lion seized him by the seat of his trousers and pulled him back, carted him across the ring before dropping him flat on his face. At this point, the spectator-clown lost his patience, because while he could accept the prospect of being devoured by a lion, the idea of being dragged about in such an undignified pose, of being reduced to a joke was too much. He jumped to his feet and landed a tremendous blow on the lion's nose, at which the lion let out a mighty roar and drew back. The other lions seemed equally terrified of him and started leaping about the cage. When the lion-tamer stepped in to defend the animals, he too was assaulted in his turn. Finally the clown started to imitate the lions, repeating the very exercises they had done but outdoing them in agility and even in the volume of the roars. He clambered up the bars of the cage and jumped through the flaming hoop. The moral twist could not be more plain: 'You can lose everything, even your life, but, by God, never your dignity.'

The Cavallini on the Knife-edge

Another perspective on the clowns' act is provided by that touch of the surreal which defies every rule and every law of physics. The Cavallini have a superb routine which illustrates the point I am making. A particularly elegant, beautiful acrobat executes a dance on the tightrope, while down below a clown sweeps away the manure left by the horses who had done the previous number. With his foot he kicks a ball of horse manure towards the exit, just at the moment when the artiste on the wire completes an especially intricate movement. The audience breaks into applause, and the clown, thinking the applause is meant for him, takes a bow. He begins to prance around the ring like a thoroughbred, throwing his head as he goes. Meantime the artiste executes even more breathtaking acts, the audience grows more and more enthusiastic and the clown, continuing to believe that the applause is directed at him, goes into his horse-act with greater and greater conviction. Finally he notices the tightrope artiste above him and stops, enchanted, to watch her. He gets carried away to the point where he falls madly in love with her. He has to be with her, come what may, and he goes off in search of a ladder to climb up beside her. The first ladder he comes across is too small and, when he attempts to climb up, he falls back, then he has another go with a longer ladder which he rests against the wire on which the girl is performing.

He starts his climb, but, one by one, the rungs give way under him. The clown, overcome by passion, does not even notice. He continues his climb – and this is something that now requires quite extraordinary strength and agility, because he can use only his arms. The artiste on the high wire has a parasol, and, before starting his climb, the clown had procured for himself a tattered umbrella which he stuck under his arm. He saunters along the wire with his hands in his pockets, making eyes at the girl. He happens to look down and, all of a sudden, he collapses in a heap. In a state of panic, he slides, waves his hands in the air, and falls off, but the handle of the umbrella under his arm catches onto the wire. After whirling about on the umbrella handle, he manages to regain his balance and clamber back on to the wire. As with all great clowning numbers, and this was very definitely one such, the situation touches and indeed transcends the surreal, the impossible.

The Tale of the Piglet and the Cabbages

Clowns and storytellers have an almost magical ability to manipulate things and situations so as to make seem possible what is impossible and false what is true. The anecdote of the non-existent pig, in the medieval morality tale of the thief saved by St Rocco (later found in the standard repertoire of many clowns) illustrates this point perfectly. The story is first found in a collection of Sienese morality tales of the fourteenth century, and deals with a thief, who is also a liar and boaster, who steals a pig and conceals it in a bag. The gendarmerie, investigating the case, catch up with the robber and demand to know what he has in his bag. The thief replies that he has only some cabbages, but just at that moment the pig grunts. The storyteller makes out that it was he who groaned because he has hurt himself. The officers, noticing other suspicious characters nearby, go off. Left on his own, the thief decides to slaughter the animal, but finds it difficult because the pig gets agitated and flaps about. He tries everything – beating it with a stick, slitting its throat with a knife, and even strangling it. Each time the pig, which had seemed to be dead, comes back to life and the struggle starts up again.

In the meantime, the peasant who is the owner of the stolen pig arrives on the scene. With the aid of the gendarmes, who had doubled back, he has the thief arrested and dragged before the judge. On the way, the group pass in front of a chapel dedicated to St Rocco, and the thief, giving the guards the slip for a moment, throws himself on his knees in front of the saint and begs his assistance. As he well knew, the law for recidivist thieves like him ordained that their ears be chopped off and their bones broken at the joints. Hauled before the judge, the thief continued to plead his innocence, protesting that there was nothing in the bag except cabbages. The bag was duly opened and . . . Miracle! . . . inside there are indeed three large red cabbages.

Often at the end of such a performance, a highly animated discussion would follow. One part of the audience would be convinced that there had indeed been a pig in the bag during the performance, and that it had been slaughtered. Therefore the replacement of the pig by the cabbages must have occurred at the moment when the storyteller threw himself to the ground in front of the saint, taking advantage of the cover offered by the guards when they, seemingly trying to drag him back to his feet, shielded him. The storyteller assured them that it was not so, that there never had been any animal inside the bag, that it had been him all along who, with his command of mime, with hand and foot gestures, with his voice, had made people believe there was a pig there. But the audience, almost to a man, would not give in and often accused him of being an empty braggart, so much so that one day the storyteller got up on stage with a real pig and attempted the slaughter scene. This time the reactions of the pig strained belief, because its grunts and thrashings were all out of time and lacking in plausibility. The audience rose to its feet, yelling 'Cheat! You've got cabbages in the bag this time, and you're doing all that whining and groaning by yourself!' The storyteller abandoned the performance, opened the bag and – miracle of miracles!

inside there was a blood-covered pig. Moral: The spectators thought the real pig was a fake, and only when the storyteller tricked them with his own squeaks and gestures, reproducing the desperate kicking of the animal, did it seem true. On this basis, we can reassert the old saw: in theatre, only the false is authentically real.

The Indian Clown

Clowns can be found at all times and in all countries. In the Chinese theatre, I saw a group of tumblers carry out the famous sarabande with the chair. Two or three clowns vie with each other for possession of the only chair on the stage. They pull it away from each other, falling to the ground in turn as the chair is pulled from under them. At the beginning, they limit themselves to tricks to distract the attention of the person with the chair, but quite soon they pass on to acts of ferocious violence. The clowns roll on the ground, jump considerable distances with the chair stuck onto their backsides, anything not to yield possession.

I used an altered version of this game in my production of Stravinsky's *Histoire du Soldat* for La Scala, Milan. The theme was the struggle for the most important positions in the government in the scene set in the parliament of the happy island. The sarabande in this case was performed by fifteen mini-clowns, all after the possession of the seven seats in a sequence of falls and tumbles of great comic effect.

It is well known that in the comedies of Aristophanes a broad clowning routine, including knockabout, a wide repertory of slaps and punches not to mention an array of the most obscene jokes, were the order of the day. In his *Parliament of Women*, there is an outrageous comic in the dress of a puffed-up old fool in his second childhood, his penis hanging out from under his 'skirt'. Every time the fellow sits down, he lets out a yell, since his 'pendant' has ended up underneath! With enormous care he places it on a bench beside him, only to see an energumen come along and sit right on top of it.

In *Lysistrata*, clown-like characters, with erect penises of improbable dimensions, play their part. One of them, the gigantic Lacedon, with his huge prick, literally shafts a bothersome old man who, thinking that he is on the back of a sea-monster, finds himself astride the stranger's penis. In street theatre in every time and place, tumblers, clowns and minstrels offer very similar types of entertainment. In every country, one can find clowns who undertake grotesque contests with real or imaginary animals, like, for example, the wrestling matches with tame bears that are common among clowns and minstrels from Armenia, Persia and the Caucasus. At other times, the same figures put on extremely funny encounters between

178

themselves and giant bears played by two clowns one on top of the other, with a huge skin slung over their shoulders. Acting in pairs, the clowns disguise themselves as camels, donkeys, horses, tigers or lions.

In the sixteenth century, the German Puritan poet, Thomas Kirchmayer, wrote a sonnet, in tones of palpable disgust, on how the clowns of his time disported themselves in the carnivals:

> Bedecked in brightly coloured skins they imitate
> Wild lions and wolves and fierce-eyed bears
> And maddened bulls. Some mince around
> As long-legged, wide-winged cranes.
> Others take the unclean appearance of apes
> While others prefer the guise of clowns.
> With such shameless rites is Bacchus celebrated
> By these obscene Papists.

In our most recent work on Harlequin, we experimented with putting people inside a donkey and a lion-skin. Obviously, it was all based on what we had seen in the circus, both Italian and Eastern, especially Chinese.

Disguise linked with a deliberate set-up is the essential characteristic of displays given by travelling clowns in India. I recently had the good fortune to see a documentary made by John Emigh of Harvard University on an amazing family of Indian comics. They appear singly or in pairs in the midst of crowds of thousands of people at markets during the great religious feasts. Initially they turn up disguised as holy men and proceed to perform a kind of parody. Many of the crowd, convinced that they are the genuine article, treat them with reverence and respect, but gradually the pieces turn irreverent and subversive, arousing the laughter of the more alert members of the audience and the indignation of the more blinkered or fanatical. On other occasions, they play different sorts of madmen, from the man besotted with love who sees in every woman in the crowd, no matter how elderly and wrinkled, the very image of his loved one, to the dutiful follower of the politician most in the public eye at that moment, who goes around spouting the most oily praise, to the point where no one could miss the jibe. At other times, they dress up as women.

An especially arresting piece was the disguise as a woman whose husband had just cut off her nose. Obviously the clown excoriates, in his bitter little sketch, the vile practice still current in many parts of India of chopping off the nose of an unfaithful wife. With blood on his face, and a little leather hood supposedly covering the place where the nose should be, the clown races howling on to the square. Some of the audience are convinced that this is no fiction, and they divide into those who sympathise with the poor woman so barbarically treated, and those who jeer at the wretched whore who has received her just deserts. The woman-clown picks on some men among the spectators, usually the more obtuse and reactionary among them, accusing them of being her lovers. She shouts at them to return home at once and to do the same to the females in their life, not ignoring their aged mother, the bitch in the kennel and the songbird in the cage, all of whom are guilty of the same whorish behaviour. Some are taken in and hurl themselves on the clown, who calmly removes his disguise, to the delight of the crowd who jeer at the unfortunates who had been taken in.

This mixture of the set-up with moral sting in the tail can be found in a considerable number of medieval plays, starting from those which provided inspiration to Boccaccio. Many comedies of the sixteenth and seventeenth centuries were based on seemingly innocent situations set up by amateur or professional actors in the piazzas all over Italy.

It's a Hit! The Theatre's on Fire!

One of the most amusing of Elizabethan plays, *The Knight of the Burning Pestle* by Beaumont and Fletcher, is based on a device of this sort. During the performance of a chivalric play, two well-to-do grocers, husband and wife, seated in the front row, declare themselves fed up with the unduly predictable course of these dramas: same old heroes, same old damsels, same wizards and monsters waiting to be slain, so they propose, or more precisely impose, that their apprentice, a half-witted, semi-literate lad, be given a part. The new knight of the burning pestle (the pestle is the symbol of grocers, but here it clearly refers to the boy's phallus) perpetrates a series of disastrous gaffes, which, while recalling Don Quixote, reduce the whole plot to tatters. The comments of the two grocers, who emerge as the directors, indeed the joint *deus ex machina* of the piece, are juxtaposed to the unfolding of the plot. The satire on the vulgar arrogance of the *nouveaux riches* is plain to see, and indeed its shock value was so effective that after only a few performances the theatre was burned down by the merchants of the City of London.

The Actors' Pay

Nowadays, when you say actor, you mean professional actor, but in other days the number of professionals was extremely limited. The majority were either amateurs or people who performed only very occasionally. Machiavelli's *The Mandrake* and Giordano Bruno's *The Candle-maker*, two key works in the history of theatre, were never performed by professionals, but only by groups of amateurs. Machiavelli himself took a part in *Clizia*. Shakespeare's company was made up, in large part, of amateurs who never received a fixed salary, but only one-off payments, plus a bounty when they performed at the feast of some great lord.

Moreover, unlike today's big successes, they very rarely managed a run of thirty performances, and even then these performances would in all probability be spread out over two or three years. A play which lasted a week was considered a triumph. *Hamlet* did not have more than twenty performances. *King Lear* even fewer, and *Measure for Measure* only five. Even the most successful of actors had to make shift and take other jobs as a safety measure. Flaminio Scala sold perfumes in Venice, others sold quality materials, others sang at weddings and others again accepted commissions to direct the arrangements at grand banquets and to organise songs and dances for the arrival of each course. The great Ruzante himself – as did others – performed during the weddings of the upper classes.

Payment was partly in kind – cuts of cloth, pieces of silverware – and partly in cash, but the sums were invariably modest. The best-off were the actors of some lord's private troupe, since they received a respectable and more or less fixed salary, but at the cost of accepting demeaning conditions of servitude. Molière found himself subjected to this kind of regime when, with his company, he contracted to play in the service of a prince.

Minstrels, clowns and all other strolling players who played the city and rural fairs were as free as the air. They were paid in kind, and had to accept every type of taxation and vexation at the hands of the civil and religious authorities. In some cases, the authorities used the trick of holding up their permission to perform with a series of bureaucratic quibbles, so that the company 'being unable to remain in town without an income, will be obliged to pack up their tents and move on'. This phrase is taken from a letter from the arch-priest Ottolelli to Cardinal Borromeo, in which the prelate offered valuable advice on how to get the players off the streets by bureaucratic means alone, without taking any specific action, just by driving them to hunger.

At times the players managed to strike it rich by coaxing princes or merchants to advance vast sums of money or even pieces of jewellery (see the famous pearl necklace which the Harlequin Martinelli was able to persuade King Henry IV of France to part with), but these were the exception. It was not easy to grow fat on an actor's pay.

Strasburg Library has a collection of letters issued by the city fathers in the years 1450–90 in which they lay down the maximum duration of the performances, the permitted subjects and the average price that spectators may be charged, and from these it becomes abundantly clear that a theatre company could, on a good night, just about make ends meet. Katrin Koll has gathered together many of these documents, and has calculated, as accurately as may be, the income of many itinerant actors from the Middle Ages to the seventeenth century. In some cases, minstrels or clowns were hired by communities or guilds to perform in sacred dramas, in comic or even straight roles. Every community or guild would undertake to attend to a 'station', that is, to put on a scene from the Passion of Christ or from the life of the patron saint of the city.

Each group was allocated a space in the itinerary of the spectacle and when the procession reached that spot, it stopped in front of the platform which had been decked out with appropriate pieces of scenery, and watched the performance of that episode of the drama, before proceeding to the next. In these cases, the community or guild offered hospitality to the minstrel and his company for the whole period of the rehearsals. The minstrel undertook to coach the amateurs and to co-ordinate the whole production; that is to say, he directed the play, and for these services he received special gifts. If the performance at their station was successful, the members of the community awarded prizes to the minstrel, who for at least a week would be invited by all the families involved to receive presents and food.

Throughout the Middle Ages, an organising committee was elected in every town to take command of the arrangements for the carnival; this still happens in Valencia and in Siena at the Palio. Every citizen taxed himself to defray the expenses of the minstrels and clowns. In particular, the most highly regarded of the minstrels was chosen in secret to play a caricature double of the bishop, mayor or prince, as the administrative structure of the place in question dictated. All over Lombardy, for example, every year on the Feast of Fools, the chosen minstrel presented himself in a caricature mask of the local bishop. Accompanied with great, if deliberately grotesque, pomp into the cathedral, he was met there by the bishop in person, who was required by custom to hand over his own vestments to the minstrel. Suitably attired, the minstrel ascended the pulpit to deliver a tongue-in-cheek sermon, in which he mercilessly mimicked all the homilies and actions of the bishop during the preceding year. It was a conscious effort to mock the highest authorities in the land, and when the minstrel had the necessary talent, these exercises could hit the mark. When the bishop was restored to his pulpit, he was liable to face howls of barely repressed laughter at every word he uttered. It was said of Archbishop Guido of Brescia that after having been the butt of a minstrel's gibes, he had no further inclination to return to the pulpit, and even tried to have the Feast of Fools suppressed. They burned down his curia, he was forced to flee the city, and he was allowed to return only when he promised to restore the feast in all its glory.

Any minstrels involved in mockery of a bishop, mayor or prince were running a considerable risk, and for this reason entered the city only at night, in disguise and under protection, once the festivities were under way. Similarly, once the performance was over, they were smuggled out among the groups of farm-workers returning to their land. If they had the misfortune to be picked up by the official guards, things were likely to go badly for them, and they would be lucky to get home in one piece. For this reason minstrels on such occasions were paid handsomely. The risks were high.

The position of the actors in Greek tragedy was entirely different. In their theatre, professionals received substantial payment for the initial performance, followed by a lower, but still reasonable, figure for subsequent performances in provincial towns. Authors, by contrast, received next to nothing, and some people have been malicious enough to suggest that that is why so many of them acted, or even took the leading role in their own works, as was the case with Euripides and Aeschylus. But this is a matter that requires more detailed treatment.

A Play with a Problem: It Reads Too Well

For years now, conscious of being both paradoxical and provocative, I have been saying that the only way to successfully renovate theatre is to force actors and actresses to write their own comedies, or, depending on preference, tragedies.

It was not said lightly. First of all, it would lead to a considerable increase in the general culture of our theatre practitioners, since, at the very least, they would be encouraged to read or even to study more, and to master the syntax and language of theatre. We would finally have actors who would be more at their ease in discussing the works they were performing and ideologically better educated.

Actors must learn to create their own theatre. What is the purpose of improvisation? To weave and shape a script with words, with gestures and off-the-cuff situations, but above all to rid actors of the false and dangerous notion that theatre is no more than literature that happens to be staged, acted and adapted, rather than simply read.

It is not so. Theatre has nothing to do with literature, even when, by fair means or foul, people go out of their way to force it into line. Brecht once said, rightly, of Shakespeare: 'A pity it reads so beautifully. It is its only defect, but a great one.' And he was right. However paradoxical it may seem, a genuine work of theatre should not at all appear a pleasure when read: its worth should only become apparent on the stage. They can say what they like, but it was only when I finally saw works like Molière's *Don Juan* or *Tartuffe* performed on stage by live actors that I fully realised that these works were indeed masterpieces. Some time ago, I saw a performance of a play by Goldoni that I had always considered one of his lesser works, or at least that was the impression I got when I read it. The play was *Last Night of the Carnival*. The director limited himself to the most straightforward staging, the actors were no more than mediocre, and yet rarely have I felt myself more caught up in a theatrical experience. This is all the more remarkable when you consider that normally the theatre of Goldoni does not excite me unduly. What can you say about the work of Ruzante? Show me the hypocrite who will say that this is a great literary production. For centuries, his scripts lay neglected precisely because they could not be accommodated in the standard literary genres. What were they – mere dialect works which dealt with topics like hunger, sex, poverty, violence, with no savour of the 'sublime' of high art.

The conflict between dramatists and littérateurs is an age-old one. Diderot, as we have already seen, was full of contempt and resentment towards professional actors. If you are on the lookout for a spot of light entertainment, you should look up the bitter articles which Gozzi and Ferrari (two second-rate men of letters in Venice) wrote against the great man of the theatre who was Goldoni. Entire volumes could be filled with the spleen and bile which academics down the ages have poured out in their attacks on people who write for the stage. Shakespeare himself received torrents of abuse from fastidious scholars with rings on their little fingers and the scent of laurel in their nostrils. They called him the 'Shakescene, the spewer of words, the fashioner of coloured windows'. The same happened to Molière, while Euripides was berated by that reactionary not bereft of talent, Aristophanes.

The advantage an author-actor has is that from the moment he writes the first line, he can hear his own voice and the reaction of the audience. He writes an entrance or a piece of dialogue with other actors, and while he cannot imagine the scene as seen from the stalls, he can see it directly as acted on the stage and projected towards the audience. It may not seem a great deal, but Pirandello's great discovery was 'to learn to write on stage'. Pirandello never acted, but he developed a kind of symbiosis with actors. To have his plays produced, he transformed himself into a director, and often had as leading lady someone with whom he had a relationship. He put everything into the theatre, down to his last penny. He was not one of those writers who dropped by with the finished script under his arm and handed it over to the producer. He created on the spot, writing and rewriting in the dressing-rooms, during the rehearsals, right up to the last minute. His quarrel with the actress Borboni attained a certain notoriety, because this madman wanted her to learn a new speech three pages long a few hours before going on stage on the first night. The older generation of actors recall that even after the opening, Pirandello carried on thinking about his play, rewriting and making changes, right up to the end of the run.

Sixth Day

Ulysses Couldn't Care Less

There is no getting away from the thought of death, or, as certain intellectuals would have it, the problem of death. However, to be conscious of death is one thing, to brood over it quite another. In Greek theatre, for instance, death is the constant counterpoint to every story; in the grand scales of every life, destiny, unrelenting and unshakeable, stands as its great pivotal force. Nothing, for whatever reason or by whatever effort, can ever shift or modify it. Destiny is above even the gods, and death has a skull with no ears. Fate and death are the essential elements of every tragedy, but mankind, in his unreason, never heeds the rules. Euripides, in his tragedies, introduces the subversive element produced by human will, a will so determined and forceful as to overturn the very laws of destiny. 'The high emotions of mankind', as Euripides calls them, induce the gods to modify their edicts and accept even the impossible and the illogical.

The great switch between Euripides and Sophocles lies in the fact that Euripides presents his heroes as hurling themselves with desperate passion into situations whose outcome is already decided. They know that the wager is lost, but they need to gamble to the last throw. Often, faced with such stubbornness and generosity in opposing destiny, the gods relent and the *deus ex machina* is brought into play. The gods descend from heaven on a piece of stage machinery to alter the pre-ordained fate.

Something of the sort happens in *Philoctetes*. The hero, Philoctetes, pursued by the gods and by destiny, is bitten on the foot by a poisonous snake, and gangrene, with its attendant stench, sets in. Howling with pain, he is left to die on an island by his friends, Menelaus, Agamemnon and Ulysses. (Now there's a right lot to call friends!) He fights back not only against the gangrene but against loneliness, but is powerless against the trap that Ulysses and Neoptolemus, son of Achilles, set for him when they return to the island. They arrive with the express purpose of removing the magic bow which this early version of Robinson Crusoe uses to catch his food. So faultless and generous is the conduct of Philoctetes that the son of Achilles begins to feel a worm. (Ulysses couldn't care less.)

The young man begins to feel the pangs of remorse (Ulysses couldn't care less), rebels against Ulysses and refuses to have any more to do with the scheme. He reveals the plot to Philoctetes, but Ulysses, every inch a politician, calmly plays his own hand. He admits that they had intended to cheat him, but not for personal gain: 'Without the magical bow, Troy, so the oracle has declared, will never be defeated. Thousands of young Achaeans will die in vain.' He spouted a great deal more in the same style, but Philoctetes was no fool. He listened with an ironic smile, gave as good as he got, and at the end gave way, not out of exhaustion but with a sense of rationality and detachment: 'Take my bow. My part is played.' At this point, the heavens open and the gods descend *en masse* in the famous ship. 'Hold it, we cannot allow this man to sacrifice himself in this way! You are a more worthy being than any of us!' In this lies the great catharsis. The reversal of fortune arrives at the final moment but the audience has been led to demand this type of solution. It needs to be reassured that 'hope surges over the misery of man, like the spring floods which make fertile the fields'.

There is the other solution, to accept with pessimistic logic, with songs to impotence and abandonment, the reality of defeat. That is indeed the elegy of death, but it is not something that I am disposed to accept, and not only in theatre.

The Croatian Passion Play

I saw in Zagreb a mystery play in Serbo-Croat: *The Death of the Peasant*. It is the story of a peasant, still in his youth, harassed endlessly by a group of powerful men, against whom he rebels with great courage. He resists as far as he is able but eventually has to succumb. On the point of death, he entrusts his closest friend with the task of performing the valediction, an ancient rite in which the designated friend must identify with the dead man, take his place and almost his appearance. He is required to dress in the dead man's clothes and to attempt, as far as is possible, to imitate his voice and gestures. The friend will even sit astride the coffin and recount, always in the first person, the events of the dead man's life. It is the friend who speaks – addressing the mother, thanking her for bringing him into the world, kissing the father's hand, recalling the first time he took him hunting, turning to the elder brother, and recalling when he taught him how to ride a horse. He even rises to his feet, miming falling off the horse and rolling on the ground.

The other friends stamp their feet and hands, in imitation of the neighing of the horse, seize hold of the young man and throw him in the air. The game is transformed into a dance, with everyone present raising a cup of wine and drinking. An accordion and two guitars back up the shouting and singing, while people start dancing round the coffin. The young man who is acting as the double of the dead man meets a girl, the dead man's wife. Together they sit on the coffin, talking and laughing. The young man repeats the old declaration of love, they pretend to quarrel until friends have to step in and the two return to the dance. Even the local lords who had persecuted the young man take their part in the fiction. They declare their contrition for their wickedness, although the mother refuses to allow them into the circle and snatches away the flask of wine from the hands of the young man who was about to offer it to them. She cries out: 'You have altered your feelings, and I do not doubt your word, but make time turn back and my son live! Only then may you be part of the feast.'

The stage is on two levels, with the landowner, the bishop and the prince on the upper level. The dance grows more and more frenzied, and the grandees disappear from the upper level. The whole party climbs up, with the coffin carried on the shoulders of some members of the group, on to the platform and there the coffin is laid down. Everyone exits to the wings and returns dragging a tree, complete with branches and roots, which is placed on the tomb. The roots begin to move and stretch down towards the lid of the coffin. The device is simple enough. All the characters in the play lie face down, placing their hands inside the roots and pushing downwards. Even their arms have become branches. The lid of the coffin is removed, the corpse is raised and, held in an embrace by the branches, slowly rises up inside the trunk until it reappears seated astride the tree.

This myth is, I am assured, older than that of Dionysus. With the body changed into fertiliser, life is reborn inside the tree. Nature is mother of humankind and offers them the possibility of new life as leaf, fruit or branch. It is not a simple question of catharsis, but rather an insistence that there is no ending. The rite serves to preserve the presence of the deceased in the memory of the society. A man or a woman, in this view, only really dies when they are forgotten and no longer spoken about, and to be remembered it is essential to give life to stories worth repeating. The deceased lives in the tree, but it is clear that he lives equally in the mind and body of each man and woman with whom he has exchanged love, friendship, solidarity. This is the view of death that attracts me, and it is no accident that it is to be found in popular theatre, for this is a theatre and a culture capable of facing, with a sense of irony, the whole question of divine laws, including free will.

Dialogue with Lucifer

Bonvesin de la Riva is an author of such success in popular culture as to be relegated to recondite entries in anthologies of Italian poetry. Who ever heard of such a thing? Someone who writes in an unfashionable dialect – Lombard! In spite of that, he remains one of the most interesting poets of the Middle Ages, principally because he established himself as the logician *par excellence*, as the figure who fired shafts of ferocious doubt against the immovable principles of scholasticism and invented the dialectic of humanism. His dialogue between the Madonna and the Devil, in which he has the extraordinary idea of arranging an encounter between the Mother of God and the enemy of mankind, is almost unknown. Once you allow the enemy to have his say, we have attained a point of hyperdemocracy. It is worth bearing in mind that we are at the halfway point in the Thirteenth century, in other words, well before the age of Dante. Further, if you pay attention, you will note that the Devil has an uncanny resemblance to mankind and that the reasoning of the one is identical to the reasoning of the other. Lucifer speaks for himself:

> Da po' ke De' savea
> avant m'aves creao
> ke per un soleng pecao
> eo me sare perduo
> crear no me dovea
> no me dovea crear

Translation: 'Since God knew, long before He created me, that for one single sin I would be damned, He should not have created me, He had no right to create me.' It continues (freely rendered), 'He could have saved me, had He wished, by making me holier and wiser, or as strong and incorruptible as the tower of ivory, but instead He infected me with the will to prevail, only to make me fall at the last.'

In other words, God stands brutally accused of having cheated, of having dealt a pack of marked cards, of preparing a sting. But why? To what purpose? Why create an enemy? Could it be that God himself needs an antagonist, needs the black to make the white stand out, the evil to set against the good? There is nothing more tedious than the sea without wind and waves, that is without contrast. So we can imagine this Almighty Father immersed in a creation without contradiction, bereft of all buffets and all dialectic, in a geometry free of angles, where straight lines run unimpeded towards eternity. So what is to be done? He puts on a comedy with grotesque and tragic passages, with actors convinced that they improvise as they go, but with a script already printed ahead of the show.

The Epic Conjuror

Before taking my leave of you, I must file a complaint about an unprovoked assault of which I was victim while innocently chatting, in the foyer of the Argentina theatre, to a group of people who had been following these 'days'. The subject was the so-called 'fourth wall', and more particularly the devices employed to shock the audience out of their passive condition as mindless spectator, when a good-looking, dark-haired young lady began berating me. She started by accusing the whole La Comune company of organising events that are often coldly mechanistic, and have little to do with theatre, and do not reach out beyond the stage. As if that were not enough, she went on to add that in *Trumpets and Raspberries*, for instance, the barbs were rarely aimed at political targets but at incidents and accidents, and my aim was to distract the audience with the same techniques as some conjuror who prepares, away from the audience, the wonderful tricks which will have them all gasping with amazement. Tell me if this is not the equivalent of a public flogging?

Still thirsting for blood, she repeated the same ideas in the conference hall and, ignoring my pleas at least to stop short of flaying the soles of my feet, she replied that she had learned the art of gutting people from me. From me! Then she begged me (I use the term loosely) to explain if I still considered it 'epic' to address the audience while having a good time along with them and while making them part of my deliberately provocative style of presentation. Bang! Collapse of stout party, wouldn't you say?

In any case, I thanked the young lady because this gives me the ideal opportunity to bring on Franca Rame, and leave her with the task of dreaming up a reply. From now on, she will do the talking.

Born and Bred to the Theatre

First of all, a brief preamble. Dario has already told you how I was born into a theatrical family. I started acting at eight days old, in my mother's arms, in the part of the son of Genoveffa di Brabante. I didn't have a lot to say, and, not being too well up on epic theatre and alienation, my style was heavily naturalistic. Fortunately at a later stage, when, as a young girl, I found myself performing classical parts like Juliet in *Romeo and Juliet*, I discovered that all our training and instincts led us to abhor over-emphasis, and that we never sought melodramatic or rhetorical effects. For us, acting never involved problems of stylistic research, because it was based on simple models and on more or less natural practice. I learned to move and speak on stage, quite unselfconsciously, and picked up the parts by listening to my mother and older sisters act them out night after night. Acting for us was as simple as walking and breathing, and only much later, while working with the supposedly leading companies, did I realise that ours was an infinitely more pure and productive style than the chaotic, mannered diction spouted by actors in those companies. We were no more than jobbing actors with a gift for communication. No words were ever allowed to disappear between the boards of the stage; they were all projected towards the audience.

In the early days of my contact with the grand, official theatre, I was a bit embarrassed by our continual tendency towards improvisation, and more than one person tried to convince me that ours was an uncultured, second-rate style. Only much later did I realise the great advantages of being born a player in the tradition of popular theatre. I felt enormous affection and gratitude for Bertolt Brecht when I happened to read a famous remark of his: 'In art, the people can express profound things with simplicity, whereas the muddled complexity of certain intellectuals expresses no more than profoundly vacuous ideas.'

For all the wealth of experience I had acquired, I was not accustomed to techniques of directly upsetting or disturbing an audience, for it formed no part of our theatre. Yes, we were naturally 'epic', in that we represented characters and did not clothe ourselves in them, but only my father, who was actor-manager and company director, knew how to address the audience directly, to entertain them, to crack jokes or to provoke them in the prologues – and never during the performance itself – which he alone presented. We women of the company acted – we prepared the costumes, we were given charge of the box office, we were allowed to assist in putting up sets, we were expected to attend to the household chores and the cooking, but on stage we never appeared up front to speak directly with the audience. And even after forming a company with Dario, I went on accepting the role and logic of the humble performer who shied away from directly entertaining, or provoking, the audience.

Only when we made the great leap, that is to say when we decided to abandon the official theatre circuit, did I find myself compelled to learn to hold an audience by speaking directly to the stalls. It was no easy task, and at the beginning I simply refused to fill that role. Today I can assure you that it was an enormous backward pirouette. The first time I felt awkward and inhibited, because to address people directly, to look them straight in the face and talk to them, is much more difficult than to act any part whatsoever, either on your own or with a company, or at least it was for me.

Here I would like to give my answer to the girl who questioned the value of dialogue with the people in the theatre. It all depends on how it is done, on whether it is an attempt to talk down to people or whether it is done with inventiveness and style. As to the comparison with the conjuror who has nothing else in mind than to amuse people with his tricks, I reject vehemently the suggestion that carefully crafted effects must necessarily be void of political content. We staged two plays, in which politically disturbing cases of some substance were mounted step by step.

The Politics of the Hoax

Let me talk about one of these works, in which the twists of the plot were deeply integrated into the work itself. The title was *War of the People in Chile*, and it was staged immediately after the *coup d'état* in Chile which led to the death of President Allende and to the massacre of thousands of members of the democratic opposition.

Many authentic, highly dramatic documents were used in the preparation of the script. A Chilean refugee obtained for us a copy of the last broadcast of Radio Mir, an ultra-left group whose headquarters were attacked and destroyed by Pinochet's *carabineros*. Two broadcasters, a man and a woman, continued to broadcast right up to the last minute, giving the position of the troops and information on the roads still free. The thump of a door being battered down and the rattle of gunfire are the last sounds on the tape.

At that very moment, Italy was in the grip of fears of an imminent *coup d'état*, and every day there were reports of plans of armed insurrection by some special corps, of plans for mass arrests and for the establishment of concentration camps in Sardinia. From the recent inquiries into the P2 Masonic Lodge, evidence of such blueprints, supported by identified political forces, has come to the surface, and has established that it was no laughing matter. The fact is that at that time, many trade union and Communist leaders were advised not to sleep at home, for fear of the consequences. Obviously the responsible organs of government rushed to assure the public that there was no truth in those rumours, which they defined as the work of irresponsible agitators.

In that climate, we put on our play in support of the victims of the military repression in Chile. The play was conceived as a series of monologues, of songs and sketches, one on top of the other. In one of these monologues, I myself played the Chilean Christian Democratic Party as a kind of *grande dame*, all uncouth gracelessness, crocodile tears, and broken promises, proclaiming her innocence while bounding between piles of corpses, wavering all the time between reactionary forces and the display of a democratic sentiment overlaid with much hypocritical tut-tutting.

We had to perform in huge spaces like sports centres and big cinemas, both unequipped with decent acoustics, and were compelled to use microphones, radio-microphones and high-power amplifiers. The advantage of this arrangement was that each actor was able to move freely around the stage, but the disadvantage was that often we picked up radio messages from police cars outside. They would start off with something like this: 'Hello, hello, black panther to red dragon, are you receiving me, over. Drunk setting fire to the bar of the sports centre, please attend, over.' This interference invited a reply, which we could hardly resist. We invented wild and fantastic names of our own, for example: 'Crazed gorilla to baboon on the loose, are you receiving me? Mad lion eaten guard . . . bring medical personnel . . . lion experiencing digestion problems . . . make your way to the spot with alka seltzer, over.' The odd policeman with a sense of humour had a good laugh over it, but the majority were harder to please. Our audiences became accustomed to the regular interference and thoroughly enjoyed the whole thing, and it provided us with the basis of a plot, involving the type of deliberate provocation we were discussing.

We faked police voices and recorded a few messages as though they came from HQ. 'Calling all cars, calling all cars . . . return to base, over!' 'Green dragon on patrol . . . confirm if order applies to us, over!' 'HQ, here, emergency call . . . idiot! Why the delay? Over and out!' Even in this case, we meant it as a spoof exchange with the police HQ, but we had uttered, in the hearing of members of audience, the dread word 'emergency'!

Among the spectators, even though we made sure we delivered some throwaway line like 'It's Saturday, and nobody organises a *coupe d'état* on a Saturday,' to reassure everyone, there was always someone who would get upset. The show went on from the point where it had been interrupted, but shortly afterwards there would be a further disturbance. A girl, with an air of embarrassment, came on stage with a piece of paper containing a number of registration numbers belonging to cars that were blocking her exit. 'I'm sorry to be such a nuisance, but I must get home and I can't get out. I phoned home, but the lines are down, or something. There's a funny noise on the phone.' Another spectator broke in: 'Same with me. My phone's not working either. The phones must be cut off in the whole district.'

Obviously the whole thing was a set-up. That afternoon, we had had a meeting with the organisers of the show in that locality and had got them all involved. One of the actors, heavily disguised, sat in the middle of the audience and co-ordinated the action. Following the appearance of the girl worried about the telephone, we took over from the stage, joking about the possibility of a road block, suggesting that if the telephones were cut off in the houses, then obviously they could not be working in the army barracks, in the police stations or the bishop's palace, so the planned *coup d'état* was already cocked up. An actor, dressed up as a particularly fierce-looking extremist type, got up to make a few provocative remarks about the tranquil rest of the Communist leaders being disturbed by bad dreams, and how it served them right for spouting all that pap about how nonsensical was all this wild talk of brutal military moves, before going off to sleep at Mummy's place. Without fail, this speech gave rise to a heated debate on social democracy and revisionism, and we let it go a while before restoring calm and getting on with the show.

At that moment, a roar from outside froze us all in our seats. We had fixed up some loudspeakers outside the theatre and at that point tapes with recordings of caterpillar wheels were switched on. One of our people came running in to announce that he had seen armoured cars and tanks on the street. We continued to play the whole thing down, but allowed a discussion to get under way. Someone announced that there were police agents in plain clothes in the audience, something that was illegal in a private circle such as ours. A policeman (once again an actor in disguise) was identified and asked to leave, and when he declined the discussion grew more intense. The real play was by now taking place in the stalls, with everyone keen to join in; meanwhile we were relegated to the role of moderators. Finally the policeman left.

Shortly afterwards, one of the organisers came striding into the hall to announce that the police had arrived and were asking to speak to someone, perhaps Dario. Dario made his way out across the stalls, joking as he went about the forthcoming interview with the highest authorities in the land. In the meantime, I was left to entertain the audience and keep things going until Dario came back with the news that the police wanted to carry out a search for someone, probably a petty criminal, who they had reason to believe was among the audience. This provided the cue for a sequence of gags and buffoonery, and the show got under way once again, but not for long. The police made an official request to be allowed in. Tension rose. There was a brief debate, before, accompanied by a group of henchmen, a senior policeman (once again a member of our company) entered. He was invited on to the stage, where, visibly embarrassed and tense, he took the microphone. He uttered a few reassuring words, said there was no problem, then took out a sheet of paper and read out some names of people present in the theatre. These people were invited to go to the police station for routine inquiries. We always warned these people in advance and received their consent.

A silence you could cut fell over the place, with only one or two of the bolder spirits daring to make sarcastic remarks about the nature of these routine inquiries. As the officer read out the names and the people designated climbed on to the stage, someone in the audience began to sing quietly the Internationale. Everyone in the theatre got to their feet and joined in, including, to general astonishment, the police officer who gave the clenched fist salute. After the initial astonishment passed, there was an explosion of indignation and amusement. 'You mean it was all a joke!' Yes, it was, we told them, to let you see that all this talk about *coups d'état* is not just hot air. 'After all, you were all taken in!'

A general hubbub of laughter and applause – the classical signs of a release of tension or of awakening from a nightmare – broke out, but the show was not allowed to end on a note of hilarity. Invariably, and this was exactly the response we were after, the laughter was followed by heated, almost violent, discussions. Some agreed with us for having goaded people out of apathy, while others accused us of low trickery and screamed that far from being theatre, all we had done was to play on irrational emotions, or in other words, that ours was the very opposite of epic and popular theatre.

Some evenings produced moments that were both exhilarating and dangerous. In Turin, Paolo Hutter, a journalist who had just returned from Chile, swallowed page by page his diary containing lists of telephone numbers, and other comrades barricaded themselves in the toilets; in Bolzano, two conscripts, terrified of being arrested, threw themselves out of a window twelve feet up, and it was only by a miracle they avoided breaking both legs; in Parma, an elderly member of the Communist party, an ex-partisan, as soon as he heard his son's name among those read out, got up on stage, shouting, 'No, no, I insist on going to the police station too, and if any of you in the audience have any self-respect, you'll come as well.'

On the other hand, some people had no hesitation in showing their true colours. The police officer announced that anyone with a party card of any of the parties in the government coalition was free to leave the theatre, and there were always some who rose immediately to their feet, and waving the precious meal-ticket card in the air, demanded to be let out at once. As soon as it became clear that it had been a hoax, they were exposed to the cruel jeers of the others.

The ensuing debate tended to be heated, and since the resentment arose from a sense of having been fooled, people tried to turn the subject round and lecture about aesthetics and taste. The standard accusation levelled against the object of their annoyance was of mere hoaxing. We counterattacked by putting the whole thing in a historical context, recalling that popular theatre had always made use of hoaxes as a provocative device, not for its own sake, but with a didactic moral purpose. I remember seeing a documentary in Iran which dealt with hoaxes put on by actors during fairs, and features an actress pretending to be pregnant. She made out that she was in labour, and when the passers-by did their best to have her taken to hospital, she would have none of it, insisting that she wanted to have her baby there, in the middle of the market place. Amidst her groans, she let it be known that one of the bystanders was the father of her child, so the men stood there, casting suspicious glances at each other. Nearby there were other members of the company, who stirred up the situation, intervening as policemen, as priests or as officials. The disputes they created led to the formation of factions, each one opposed to the other. People got up to explain their own point of view, to reveal their own mean-mindedness or generosity, so that when the fiction was revealed, each person found himself naked in the face of the truth about his own behaviour.

Women as Clowns, Fools or Minstrels

I would like to consider the position of women in the comic tradition, with some specific historical references. It has been established that in ancient times the only women allowed to get up on a stage were the women-minstrels. In the Christian period, we have information relating to certain famous dancers such as Theodora of Byzantium.* From the frescoes at Knossos, we know about the girl acrobats in the island of Crete some three thousand years before the birth of Christ, but for the entire Graeco-Roman period there is precious little mention of actresses. Only from the Middle Ages is there any pictorial evidence from which it is possible to deduce the presence of real women on the stage. We know of French medieval tales, the *fabliaux*, which were recited by very able female storytellers. In Boccaccio,† it is the women who are in charge of the situation in the *Decameron*, and it is they who speak more than the men in the cyclical recitation of the stories. Generally, the women's stories are more erotically entertaining and spicy than those of their male counterparts.

Boccaccio was not the inventor of the custom of storytelling. Until about fifty years ago, among peasant peoples, it was common for the higher-ranking women to gather others together in the stables, and recount fables and moral tales until the children went to bed and then to get down to more obscene stories. The obscene has always been, as I will never tire of repeating, the most effective of all weapons in the struggle to free people from the disease with which Power infected people when it planted in their minds a sense of guilt or shame, and an anxiety over sinfulness. What a splendid device that

---

* Theodora, Empress of Byzantium, had been a professional drama and circus performer before marrying the Emperor Justinian in AD 523.

† Giovanni Boccaccio (1313–1375), writer and humanist, author of *The Decameron*.

was to have us all born guilty, with a sense of sin (original) to be cleansed or of a penalty to pay. Machiavelli advised the Prince: 'Give the people a sense of guilt, it doesn't matter of what, and it will be much easier to govern them.'

To destroy this anxiety through laughter has always been the principal task of comic writers and performers, especially the women among them. *La Celestina** by Rojas is the very symbol of the female comic spirit. Who is Celestina! A cynical, passionate, generous-minded old bawd, with the secret of plastic surgery, who uses her knowledge to renew the genitals of young women who have lived not wisely but too well. She offers advice to young women of too candid a disposition, trains them in the school of the old procuress in Ovid† and teaches them not to be embarrassed by their inexperience. 'You blush, maiden, if a man touches your hand? You turn as white as the veil which covers your head if he talks of love? Do not be ashamed, but take full advantage of your coyness. If you only knew what effort it will take within a few years to feign that comely coyness of yours!'

In his *Anconeta*, Ruzante makes use of another bawd, as does the anonymous author of the *Venesiana* (not to be confused with *La Venexiana*). In this work, the bawd has to make it impossible for two merchants, fathers of two beautiful girls, to make love to each other's daughter. The two men, both in their maturity, are indignant over the swarms of handsome suitors drawn to their daughters 'like tomcats on heat, drooling over the tasty morsels offered them'. They have received information that the two girls, already head over heels in love with two young men, have fixed on Carnival night in a gondola, when everyone is masked, as the time and place when they will make merry with their young lovers. The two solid merchants are convinced in their own minds that it would be altogether more appropriate if they themselves, rather than some random swine given to running off with delicate maidens, were left to enjoy their own daughters, but the morality of the race would have it otherwise. The father's lot is to raise his daughters, to protect them and then to hand them over, intact and accompanied by a fat dowry, to the first cretin who comes along.

The two decide, with the aid of the bawd, to disguise themselves with the very costumes the lovers intend to wear the night of Carnival, to swap daughters, and to lie with the girls in the gondolas. There never was a more ferocious satire against the culture of the consumer society and of nascent capitalism. The task of the old woman is not merely to manufacture a trap for the two daughters, but also to deliver a commentary on the unfolding action and on the logic of the market for which even the sexual organs of the girls are

* A novel in dialogue (*c.*1499) by Fernando de Rojas.
† Ovid (43 BC–18 AD), Roman poet whose works include *Ars Amatoria* (The Art of Love).

no more than an object of trade. At the same time, the unfortunate girls thus traded will be compelled to remain inside the family, or at least inside the family circle.

The bawd, a woman still young and passionate, sets up the situation, but it begins to go wrong when she herself falls in love, alas, with the captain, one of the lovers of the girls. In the change-over, she arranges for the captain to be in the same gondola as her, but she is unable to disguise her feelings. It is not enough for her to be kissed and embraced; she wants to talk, to confess her love, so she ends up unmasking herself and undoing the entire plot. I saw this play staged some years ago, and while the actress who played the bawd had talent and the right temperament, and even the ideal physique, she had no idea how to employ them to the best advantage. She remained unduly restrained.

At the opposite extreme, I have too often seen displays by female comic actresses that were right over the top. There is nothing worse than seeing women reduced to making funny faces and teasing movements, swaying their hips and wiggling their bottoms for no good reason, stroking their breasts and patting their buttocks, all to show how uninhibited and provocative they can be – anything, in other words, to raise a laugh or win another round of applause. It is possible to provoke and shock an audience while maintaining a sense of measure. Every actress should remember that for a woman dignity is more important than anything.

A monologue in *Female Parts*, entitled 'Same Old Story' begins with a woman miming sexual intercourse with her man. The woman complains about the lack of consideration and tenderness shown by her partner; she expresses her disappointment and they begin to quarrel. After a while they make up and continue making love. This action is also mimed. In my travels around Europe and America, I have seen this monologue performed by many actresses from many nations: British, Finnish, Swedish, French, German and American among others. Some, like Yvonne Bryceland in London acted with a sense of measure and balance, but the great majority forced the pace, and in their attempts to be realistic, described every gesture with traits of a naturalism which were frankly unpleasant. They bent their hips then jerked their pubic regions with a violence that would have snapped the bronze penis of a statue. While flat on their backs, they executed a belly dance. They passed easily from grips taken from Graeco-Roman wrestling to grips that would have honoured a contender in the mythical Korean wrestling which ends with the obligatory sodomising of the loser. There is no denying that the audience enjoyed themselves, but the laughter was at the expense of the basic sense of the play and undermined both its theatrical thrust and the value of the character. The tenderness, the delicate sentiments that appear in the dialogue were gutted by the preceding, unbridled pantomime.

It is not a matter of prudery. I am in complete agreement with those women who are struggling for liberation, once and for all, from those senseless inhibitions on sexual matters which have been inculcated into us over the years, but I would always, even when dropping my knickers, like to achieve that with a minimum of style.

On the other hand, some women, determined not to overdo eroticism and finding it vulgar of women to make people laugh by a grotesque treatment of their own bodies, will have nothing to do with sex in any shape or form. There are schools for clowns where the articulation and gestures taught amount to a castration of all femininity. The clown is unisex, they say, that is, male. In the clown's act, the presence of women is secondary; they have the role of the entrancing figure on the high wire; they are akin to a poetic symbol, but never more than a symbol. Speaking personally, the role of symbol holds no attractions, indeed it drives me into wild rages. There are women clowns who dress as men, and even try to put on a man's voice. An amazing hybrid, this, but a blind alley.

If anything, the situation of women mimes is even worse. Almost all the great masters of mime are men, with a male approach to mime, which tends to be sexless. The classical mimes tend to exclude sex and eroticism, preferring the blanched, moonlike figure of Pierrot. Marcel Marceau has as his prototype a kind of seaside Pierrot (a mixture of ice-cream vendor and sailor dipped in white flour), ready to be popped into the frying pan. Artless, dreaming, carefree, he is never agitated, unless it be over the sight of a cloud or a dragonfly. He may chase after a red balloon, but the thought that it might resemble a woman's buttocks would never enter his head – or if it did, it would be him, and not the balloon, who would burst. The result is that when a woman plays the part of one of these Pierrots, it becomes even more unbearable. A sexless man is acceptable but a sexless woman . . . never!

I once had occasion to speak with a woman in New York who had dedicated a great deal of study to mime and the art of the clown. In addition to being a talented acrobat, she had a splendid singing voice and could accompany herself on the guitar, but she was going through a personal crisis because she realised she had lost her own identity. A woman must play female roles. A man can take the part of a transvestite, and can, through caricature, find delightful accents, but a woman 'transvestite' has no meaning, unless it is an explicit travesty, put on in the context of a theatrical fiction and, in consequence, made totally explicit and public. It must be one hundred per cent clear that the character is playing a game.

The recourse to open disguise was a device employed in Commedia dell'Arte, but the switch worked because the actress had demonstrated in advance to the audience her authentic feminity, had managed to convince them that she possessed the requisite feminine charm and female features, with especial reference to the rotundity of the breasts and overall womanly grace. Then, and only then, could she permit herself to dress up as a man, but even this was no more than a pretext for showing off more clearly her own attributes. In one cross-over scene, Isabella Andreini dressed in the clinging tights which were the height of fashion among young aristocrats of the day, but did so in such a way as to reveal her figure more plainly than if she had appeared completely nude. In another scene, the same actress played the part of an insane person, talking wildly, cackling, pulling her hair and ripping her clothes. With her dress in tatters and her skirt ripped, her breast is uncovered and her legs can be glimpsed, as can, once she turns round, her jaunty little buttocks. The audience went wild. The moral is clear. As an innocent little creature, she has no wish to expose herself; it is the madness that makes her do it. It is not hard to work out the reasons for the enormous success of these pieces. It was the first time in centuries that real women, and highly attractive ones, were permitted to appear on stage.

Until then, women actresses could be found only in some taverns in the double role of entertainer and prostitute. Up to that time, female parts were played on stage by boy actors. As late as the seventeenth century, women who worked in theatre were viewed as prostitutes, high-class prostitutes undoubtedly, but prostitutes just the same. I do not know if any irony was intended in the designation given them of 'honoured courtesans', for even if intellectuals and princes bestowed gifts and honours, their status was unchanged.

There exist a certain number of plays written by women and performed by women alone. The nuns of a convent in Brittany in the fifteenth century staged plays, part comedy and part tragedy, written by the Abbess. In one of them, a nun falls in love with a young Ganymede and falls pregnant; it could be the story of the Nun of Monza, except that this time there is a catharsis. Abandoned and in despair, the nun is on the point of hanging herself, when, having received a sign from the Virgin Mary, she decides to face up to the scandal and to accept the reparation she will be required to make. In her terror, she throws herself on her knees before the Virgin, prays for help, and the following morning has a miscarriage. The sisters bury the little corpse, and when the nun presents herself for the judgement of her superiors, who had planned to use the scandal as a pretext to close the convent, she shows that it was all a frame-up and her accuser is led away for punishment.

If we analyse this morality tale with the slightest attention, we cannot fail to notice that it embodies an odd anti-morality. If the abortion had been the work of some old hag, it would have been an unspeakable crime, but since it followed the nun's devout action in prostrating herself on the floor of the church for a whole night, it could be regarded as a miracle, while the fruit of the sin comes to merit pious burial. What matters to us is the note that nuns in a medieval convent were able to stage and discuss troublesome topics, like sex in the convent, the problem of sexual desire, and even abortion, albeit holy abortion.

We have no idea if these works were produced. We know that the nuns themselves acted the parts, that virtually all the roles were female and that the audience was made up of women. The male parts are few and secondary. When male roles were indispensable, to the great delight of the novices and of the remaining nuns in the audience, certain carefully selected sisters were chosen and decked out in male attire. It must have been an exercise that aroused the most morbid of fantasies to see men, even if only make-believe ones, appear in an environment to which they never had access, except illicitly.

In ancient times, among the Attic and Achaean peoples, women often went out of town to put on orgiastic plays in sacred places, to which men were denied access. Ovid describes such an incident in his *Metamorphoses*, while in *The Bacchae* Euripides explains that any unwary male turning up in the wrong spot runs the risk of being devoured by those frenzied, possessed females. The women of Bali even today, just like the Bacchae of old, draw apart on special feasts to perform grotesque tales in which men, in caricature guise and represented by actresses in men's clothing, are ridiculed. Once again, the leading parts are female. It is worth repeating that the first comic actors, at the very dawn of mythology, were women, and that some form of comic spectacle was a fundamental element in every initiation rite. To make the site of the feast sacred, comic actors, with a comic actress at their head, were the first to enter the space set aside for the rite. Only when they had produced laughter from people around, did the god bestow sacredness on the place and feast.

Arab peoples, long before the advent of Mohammed, celebrated a special rite to induce the god of rain to make the clouds open. The community sat a puppet on a chair placed in the middle of a square; the puppet was covered with flour, had its eyes wide open, but the eyebrows and mouth – drawn with a single line – had a downwards curve, to indicate great sadness. This frowning puppet (the modern term would be 'depressive') symbolised the son of the god of the rains, and since in those times women had not as yet been relegated to the *gynaeceum* they were free to participate in the great rites. In particular, they took part in the acts of buffoonery that were organised during droughts to persuade the god of the rains to assist mankind and save them from catastrophe. Groups of real clowns did dances with bits of knockabout, tumbles and mock clashes; the women padded out their bosoms, thighs and buttocks with no half measures; they bumped bottoms during the dances, and, with these great protuberances, they knocked into the clowns and pushed them to the ground. They grabbed hold of the men by the head and, still dancing, buried their faces in their enormous bosoms until they were nearly suffocated. Once again, it is plain that a parody of courting customs and a satirical use of obscenity were at the basis of the rite. When the excitement of the whole community overflowed into wild laughter, the puppet's mouth was turned up in a strange smile, and at that very moment the rain began to fall from heaven. The drops of rain were the tears of a god moved by the love shown by men who had gone to such lengths to amuse his son.

Among Arabs nowadays there is a poem which women storytellers mime and sing, but with deep irony. Here is a sample:

> At the first light of the moon
> I have decked myself in my finest array.
> I await the sounds of the camels' hooves
> Carried in from beyond the city walls.
> My heart will hear them before the dogs
> Standing guard at the city gates,
> And in time with the rhythm of the hooves
> Beating on the roadway
> My heart will tell of your coming,
> Curly-haired guide of Hassan's caravan.
> I will hold you, still covered with dust
> And damp with the sweat of the journey,
> In my arms, and kiss your lips.
> Were you a son of the gods
> I could not deny that you are
> A smelly lover.
> But I have so long awaited your coming
> That you seem like the lamb scented with roses.
> My lavender-perfumed hands
> Slide smoothly over your body.
> I bathe you, I wash you, I wrap you in linen clothes
> I sprinkle your chest and strong shoulders with fresh thyme.

Gently, gently, my dark-haired lover.
Do you imagine you are still astride your horse?
The beast is in the stable,
Wild love fills my heart
And you are already on your way.
When your camels are a distant outline
On the far horizon,
My heart will be stilled
And I ready for the shroud of death.
But have no fear, my gentle lover.
I will again deck myself in my finest array
At the sound of camels' hooves
From the next caravan.
For they bring, upright in the saddle,
A young man with eyes as clear as rains in springtime.
Forgive me, but I cannot resist
The delight of feeling my heart break
When he too makes ready to depart.
The next moon will again see me ready for
The shroud of death,
When the camels are
A distant outline on the far horizon.

In the original, the song has repeated cadences and an African sound, reminiscent of the rhythmic plod of camels' hooves. The singer had round her neck a drum a little larger than a half-melon, on which with her fingers and the palms of her hands she beat out the non-stop movement of the camels, but with no descriptive gestures. At times the drum beat stopped, giving way to the sound of wind instruments, and a flute played continually in time with her singing. To indicate the passage of time or change of action, the flute played solo, while the woman danced silently on the one spot. Perhaps it would be more accurate to talk of a mime rather than of dance, for she seemed to caress her lover and to throw back her head and bust as though about to fall under his embrace. Her pelvis was allowed to tremble slightly and delicately before the drum took up again and she raised her legs, bending the knee and stretching it out in a beautiful, swaying movement, the very re-creation of the camel's step.

The same extraordinary irony can be seen in an Occitan* poem from the fourteenth century. Called *The Farewell at Dawn*, or *The Verse of the Queen of*

* The language of medieval Provence.

Navarre, it too was certainly performed by a female minstrel who perhaps acccompanied herself on an instrument and mimed the various characters.

(With her forearm, Franca covers her eyes and, although still standing, pretends to be asleep. Her voice has a sleepy tone.)

At first light, inside the sheets, I lie stretched out;
You rise from my bed and turn your back
To put on your trousers.

(She sits down slowly, crosses her legs.)

How odd this modesty of yours!
All night long, naked in my arms I have held you.
I have known you for many months.
Why hide now from my glance?

(Slowly she rises to her feet.)

I hardly see you
As you pull away the sheet.
You want me to hold you
And cry after you:
'Stay awhile, it is too early,
It was so beautiful, when will you return?'

(She goes over to the side of the stage, as though she were accompanying her love to the door.)

But you will not have this feather to put in your cap.

(She moves to the centre stage and sits down.)

You wear your bright jacket and your boots
And I watch you fumble noisily with your laces.

(She rises suddenly to her feet.)

Let me race to the door,
Put my shoulders against the exit
To bar the way, crying out:

(Stretching wide her arms.)

'One more kiss, tell me you love me still.'

(Slowly returning to her seat, relaxedly.)

No, I shall not move.
I will let you go.
No more plumes for your hair.

(*Raising her head slightly.*)

You have descended the staircase
And are waiting at the half-opened doorway.
You hope to see me throw my arms round your neck,
And to hear my plaintive cry:
'I need you at my side every night.'
But no, I have not moved from my place,
I will not let you wear any of my plumes
In your hair.

(*Rises slowly.*)

You are astride your horse and you make it paw the ground.
Its hooves drumming on the cobbles, just to signal your presence
At the courtyard corner near the kitchen.
I stand in the kitchen, pouring a glass of wine.

(*Makes the gesture of raising a glass to her lips.*)

I drink to my own health and to my prowess in making love.
You will go off, my love, without my feather,
Like a plucked cockerel!

I have always found that this ballad went down well with women and young girls, but rather less so with men, of any age. Normally men have no ability to laugh at themselves. In our play, *Open Couple*, there are certain passages in which women laugh happily, but where the men sit in stony, tight-lipped silence. However, I took to commenting on this situation in the prologue, and after that, while the women continued laughing as before, the laughter of the men took on a forced, strident quality that was downright inhuman. Every so often, at certain moments of particularly pointed satire, you could hear loud whispers from some woman to the man sitting next to her, 'Do you recognise yourself, you idiot?' There were other men who burst into applause even earlier than the women round them, congratulating themselves that they had no reason to feel any embarrassment, because the character on stage had nothing to do with them – 'After all, I'm a feminist myself!' Male feminists should be strangled at birth!

On the subject of feminism, things seem to have taken a turn for the better, now that certain forms of hysterical extremism have been done away with. Many of the women who, in the early days of passion and fervour, celebrated their emancipation with witches' dances leading up to the final rite (thankfully merely allusive) of castration of the male, have now returned to humdrum normality as home-owners, happy mothers and smiling brides. There must be some explanation of why in any struggle it is always the most perfervid and hot-headed who burn themselves out most quickly, and most permanently. I still come across groups of feminists with, as they say, radical views on relationships with men, but many of them remind me of certain political associations that sprang up in the aftermath of the 1968 movement and wanted to cut everything with an axe: the bourgeoisie are always treacherous, exploitative, and ratlike while working people are invariably clean, bright and revolutionary-minded.

During a performance in Sicily a young woman got up and walked out of the theatre, denouncing me as she went because I had had the temerity to satirise the language of romantic fiction, and because I had, she said, dramatised a condition, that of a woman not in charge of her own life and compelled to remain housebound by her lord and master of a husband, which did not exist. I managed to trace her after the show and suggested that she come to dinner with the company to talk things over. She replied that she could not, because if she was not home within half an hour her father would kill her. It was only ten o'clock. In spite of that, that girl was firmly convinced that she was liberated and mistress of her own life. I really believe that facing any question without a minimum of critical self-irony is always dangerous.

Consider the judgements made by certain sections of feminist thought on some masterpieces, such as Euripides *Alcestis*. The plot is well known; Alcestis is the wife of Admetus and lives happily with her husband until one evening when she receives a visit from a strange, kindly, if somewhat doleful individual, who turns out to be none other than Thanatos, death, who in Greek is male. Thanatos has not come for her, as Alcestis initially believes, but for her husband. Alcestis is driven to despair and manages to move Thanatos with her tears, so that he offers a bargain. If someone offers himself in the place of King Admetus, that will do nicely for him. Alcestis makes her weary round of her husband's friends, relatives, brothers and in-laws, but they all decline. She insists that the very survival of the kingdom is at stake, that never had there been a king of such proven honesty and competence, that his death would be an irreparable loss for one and all, and that once he, who had kept the enemies of the state at bay, was removed from the scene, the country would be subject to invasion and that the most treasured of liberties would be in jeopardy. No deal; no one is prepared to make the ultimate sacrifice.

Alcestis plays her last card. She goes to his parents, two aged, infirm people. For them the sacrifice could involve no more than the loss of a couple of years, perhaps of months, but both reply that precisely because the time left to them is so short, it has become all the more precious. The only alternative left to Alcestis is to offer herself. Naturally her husband refuses, especially since there are the children to consider, but Alcestis raises so many persuasive arguments that at the end, he gives way. Thanatos carries off the woman. Admetus feels his heart burst within him, and the man who had 'appeared a lump of unmoving rock to the world' cries in the deepest despair. Hercules intervenes from the underworld, snatches the gentle Alcestis from the clutches of Thanatos and carries her back to the arms of her husband.

In the eyes of certain hard-line feminists, the brutal moral which clearly emerges from this myth is that a good mother must always be prepared for self-sacrifice, or, more precisely, that sacrifice in the interests of men is the highest peak and the supreme honour and privilege a woman can aspire to. A wife and mother worthy of the name must offer herself for her husband and children. This judgement may have a certain partial credibility, but I think that an approach of this kind is tantamount to looking at things with one eye, and a short-sighted one at that. The author in question is Euripides, and a writer so roundly mocked and jeered by Aristophanes for his excessive sympathy for movements of emancipation of Athenian women in the fourth century BC was not likely to have fallen into such an obvious and hypocritical over-simplification.

Going more deeply into the matter, we must be struck by the fact that the prime moral act of the play is the accusation that Euripides, through Alcestis, levels at a fundamentally egoistical society, where public values and the problems of the collectivity are overlooked. His next attack is on hypocrisy. Where is that much-vaunted maternal love, not to mention the love of family and friends? Alcestis finds herself alone. Her gesture of self-sacrifice is an act of condemnation of a whole society. It is worth recalling that Euripides was an expert practitioner of theatre and not likely to fall into any act of tawdry catharsis. The husband refuses right up to the end, for he is no coward. He does not accept the substitution, holding fast to the pretext that destiny has to be accepted without demur. Far from being someone who wavers just for effect, he is completely decisive. At the end, he is convinced by the arguments of Alcestis and agrees to the sacrifice of the dearest part of himself, his Alcestis. You may say that this is another act of cunning, but his despair, which pushes him to consider suicide so as to rejoin his wife, is there to prove the opposite. For him, the most intolerable of options is to remain alive without his love. The intensity of tragic feeling requires the intervention of a *deus ex machina*. The audience demands nothing less. Hercules arrives on the scene like the US cavalry to dispel a pain now shared by the spectators. I believe this is the correct reading of the tragedy of Alcestis. You may accuse me of naiveté, but I remain to be convinced.

None of this should be viewed as an attempt to redefine judgements on the behaviour of men in general, or on their phallocratic culture. It is sufficient to consider the weight, the value which men give to that magical little attachment of theirs, and, if you examine it carefully, what does it amount to? A tiny tail. The Devil has his behind, the male of the species in front. Thanks to that tiny tail, which is presented to us as the very hinge of the universe, man feels himself invincible. To tell the truth, we women, and there is no point in denying it, are by comparison very imperfect creatures. We can produce children with all their organs in working order, with ten fingers and toes, two eyes, two ears, one nose and so on, but without the little male tail we are inefficient, useless beings. And do not forget the great miracle of miracles – the erection! At one moment you see a minute snail of a thing, depressed and defenceless, then all of a sudden, Wow! it rises in all its glory. It is a phenomenon that can occur in the most diverse of circumstances ... in particular atmospheric conditions, on land, under water, provided it is warm enough. I once heard of a pilot who had an extraordinary erection as he went into a nose-dive over the target of his bombs. A miracle! It is never going to happen to women, not even if we pack ourselves full of TNT and launch ourselves headlong at the target.

You have to agree that from the very dawn of time, men have always given the most grandiloquent of names to their organ ... but that word organ always sidetracks me. It makes me think of St Peter's. Anyway, the anatomical details of the male organ have always rejoiced in high-sounding names. Phallus! What a ring it has to it. Prepuce! The prepuce could be anything except what it actually is. Just imagine: 'How quite outstanding was yesterday's preacher who, from the top of his prepuce, addressed the flocks of the faithful!' Gland! This could be the name of some exotic flower. 'Here, darling, take this sweet scented bouquet of glands, and clasp it to your breast.' There could be a Sophoclean epic constructed with this terminology:

> They sighted great Hercules,
> The unconquered prepuce,
> His fearless brother Gland at his side
> A priapic helmet on his manly forehead
> They strode over the untamed scrotum.

Nothing of the sort could be attempted with the terminology foisted on us women. They have imposed on us the most revolting expressions: 'Vagina'! The best you could do with a vagina is slip on it. 'I broke my ankle when I slipped on a vagina skin . . . just look.' The word uterus is even nastier. What an expression! It sounds like an insult, or an offensive weapon: 'I'll break your head with this uterus!' And I don't want to hear about the 'vulva'! I agree, the Volvo is all the rage, but that is a different kettle of fish. Vulva could be the name of a species of Mexican porcupine, crossed with a Peruvian anteater. In any case, it is unquestionably poisonous. If the vulva bites, the only known antidote is the substance injected to counteract the bite of the black widow.

There can be no serious doubt that men deliberately dreamed up these terms to mortify women. Far from being the stuff of heroic poetry, these words are only fit for horror stories:

> The bats flew at night-fall
> The vaginas croaked at the edge of the stagnant pond
> As they laid their fantom ovaries.
> A fearsome uterus raised its slimy head
> And the tiny spermatozoids fainted with terror!

The first prize must go to another term, one that I can hardly bring myself to utter – orgasm! It is a word addressed almost exclusively to women, but what a word! Men experience pleasure, but women orgasm. The very sound is enough to make the hairs stand up on the back of your neck. It summons up monsters. I imagine it as the cross between an orang-utan and a mandrill. Can you see the headlines in the morning paper: 'Giant orgasm escapes from city zoo!' or even 'Nun assaulted by mad orgasm on run from American circus'. When they ask you: 'Did you reach orgasm, dear?' I always have this image of some poor old soul running madly behind a moving bus and jumping on board at the last minute.

Earlier, I was saying that at the time of the Greeks, women were not allowed on the stage, but this ban only came into force from the seventh century BC. In more ancient times there were many cases of women acting and writing works in which they figured as the undisputed protagonists. With a certain pride, I can state that tragedy itself, in its most ancient form, was invented by women. What is even more surprising is that these tragedies were worked out in a comic, or even burlesque, style.

The Eleusinian rite, the primary form of tragedy as it has been pointed out, was originally conceived to celebrate a burlesque game invented by a particularly highly-spirited girl in an effort to rescue Demeter from her despair. Mother Earth descended from Olympus where she had been having an argument with the gods over their refusal to satisfy the requests of the mother of Dionysus and Koré. The goddess wanted the gods to restore Koré who had been snatched away by Pluto, but, to her dismay, they would have nothing to do with her, and even made fun of her. In high dudgeon, Demeter came down to earth and stopped off in Eleusis at the house of some kindly, well-meaning people, but she kept herself to herself. Such was her unhappiness that she even refused a glass of wine offered by Baubo, the high-spirited girl already mentioned. Baubo, who in the Eleusinian rites is referred to as the 'daughter of the earth', stripped herself naked and painted on her stomach two big eyes, a nose and, just above the pubic hair, a mouth. The navel was to be the third eye. She concealed her face and bust with a huge mask of reeds which seemed like a shock of hair covering a round face and, swaying her hips and moving the folds of her stomach, she improvised, in front of the goddess, a dance with obscene passages and a song with bawdy verses. Demeter smiled, then laughed contentedly. The daughter of the earth succeeded in freeing Mother Earth from sorrow, and this marks the return of joy and life to the world of men.

Noh drama in Japan has a similar origin. In this case, too, there is a divinity, no less than the Sun in person, at odds with the rest of the gods. The Sun shuts himself up in a cave and refuses to come out, leaving the Earth in the deepest darkness. The gods gather round a fire in front of the cave, hoping that the rage of the Sun will subside and that he will at least listen to them. In the meantime, a pretty demigoddess, a girl (note that it is always a woman who invents these comic-obscene games) climbs on to a slab of stones near the fire and begins to sing. She moves slowly, making everyone aware of her astonishing physical beauty; she tries some tentative dance steps and begins to strip. During her striptease, the girl herself grows excited and her dance assumes a more provocative edge; the words of the song take on scurrilous but still humorous, overtones. The gods laugh and applaud and, inside his cave, the Sun hears the sound and grows curious. He peeps out through a gap and then, to get a better view, removes the giant stone which had been blocking the entrance to the cave. The opening grows wider until a ray of light falls on the young striptease artist who, flattered, steps up the erotic movements and the hip swaying – all to the accompaniment of cheers and whistles from the gods who are notoriously susceptible in these matters. The Sun, too, joins in, and the hostilities cease. Life resumes its course.

The two most ancient forms of tragedy known to the world have at their origin a catharsis of laughter and sexual obscenity, releasing light and harmony. In this way, in all forms of popular entertainment, by the use of the grotesque, hatred, fear and resentment are exorcised and dispelled.

While discussing masks, Dario mentioned the problems that women encounter with their use. I would like to elaborate a little, because here too there is a historical explanation. In the first place, for centuries women's parts were played by men dressed up. In the play *La Venexiana*, there is one particularly awkward scene, guaranteed to stir up moralistic controversy on account of a number of allusions, somewhat pointed in the script, to homosexuality. The protagonist is a widow in love with a young stranger newly arrived in Venice in search of amorous adventures. The widow dreams of holding her lover in her arms and rolling about with him on a bed. She compels her serving maid to play the part of a man, to embrace her, kiss her and cry out obscene remarks like the most chauvinistic of male braggarts, so that she can indulge in unbridled fantasies of passionate love with her stranger.

Normally, a warning was given to the audience in the prologue to the play: 'We trust that you are not a bunch of small-minded moralists who will be horrified by what you are about to see. It is true that in the second act there is a scene with a woman kissing another woman on the mouth, but there is no need to be scandalised because it is really two men and not two women at all.' It is all a pretence, which would have it that if two boys, passing themselves off as women, were to kiss, the moral system is safe. The anecdote does prove that as late as the beginning of the sixteenth century women were forbidden access to theatre, both as actresses and as spectators. During the Counter-Reformation, which brought about the exodus of numerous Italian theatre troupes, many theatres were closed down. Popes Pius VI and Paul V, under pressure from Cardinal Borromeo (the great theoretician of the Counter-Reformation), became the butchers of Italian theatre in general and Roman theatre in particular.

Women with no Masks

At the same time in France the position of women was quite different, for this was the moment when Isabella Andreini, poet, writer, actress of great acclaim, enjoyed her most brilliant success not only with the public at large but also with the intellectuals. Since Isabella was prone to playing herself rather than a character, she had no real need of a mask. The other reason for which women refused to don a mask was that they wished to be finally recognised as real women, and not just as men in disguise. There are certain female characters, like Marcolfa (whom I played in *Arlecchino*), which were normally performed by women who did not use masks. They employed strong make-up with various attachments, such as false nose, bushy eyebrows, artificial lips or warts, but never masks. No women's masks for the use of actresses have ever been found among the paraphernalia of theatre history.

Here Ends the Sixth Day

Index

36–7; sing as you row, 30–2, 40–1; and speech, 34–5; and survival, 29–30, 37–8; synthesis in, 36, 144; in work, 32–3, 39; *see also* mime

Gian-farina (Johnny-flour), 172

Giotto, 59

giullare (minstrels), 6, 70–1, 84–7, 135–6, 171, 172, 181, 182–3

Goldoni, Carlo, 4, 27–9, 88, 184; *Arlecchino, Servant of Two Masters*, 27–8, 29; *Last Night of the Carnival*, 184

Gozzi, Carlo, 184

grammelot, 34 &n, 42, 43, 44, 48–9, 56–8, 63, 64–5, 74; American, 74–5, 76–80; birth of, 61–3; lecture on technology in, 76–80; lesson of Scapino in French, 68–70; live TV broadcast in, 80–1

Gramsci, Antonio, 3, 81

Greek theatre, 2, 4, 90–1, 111, 137–43; actors' pay, 183; audience reaction to, 122–3; 'Big Mouth' (the haranguer), 25–6; death and destiny in, 186–7; epic alienation from characters, 143; *Hypocrites and Ethiopios*, 122, 143; masks and disguises, 23, 25, 137–8; mime, 143; mobile stage machinery, 140; performed in winter, 139–40; the protagonist, 141–3; reflector and foreshortening effect, 138–9; switching of roles, 141–2

Guido of Brescia, Archbishop, 182

Harlequin/Arlecchino, the whore-monger, 6, 7–8, 9–10, 29, 45–7, 50, 137, 179, 181; *Arlecchino Fallotropo*, 48–9; *Arlecchino, Servant of Two Masters* (Goldoni), 27–8, 29; hip movement, 36; make-up, 172; mask, 22, 23, 25, 26, 46; origins, 45–6; spoken words, 12–13

Harlequin-Cat, 22, 25

Hauser, Arnold, *Social History of Art*, 85

Henry III, King of France, 16–17, 47

Henry IV, King of France, 181

Het Werk Teatr, Holland, 5

hoax, politics of the, 192–6

Holy Communion, 21

homosexuality, 211

Huguenots, Geloso company captured by, 14–15

Hypocrites and *Ethopios*, 122, 143

Ibsen, Henrik, 4

improvisation, 10–11, 71, 87–8, 160–9, 183, 193; at the Berliner Ensemble, 169; minstrel's, 84; and speech, 153

Indian clowns, 179–80

Indian masks, 22, 23

Innocent XII, Pope, 61

Japanese: Kabuki theatre, 36, 141, 149; masks, 23; Noh drama, 210

John Paul II, Pope, 125; attempted assassination of, 117–19; kissing the ground at Madrid airport, 75–6

Jouvet, Louis, 147, 159

jugglers, 15, 85, 171

Kabuki theatre, Japanese, 36, 141, 149

Karacochis, 50

Kirchmayer, Thomas, 179

Koll, Dr Katrin, 85, 86

laugh, programmed or 'telegraphed', 36

lazzi, 8–10, 81

Lecoq, Jacques, 147, 148

Leonardo da Vinci, 77

Louis XIV, Sun King, 63, 65

Louis clown, 125, 129

Lu Gatto Lupesco (the Wolf-Cat), 135–6

Lucian of Samosata, 50

Machiavelli, Niccolò, 197; *Clizia*, 180; *La Mandragola* (*The Mandrake*), 63, 180

'Madonna' (character in 'Shepherds' cantata'), 91, 92–3

Maggi, theatre of the, 106–7, 108, 109, 110

'Magnifico', 42, 48, 68; mask, 22, 67, 68

make-up, 137; clown's, 172; Commedia dell'Arte, 137, 172; instead of masks, 26, 137; Moretti's, 26

Malpagas pirates, 109

mammuttones of Sardinia, 19–20, 110; pseudo-, 20–1

Manzoni, Alessandro, 154 &n; *I Promessi Sposi*, 154

maona, 42

marble quarries of Massa and Carrara, 39–40

Marceau, Marcel, 146, 199

Martinelli, Tristano, 7, 29, 46, 47, 137, 181

masks, 18–30, 66–70, 73, 137–8; animal (zoomorphic), 18–19, 20, 22–3, 135; 'breathing' of, 66–7; cave men's, 18–19; Commedia dell'Arte, 18, 22–7, 46, 67–8, 110; discomfort of wearing, 26–7, 66; and gestures, 29, 35–7, 41–2, 43–5, 68, 70; hands off, 27; Japanese, 23; make-up instead of, 26, 137; *mammuttones*, 19, 20; as megaphone, 25; minstrel's caricature of bishop, 182; modelling of, 66; 'third eye' in, 23; Thessalian, 70; women with no, 211–12; Zannone, 110

Mayakovsky, Vladimir, 29

Medrano Circus, Paris, 175

Meldolesi, Claudio, 156–7

mentally ill patients, theatre for, 130–4

Mercadante Theatre, Naples, 152

Meyerhold, Vsevolod, 29

Michelangelo, 17, 39

215

216